Birnbaum's 94
Miami
& Ft. Lauderdale

A BIRNBAUM TRAVEL GUIDE

Alexandra Mayes Birnbaum
EDITORIAL CONSULTANT

Lois Spritzer
Executive Editor

Laura L. Brengelman
Managing Editor

Mary Callahan
Senior Editor

Patricia Canole
Gene Gold
Jill Kadetsky
Susan McClung
Beth Schlau
Associate Editors

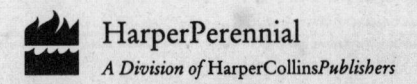

HarperPerennial
A Division of **HarperCollins***Publishers*

To Stephen, who merely made all this possible.

BIRNBAUM'S MIAMI & FT. LAUDERDALE 94. Copyright © 1993 by HarperCollins Publishers. All rights reserved. Printed in the United States of America. No part of this book may be used or reproduced in any manner whatsoever without written permission except in the case of brief quotations embodied in critical articles and reviews. For information address HarperCollinsPublishers, 10 East 53rd Street, New York, NY 10022.

FIRST EDITION

ISSN 0749-2561 (Birnbaum Travel Guides)
ISSN 1056-4454 (Miami & Ft. Lauderdale)
ISBN 0-06-278109-X (pbk.)

93 94 95 96 97 CC/CW 10 9 8 7 6 5 4 3 2 1

Cover design © Drenttel Doyle Partners
Cover photograph © C. Cordina/Tony Stone Images

BIRNBAUM TRAVEL GUIDES

Bahamas, and Turks & Caicos
Berlin
Bermuda
Boston
Canada
Cancun, Cozumel & Isla Mujeres
Caribbean
Chicago
Disneyland
Eastern Europe
Europe
Europe for Business Travelers
France
Germany
Great Britain
Hawaii
Ireland
Italy
London
Los Angeles
Mexico
Miami & Ft. Lauderdale
Montreal & Quebec City
New Orleans
New York
Paris
Portugal
Rome
San Francisco
Santa Fe & Taos
South America
Spain
United States
USA for Business Travelers
Walt Disney World
Walt Disney World for Kids, By Kids
Washington, DC

Contributing Editors
Laura Hambleton
Laura Kelly
Tracy Smith
Molly Arost Staub

Maps
Mark Carlson
Susan Carlson

Contents

Foreword ... vii

How to Use This Guide ... 1

Getting Ready to Go

Practical information for planning your trip.

When to Go ... 11
Traveling by Plane ... 11
On Arrival ... 14
Package Tours ... 15
Insurance ... 16
Disabled Travelers ... 17
Single Travelers ... 19
Older Travelers ... 20
Money Matters ... 21
Time Zone ... 22
Business Hours ... 22
Mail ... 22
Telephone ... 23
Medical Aid ... 24
Legal Aid ... 25
For Further Information ... 25

The Cities

Thorough, qualitative guides to Miami and Ft. Lauderdale. Each section offers a comprehensive report on the city's most compelling attractions and amenities — highlighting our top choices in every category.

Specific Data About Miami and Miami Beach ... 29
Specific Data About Ft. Lauderdale ... 72

Diversions

A selective guide to a variety of unexpected pleasures, pinpointing the best places in which to pursue them.

Exceptional Experiences for the Mind and Body
Quintessential Miami ... 103
Antiquing ... 108

v

Historic Churches ... 109
Miami from Another Angle: From the Farm to the Keys ... 110
Sybaritic Spas ... 111
Day Cruises ... 114
A Shutterbug's View ... 115

Directions

Nine of the best walks and drives through Miami and Ft. Lauderdale, and beyond.

Introduction ... 121

Tour 1: South Beach — The Art Deco District ... 123
Tour 2: South Miami by Car ... 129
Tour 3: Coconut Grove ... 133
Tour 4: Cruising through Coral Gables ... 137
Tour 5: Little Havana ... 141
Tour 6: Cowboy and Indian Tour ... 145
Tour 7: Palm Beach ... 149
Tour 8: Florida Keys and John Pennekamp Coral Reef State Park ... 153
Tour 9: Everglades National Park ... 161

Index ... 169

Foreword

Miami Beach — and to a lesser degree, Miami and Ft. Lauderdale — are good object lessons of how not to run towns that depend on tourists.

For a couple of decades after World War II, southeastern Florida had only to exist to attract more than its fair share of northerners seeking the sun during the winter. The temperature alone was a powerful lure, and the existence of glitzy hotels, a beckoning beach, and other such attractions was just frosting (actually, thawing) on the cake. Each year, as the final leaf fell from the last tree in the northeast, hordes of heat-seeking sun worshipers — not unlike lemmings determined to reach the sea — headed for Miami.

The vendors of travel services in southeastern Florida, long accustomed to the regular arrival of their traditional clientele, did absolutely the worst possible thing to assure their own continued prosperity: nothing! By taking their customers for granted, they let hotels run down, they allowed shops and restaurants to grow stale, and generally did little to keep the appeal of Miami/Miami Beach very high.

You can say lots of things about travelers, but most of them ain't dumb. Soon tales of equally appealing beaches in the Caribbean, Mexico, and Hawaii began to reach the ears of longtime Miami visitors, and promotional airfares and discounted package programs made these new destinations delightfully affordable. So it wasn't too long before hotel occupancy levels in southeastern Florida began to fall precipitously.

The facts were simple: Travel and tourism habits had dramatically changed, and aside from the appeal that the local climate continued to have for retirees, the bulk of sun-seeking winter travelers tanned elsewhere. A less vital and vibrant community would have packed it in and given up.

The decline in tourist traffic meant an absence of cash with which to maintain and refurbish tourism facilities, and the erection of *Walt Disney World* in Orlando in 1971 — followed by important attractions on both the east and west coasts of central Florida — created a "wall" across the Sunshine State that stopped traffic several hundred miles north of Miami Beach. Many tourism experts thought they heard the death knell of Miami for tourists.

The impetus for the turnaround in Miami's fortunes came from an unexpected direction — the south instead of the north. The influx of ambitious, energetic Cubans jump-started the city of Miami — for a long time just a poor relation to the glamour and glitz of Miami Beach. The sharpening of focus on the southern tier of the United States brought new development — commercial, industrial, and residential — to Florida, and Miami got its fair share of the new projects. Finally, Miami became the natural headquarters for virtually all financial and commercial activities relating to Latin America — whether domestic or foreign. Suddenly, Miami was a throbbing force in the expansion of the entire US economy.

Even tourism was a beneficiary of this growth; money earned in everything from banking to sugarcane trickled down to hotel building and restoration, and a new sense of civic pride caused the citizenry to re-examine local assets. It wasn't long before blocks of mostly run-down hotels occupied by pensioners became one of this nation's most compelling areas of Art Deco architecture. Concurrently came the city's emergence as an important art center, and it wasn't too long before the troubled tourists started coming back — although they are no longer the sole foundation on which the local economy depends. It made some of us — who had glibly predicted Miami's demise — gladly rethink our conclusions.

My husband, Steve Birnbaum, had a particular affinity for Florida — admittedly not always shared by me. He was a golfer and a sun worshiper. I am an indoors woman: no fairways or swaths of sand for me. And until Miami's relatively recent renaissance, for me, this "moon over" city meant sitting under a palm tree, my head protected by a broad-brimmed straw hat. Happily, the Miami of this minute represents a truly hot spot for travelers of both persuasions. And in spite of its myriad metamorphoses, everyone can continue to enjoy the one major passion Steve and I did share: dinner at *Joe's Stone Crab*.

Obviously, any guidebook to Miami must keep pace with and answer the real needs of today's travelers. That's why we've tried to create a guide that's specifically organized, written, and edited for the more demanding modern traveler, one for whom qualitative information is infinitely more desirable than mere quantities of unappraised data.

For years, dating back as far as Herr Baedeker, travel guides have tended to be encyclopedic, much more concerned with demonstrating expertise in geography and history than with a real analysis of the sorts of things that actually concern a typical modern tourist. I think you'll notice a different, more contemporary tone to our text, as well as an organization and focus that are distinctive and more functional. Early on, we realized that giving up the encyclopedic approach precluded our listing every single route and restaurant, a realization that helped define our overall editorial focus. Similarly, when we discussed the possibility of presenting certain information in other than strict geographic order, we found that the new format enabled us to arrange data in a way that best answers the questions travelers typically ask.

Travel guides are, understandably, reflections of personal taste, and putting one's name on a title page obviously puts one's preferences on the line. But I think I ought to amplify just what "personal" means. I don't believe in the sort of personal guidebook that's a palpable misrepresentation on its face. It is, for example, hardly possible for any single travel writer to visit thousands of restaurants (and nearly as many hotels) in any given year and provide accurate appraisals of each. And even if it were physically possible for one human being to survive such an itinerary, it would of necessity have to be done at a dead sprint, and the perceptions derived therefrom would probably be less valid than those of any other intelligent individual visiting the same establishments. It is, therefore, impossible (especially in a large, annually revised and updated guidebook *series* such as we offer) to have only one person provide all the data on the entire world.

I also happen to think that such individual orientation is of substantially less value to readers. Visiting a single hotel for just one night or eating one hasty meal in a random restaurant hardly equips anyone to provide appraisals that are of more than passing interest. We have, therefore, chosen what I like to describe as the "thee and me" approach to restaurant and hotel evaluation and, to a somewhat more limited degree, to the sites and sights we have included in the other sections of our text. What this really reflects is a personal sampling tempered by intelligent counsel from informed local sources, and these additional friends-of-the-editor are almost always residents of the city and/or area about which they are consulted.

In addition, very precise editing and tailoring keep our text fiercely subjective. So what follows is the gospel according to Birnbaum, and it represents as much of our own taste and instincts as we can manage. It is probable, therefore, that if you like your cities stylish and prefer small hotels with personality to huge high-rise anonymities, we're likely to have a long and meaningful relationship.

I also should point out something about the person to whom this guidebook is directed. Above all, he or she is a "visitor." This means that such elements as restaurants have been specifically picked to provide the visitor with a representative, enlightening, stimulating, and above all pleasant experience. Since so many extraneous considerations can affect the reception and service accorded a regular restaurant patron, our choices can in no way be construed as an exhaustive guide to resident dining. We think we've listed all the best places, in various price ranges, but they were chosen with a visitor's enjoyment in mind.

Other evidence of how we've tried to tailor our text to reflect modern travel habits is most apparent in the section we call DIVERSIONS. Where once it was common for travelers to spend an urban visit seeing only the obvious sights, the emphasis today is more likely to be directed toward pursuing some special interest. Therefore, we have collected these exceptional experiences so that it is no longer necessary to wade through a pound or two of superfluous prose just to find unexpected pleasures and treasures.

Finally, I also should point out that every good travel guide is a living enterprise; that is, no part of this text is carved in stone. In our annual revisions, we refine, expand, and further hone all our material to serve your travel needs better. To this end, no contribution is of greater value to us than your personal reaction to what we have written, as well as information reflecting your own experiences while using the book. Please write to us at 10 E. 53rd St., New York, NY 10022.

We sincerely hope to hear from you.

Alexandra Mayes Birnbaum

ALEXANDRA MAYES BIRNBAUM, editorial consultant to the *Birnbaum Travel Guides*, worked with her late husband Stephen Birnbaum as co-editor of the series. She has been a world traveler since childhood and is known for her lively travel reports on radio on what's hot and what's not.

How to Use This Guide

A great deal of care has gone into the special organization of this guidebook, and we believe it represents a real breakthrough in the presentation of travel material.

Our text is divided into four basic sections in order to present information in the best way on every possible aspect of a vacation to Miami. Our aim is to highlight what's where and to provide basic information — how, when, where, how much, and what's best — to assist you in making the most intelligent choices possible.

Here is a brief summary of what you can expect to find in each section. We believe that you will find both your travel planning and en route enjoyment enhanced by having this book at your side.

GETTING READY TO GO

A mini-encyclopedia of practical travel facts with all the precise data necessary to create a successful trip to Miami. Here you will find how to get where you're going, plus selected resources — including useful publications, and companies and organizations specializing in discount and special-interest travel — providing a wealth of information and assistance useful both before and during your trip.

THE CITIES

Our individual reports on Miami and Ft. Lauderdale offer a short-stay guide, including an essay introducing each city as a historic entity and a contemporary place to visit; *At-a-Glance* material is actually a site-by-site survey of the most important, interesting, and sometimes most eclectic sights to see and things to do; *Sources and Resources* is a concise listing of pertinent tourism information, such as the address of the local tourist office, which sightseeing tours to take, where to find the best nightspot, which are the shops that have the finest merchandise and/or the most irresistible bargains, and where the best museums and theaters are to be found. *Best in Town* lists our collection of cost-and-quality choices of the best places to eat and sleep on a variety of budgets.

DIVERSIONS

This section is designed to help travelers find the best places in which to engage in a variety of exceptional — and unexpected — experiences, without having to wade through endless pages of unrelated text. In each case, our particular suggestions are intended to guide you to that special place where the quality of experience is likely to be highest.

DIRECTIONS

Here are seven walks and drives that cover the city, along its main thoroughfares and side streets, past its most spectacular landmarks and lovely parks, and the most compelling tours in the areas nearby. We also suggest two 1-day or overnight drives: to the Florida Keys and Everglades National Park.

To use this book to full advantage, take a few minutes to read the table of contents and random entries in each section to get a firsthand feel for how it all fits together. You will find that the sections of this book are building blocks designed to help you put together the best possible trip. Use them selectively as a tool, a source of ideas, a reference work for accurate facts, and a guidebook to the best buys, the most exciting sights, the most pleasant accommodations, and the tastiest foods — *the best travel experience* that you can possibly have in Miami.

Miami Beach

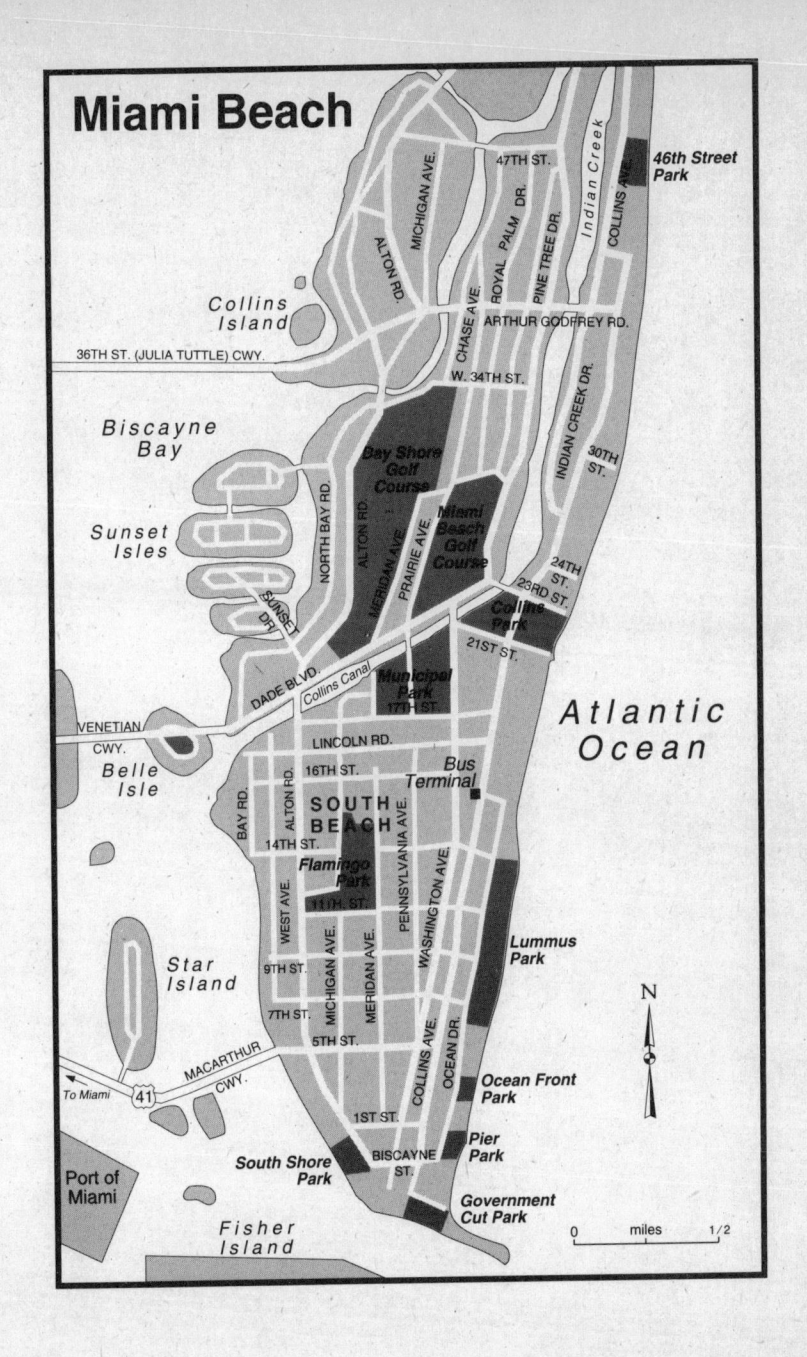

Miami

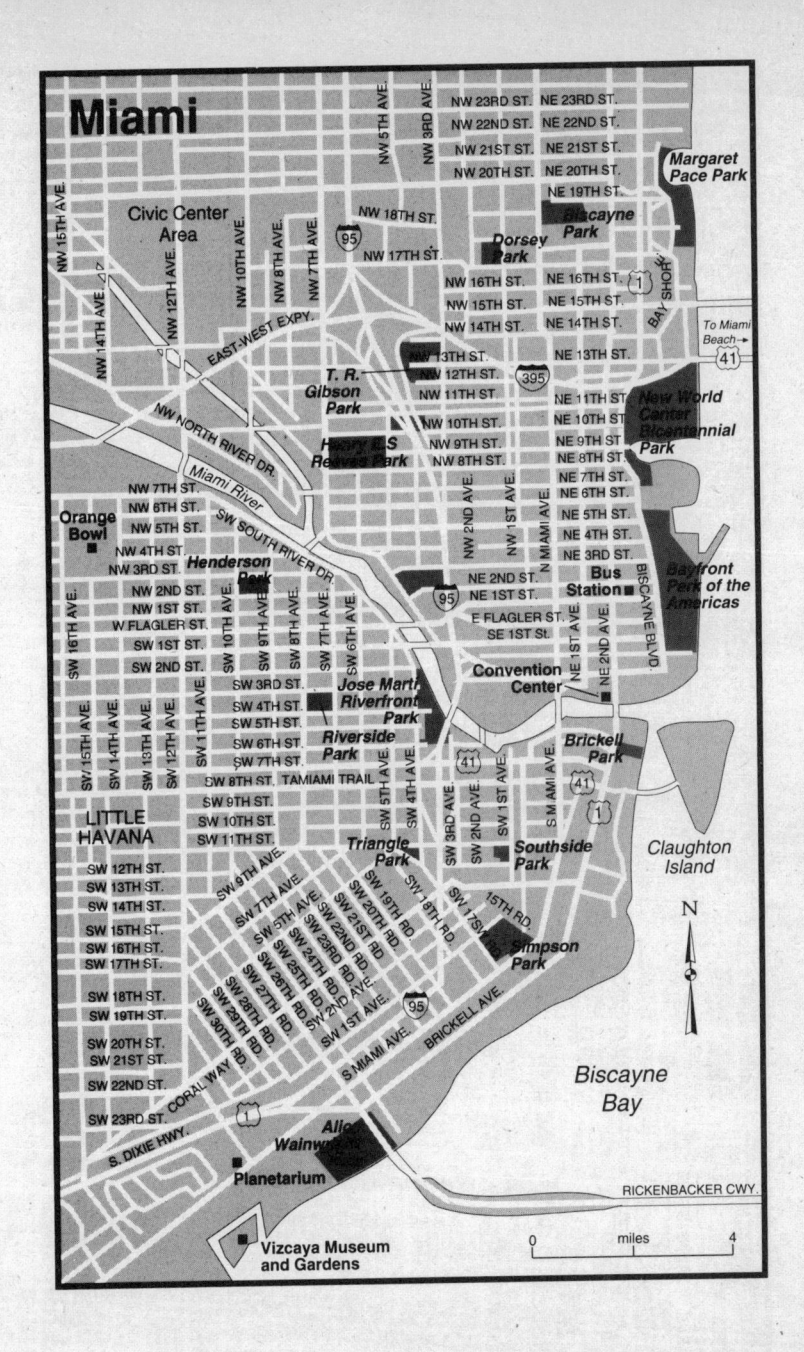

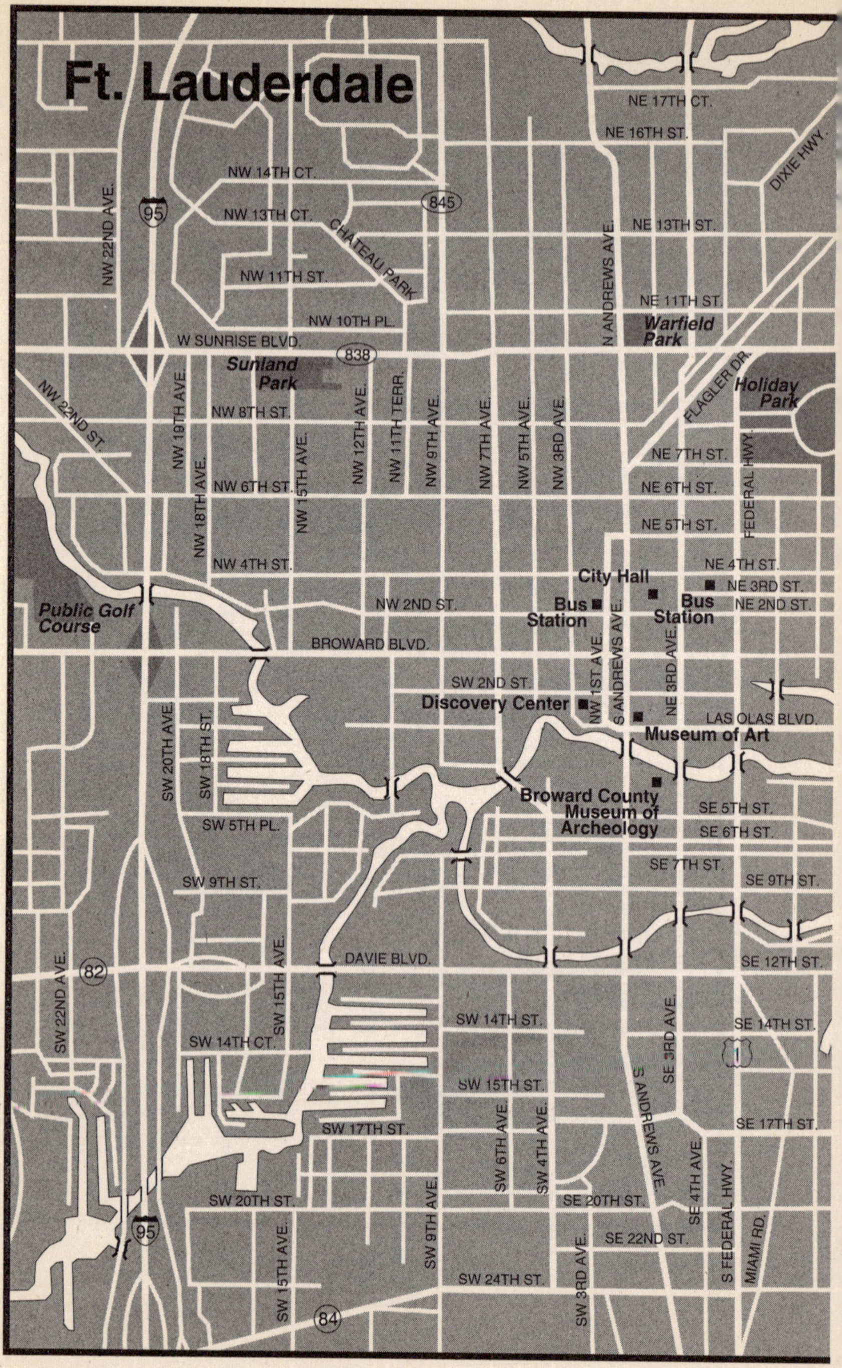
Ft. Lauderdale
NE 17TH CT.
NE 16TH ST.
DIXIE HWY.
NW 14TH CT.
845
95
NW 13TH CT.
CHATEAU PARK
NE 13TH ST.
NW 22ND AVE.
NW 11TH ST.
N ANDREWS AVE.
NE 11TH ST.
NW 10TH PL.
Warfield Park
W SUNRISE BLVD.
838
Sunland Park
FLAGLER DR.
Holiday Park
NW 22ND ST.
NW 19TH AVE.
NW 8TH ST.
NW 12TH AVE.
NW 11TH TERR.
NW 9TH AVE.
NW 7TH AVE.
NW 5TH AVE.
NW 3RD AVE.
NE 7TH ST.
NW 18TH AVE.
NW 6TH ST.
NW 15TH AVE.
NE 6TH ST.
FEDERAL HWY.
NE 5TH ST.
NW 4TH ST.
NE 4TH ST.
City Hall
NE 3RD ST.
Bus Station
Bus Station
NE 2ND ST.
Public Golf Course
NW 2ND ST.
BROWARD BLVD.
NW 1ST AVE.
S ANDREWS AVE.
NE 3RD AVE.
SW 2ND ST.
Discovery Center
LAS OLAS BLVD.
Museum of Art
SW 20TH AVE.
SW 18TH ST.
Broward County Museum of Archeology
SE 5TH ST.
SE 6TH ST.
SW 5TH PL.
SE 7TH ST.
SE 9TH ST.
SW 9TH ST.
SW 22ND AVE.
82
SW 15TH AVE.
DAVIE BLVD.
SE 12TH ST.
SW 14TH ST.
SE 14TH ST.
SW 14TH CT.
SE 3RD AVE.
1
SW 15TH ST.
S ANDREWS AVE.
SW 17TH ST.
SE 17TH ST.
SW 6TH AVE.
SW 4TH AVE.
SE 4TH AVE.
SW 9TH AVE.
SW 20TH ST.
SE 20TH ST.
S FEDERAL HWY.
95
SE 22ND ST.
MIAMI RD.
SW 15TH AVE.
SW 24TH ST.
SW 3RD AVE.
84

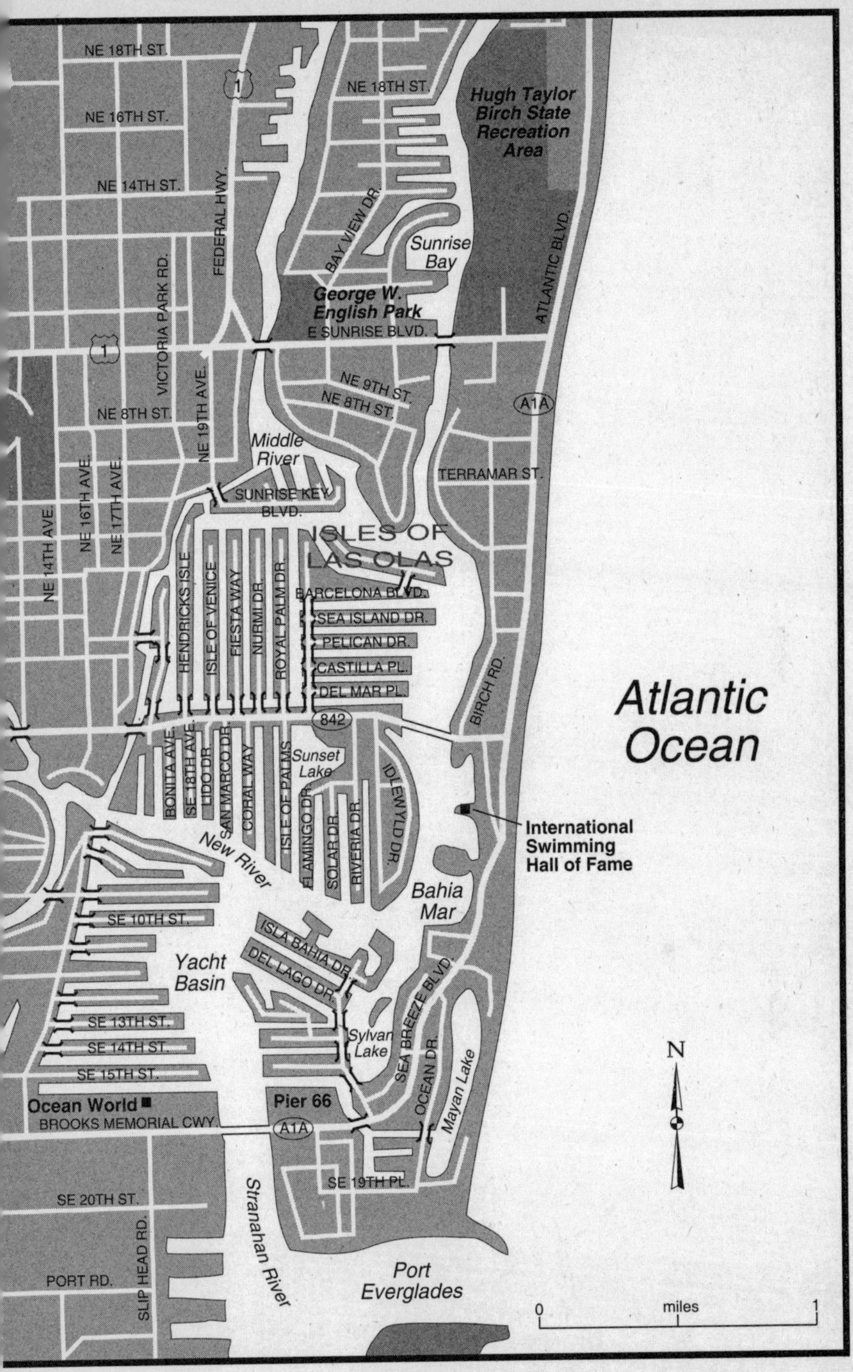

NE 18TH ST.
1
NE 18TH ST.
Hugh Taylor Birch State Recreation Area
NE 16TH ST.
NE 14TH ST.
FEDERAL HWY.
BAY VIEW DR.
Sunrise Bay
ATLANTIC BLVD.
VICTORIA PARK RD.
George W. English Park
E SUNRISE BLVD.
1
NE 9TH ST.
NE 8TH ST.
A1A
NE 19TH AVE.
NE 8TH ST.
Middle River
NE 16TH AVE.
NE 17TH AVE.
TERRAMAR ST.
SUNRISE KEY BLVD.
ISLES OF LAS OLAS
NE 14TH AVE.
HENDRICKS ISLE
ISLE OF VENICE
FIESTA WAY
NURMI DR.
ROYAL PALM DR.
BARCELONA BLVD.
SEA ISLAND DR.
PELICAN DR.
CASTILLA PL.
DEL MAR PL.
Atlantic Ocean
BIRCH RD.
842
BONITA AVE.
SE 18TH AVE.
LIDO DR.
SAN MARCO DR.
CORAL WAY
ISLE OF PALMS
Sunset Lake
FLAMINGO DR.
SOLAR DR.
RIVERIA DR.
IDLEWYLD DR.
International Swimming Hall of Fame
New River
Bahia Mar
SE 10TH ST.
ISLA BAHIA DR.
DEL LAGO DR.
Yacht Basin
SEA BREEZE BLVD.
SE 13TH ST.
Sylvan Lake
SE 14TH ST.
OCEAN DR.
Mayan Lake
N
SE 15TH ST.
Ocean World
Pier 66
BROOKS MEMORIAL CWY.
A1A
SE 19TH PL.
SE 20TH ST.
Stranahan River
SLIP HEAD RD.
PORT RD.
Port Everglades
0
miles
1

Getting Ready to Go

When to Go

Miami and Ft. Lauderdale enjoy year-round tropical weather, although summers can be hot and humid with frequent showers. The best weather is during the peak winter season. Travel during the off-season and shoulder seasons (the months immediately before and after the peak months) offers relatively fair weather and smaller crowds. During these periods, travel also is less expensive.

The *Weather Channel* (2600 Cumberland Pkwy., Atlanta, GA 30339; phone: 404-434-6800) provides current weather forecasts — call 900-WEATHER from any touch-tone phone in the US; the 95¢ per-minute charge will appear on your phone bill.

Traveling by Plane

SCHEDULED FLIGHTS

Leading airlines offering flights to Miami International Airport and Ft. Lauderdale/Hollywood International Airport include *American, American Eagle, Continental, Continental Express, Delta, Delta Connection, Northwest, TWA, United, USAir,* and *USAir Express.*

FARES The great variety of airfares can be reduced to the following basic categories: first class, business class, coach (also called economy or tourist class), excursion or discount, and standby, as well as various promotional fares. For information on applicable fares and restrictions, contact the airlines listed above or ask your travel agent. Most airfares are offered for a limited time period. Once you've found the lowest fare for which you can qualify, purchase your ticket as soon as possible.

RESERVATIONS Reconfirmation is not generally required on domestic flights, although it is wise to call ahead to make sure that the airline has your reservation and any special requests in its computer.

SEATING Airline seats usually are assigned on a first-come, first-served basis at check-in, although you may be able to reserve a seat when purchasing your ticket. Seating charts, which make choosing a seat easier, often are available from airlines and are included in the *Airline Seating Guide* (Carlson Publishing Co., PO Box 888, Los Alamitos, CA 90720; phone: 310-493-4877).

SMOKING US law prohibits smoking on flights scheduled for 6 hours or less within the US and its territories on both domestic and international carriers. A free wallet-size guide that describes the rights of nonsmokers is available from *ASH (Action on Smoking and Health;* DOT Card, 2013 H St. NW, Washington, DC 20006; phone: 202-659-4310).

SPECIAL MEALS When making your reservation, you can request one of the airline's alternate menu choices for no additional charge. Call to reconfirm your request 24 hours before departure.

BAGGAGE On a major airline, passengers usually are allowed to carry on board one bag that will fit under a seat or in an overhead bin. Passengers also can check two bags in the cargo hold, measuring 62 inches and 55 inches in combined dimensions (length, width, and depth) with a per-bag weight limit of 70 pounds. There may be charges for additional, oversize, or overweight luggage, and for special equipment or sporting gear. Note that baggage allowances may vary for children (depending on the percentage of full adult fare paid). Check that the tags the airline attaches are correctly coded for your destination.

CHARTER FLIGHTS

By booking a block of seats on a specially arranged flight, charter operators frequently offer travelers bargain airfares. If you do fly on a charter, however, read the contract's fine print carefully. Charter operators can cancel a flight or assess surcharges of 10% of the airfare up to 10 days before departure. You usually must book in advance (no changes are permitted, so invest in trip cancellation insurance); also make your check out to the company's escrow account. For further information, consult the publication *Jax Fax* (397 Post Rd., Darien, CT 06820; phone: 203-655-8746).

DISCOUNTS ON SCHEDULED FLIGHTS

COURIER TRAVEL In return for arranging to accompany some kind of freight, a traveler may pay only a portion of the total airfare and a small registration fee. One agency that matches up would-be couriers with courier companies is *Now Voyager* (74 Varick St., Suite 307, New York, NY 10013; phone: 212-431-1616).

Courier Companies

Courier Travel Service (530 Central Ave., Cedarhurst, NY 11516; phone: 516-763-6898).

Discount Travel International (169 W. 81st St., New York, NY 10024; phone: 212-362-3636; and 940 10th St., Suite 2, Miami Beach, FL 33139; phone: 305-538-1616).

Excaliber International Courier (c/o *Way to Go Travel*, 6679 Sunset Blvd., Hollywood, CA 90028; phone: 213-466-1126).

F.B. On Board Courier Services (10225 Ryan Ave., Suite 103, Dorval, Quebec, H9P 1A2, Canada; phone: 514-633-0740).

Halbart Express (147-05 176th St., Jamaica, NY 11434; phone: 718-656-8279).

International Adventures (60 E. 42nd St., New York, NY 10165; phone: 212-599-0577).

Midnight Express (925 W. High Park Blvd., Inglewood, CA 90302; phone: 310-672-1100).

Publications
Insider's Guide to Air Courier Bargains, by Kelly Monaghan (The Intrepid Traveler; PO Box 438, New York, NY 10034; phone: 212-304-2207).
Travel Secrets (PO Box 2325, New York, NY 10108; phone: 212-245-8703).
Travel Unlimited (PO Box 1058, Allston, MA 02134-1058; no phone).
World Courier News (PO Box 77471, San Francisco, CA 94107; no phone).

CONSOLIDATORS AND BUCKET SHOPS These companies buy blocks of tickets from airlines and sell them at a discount to travel agents or to consumers. Since many bucket shops operate on a thin margin, before parting with any money check the company's record with the Better Business Bureau.

Bargain Air (655 Deep Valley Dr., Suite 355, Rolling Hills, CA 90274; phone: 800-347-2345).
Council Charter (205 E. 42nd St., New York, NY 10017; phone: 800-800-8222 or 212-661-0311).
International Adventures (60 E. 42nd St., New York, NY 10165; phone: 212-599-0577).
Travac Tours and Charters (989 Ave. of the Americas, New York, NY 10018; phone: 800-872-8800 or 212-563-3303).
Unitravel (1177 N. Warson Rd., St. Louis, MO 63132; phone: 800-325-2222 or 314-569-0900).

LAST-MINUTE TRAVEL CLUBS For an annual fee, members receive information on imminent trips and other bargain travel opportunities. Despite the names of these clubs, you don't have to wait until literally the last minute to make travel plans.

Discount Travel International (114 Forest Ave., Suite 203, Narberth, PA 19072; phone: 215-668-7184).
Last Minute Travel (1249 Boylston St., Boston, MA 02215; phone: 800-LAST-MIN or 617-267-9800).
Moment's Notice (425 Madison Ave., New York, NY 10017; phone: 212-486-0500, -0501, -0502, or -0503).
Spur-of-the-Moment Cruises (411 N. Harbor Blvd., Suite 302, San Pedro, CA 90731; phone: 800-4-CRUISES in California; 800-343-1991 elsewhere in the US; or 310-521-1070).
Traveler's Advantage (3033 S. Parker Rd., Suite 900, Aurora, CO 80014; phone: 800-548-1116 or 800-835-8747).

Vacations to Go (1502 Augusta, Suite 415, Houston, TX 77057; phone: 713-974-2121 in Texas; 800-338-4962 elsewhere in the US).

Worldwide Discount Travel Club (1674 Meridian Ave., Miami Beach, FL 33139; phone: 305-534-2082).

GENERIC AIR TRAVEL These organizations operate much like an ordinary airline standby service, except that they offer seats on not one but several scheduled and charter airlines. One pioneer of generic flights is *Airhitch* (2790 Broadway, Suite 100, New York, NY 10025; phone: 212-864-2000).

BARTERED TRAVEL SOURCES Barter is a common means of exchange between travel suppliers. Bartered travel clubs such as *Travel World Leisure Club* (225 W. 34th St., Suite 909, New York, NY 10122; phone: 800-444-TWLC or 212-239-4855) offer discounts to members for an annual fee.

CONSUMER PROTECTION

Passengers with complaints who are not satisfied with the airline's response can contact the US Department of Transportation (DOT; Consumer Affairs Division, 400 7th St. SW, Room 10405, Washington, DC 20590; phone: 202-366-2220). Also see *Fly Rights* (publication #050-000-00513-5; US Government Printing Office, PO Box 371954, Pittsburgh, PA 15250-7954; phone: 202-783-3238).

On Arrival

FROM THE AIRPORTS TO THE CITY

Miami International Airport is a 15-minute drive from downtown and about a half hour from Miami Beach — longer during rush hours. Taxi fares average $12 to $15 to downtown, $22 to mid–Miami Beach. The *Supershuttle* (phone: 800-8-SHUTTL or 305-871-2000) has van service to and from Miami International Airport for $7 to $14.

Ft. Lauderdale/Hollywood International Airport is 10 to 15 minutes from downtown; taxi fares average $10 to $15. *Broward County Transit* (phone: 305-357-8400) runs a bus between the airport and the downtown bus terminal at NW 1st St. and 1st Ave.; the fare is 85¢. *Airport Express* (phone: 305-527-8690) offers transportation to anywhere in Broward County for $6 to $13.

Tri-Rail (phone: 800-TRI-RAIL in Florida; 305-728-8445 elsewhere in the US) operates shuttle bus–rail connections between Miami International and downtown Miami and between Ft. Lauderdale/Hollywood International and downtown Ft. Lauderdale for $3 one way, $5 round trip.

RENTING A CAR

You can rent a car through a travel agent or national rental firm before leaving home, or from a regional or local company once in Miami or Ft. Lauderdale. Reserve in advance.

Most car rental companies require a credit card, although some will accept a substantial cash deposit. The minimum age to rent a car is set by the company; some impose special conditions on drivers above a certain age. Electing to pay for collision damage waiver (CDW) protection will add to the cost of renting a car, but releases you from financial liability for the vehicle being rented. Additional costs include drop-off charges or one-way service fees.

National Car Rental Companies
Alamo (phone: 800-327-9633).
Avis (phone: 800-331-1084).
Budget (phone: 800-472-3325).
Dollar Rent A Car (phone: 800-800-4000).
Hertz (phone: 800-654-3001).
National (phone: 800-227-3876).
Sears Rent-A-Car (phone: 800-527-0770).
Thrifty Rent-A-Car (phone: 800-367-2277).

Regional and Local Car Rental Companies
In Miami
A-Jiffy Rent-A-Car (phone: 305-621-5566).
Delta Auto Rental (phone: 305-526-8755).
General Rent-A-Car (phone: 800-327-7607 or 305-871-3573).
Inter-American Car Rental (phone: 800-327-1278 or 305-871-3030).
Pass Rent-A-Car (phone: 305-871-6262).
Superior Rent-A-Car (phone: 800-237-8106 or 305-649-7012).
Unidas (phone: 305-530-9513).

In Ft. Lauderdale
Air & Sea Rent-A-Car (phone: 305-764-1008).
Arrow Car Rental (phone: 305-776-4500).
Enterprise Rent-A-Car (phone: 305-764-3144).
Lauderdale-by-the-Sea Rent-A-Car (phone: 305-776-4950).
Slaton Rent-A-Car (phone: 305-561-5222).
USA Rent A Car (phone: 305-635-7800).

NOTE *Rent-a-Wreck* (10045 S. Dixie Hwy., Miami; phone: 305-666-9817) rents cars that are well worn but (presumably) mechanically sound. *Prestige Auto Rental and Leasing* (1946 NE 123rd St., Miami; phone: 305-895-0854) rents exotic luxury models.

Package Tours

A package is a collection of travel services that can be purchased in a single transaction. Its principal advantages are convenience and economy — the cost is usually lower than that of the same services bought separately. Tour programs generally can be divided into two categories: escorted or locally hosted (with a set itinerary) and independent (usually more flexible).

When considering a package tour, read the brochure *carefully* to determine what is included and other conditions. Check the company's record with the Better Business Bureau. The *United States Tour Operators Association* (*USTOA;* 211 E. 51st St., Suite 12B, New York, NY 10022; phone: 212-944-5727) also can be helpful in determining a package tour operator's reliability. As with charter flights, always make your check out to the company's escrow account.

Many tour operators offer packages focused on special interests such as the arts, nature study, sports, and other recreations. *All Adventure Travel* (PO Box 4307, Boulder, CO 80306; phone: 800-537-4025 or 303-499-1981) represents such specialized packagers; some also are listed in the *Specialty Travel Index* (305 San Anselmo Ave., Suite 313, San Anselmo, CA 94960; phone: 415-459-4900 in California; 800-442-4922 elsewhere in the US).

For additional organized touring, contact *Eagle Tours and Travel* (6261 Collins Ave., Miami, FL 33140; phone: 305-864-6204) and *Art Deco Tours/Miami Design Preservation League* (1244 Ocean Ave., Miami Beach, FL 33139; phone: 305-672-2014) both offer walking tours; the *Water Taxi Historic Cruise* (Ft. Lauderdale Historical Society; phone: 305-463-4431) sails the New River.

Package Tour Operators

Adventure Tours (9818 Liberty Rd., Randallstown, MD 21133; phone: 410-922-7000 in Baltimore; 800-638-9040 elsewhere in the US).

American Airlines FlyAAway Vacations (phone: 800-321-2121).

American Express Vacations (offices throughout the US; phone: 800-241-1700 or 404-368-5100).

Continental Grand Destinations (phone: 800-634-5555).

Delta's Dream Vacations (phone: 800-872-7786).

Domenico Tours (751 Broadway, Bayonne, NJ 07002; phone: 800-554-8687 or 201-823-8687).

Funway Holidays Funjet (PO Box 1460, Milwaukee, WI 53201-1460; phone: 800-558-3050).

GoGo Tours (69 Spring St., Ramsey, NJ 07446-0507; phone: 201-934-3500).

Travel Tours International (250 W. 49th St., Suite 600, New York, NY 10019; phone: 800-767-8777 or 212-262-0700).

TWA Getaway Vacations (phone: 800-GETAWAY).

Insurance

The first person with whom you should discuss travel insurance is your own insurance broker. You may discover that the insurance you already carry protects you adequately while traveling and that you need little additional coverage. If you charge travel services, the credit card company also may provide some insurance coverage (and other safeguards).

Types of Travel Insurance
Baggage and personal effects insurance: Protects your bags and their contents in case of damage or theft anytime during your travels.

Personal accident and sickness insurance: Covers cases of illness, injury, or death in an accident while traveling.

Trip cancellation and interruption insurance: Guarantees a refund if you must cancel a trip; may reimburse you for the extra travel costs incurred for catching up with a tour or traveling home early.

Default and/or bankruptcy insurance: Provides coverage in the event of default and/or bankruptcy on the part of the tour operator, airline, or other travel supplier.

Flight insurance: Covers accidental injury or death while flying.

Automobile insurance: Provides collision, theft, property damage, and personal liability protection while driving your own or a rented car.

Combination policies: Include any or all of the above.

Disabled Travelers
Make travel arrangements well in advance. Specify to all services involved the nature of your disability to determine if there are accommodations and facilities that meet your needs.

Organizations
ACCENT on Living (PO Box 700, Bloomington, IL 61702; phone: 309-378-2961).

Access: The Foundation for Accessibility by the Disabled (PO Box 356, Malverne, NY 11565; phone: 516-887-5798).

American Foundation for the Blind (15 W. 16th St., New York, NY 10011; phone: 800-232-5463 or 212-620-2147).

Information Center for Individuals with Disabilities (Ft. Point Pl., 1st Floor, 27-43 Wormwood St., Boston, MA 02210; phone: 800-462-5015 in Massachusetts; 617-727-5540 or 617-727-5541 elsewhere in the US; TDD: 617-345-9743).

Mobility International USA (*MIUSA;* PO Box 3551, Eugene, OR 97403; phone: 503-343-1284, both voice and TDD; main office: 228 Borough High St., London SE1 1JX, England; phone: 44-71-403-5688).

National Rehabilitation Information Center (8455 Colesville Rd., Suite 935, Silver Spring, MD 20910; phone: 301-588-9284).

Paralyzed Veterans of America (*PVA;* PVA/ATTS Program, 801 18th St. NW, Washington, DC 20006; phone: 202-872-1300 in Washington, DC; 800-424-8200 elsewhere in the US).

Partners of the Americas (1424 K St. NW, Suite 700, Washington, DC 20005; phone: 800-322-7844 or 202-628-3300).

Royal Association for Disability and Rehabilitation (*RADAR;* 25 Mortimer St., London W1N 8AB, England; phone: 44-71-637-5400).

Society for the Advancement of Travel for the Handicapped (*SATH;* 347 Fifth Ave., Suite 610, New York, NY 10016; phone: 212-447-7284).

Travel Information Service (MossRehab Hospital, 1200 W. Tabor Rd., Philadelphia, PA 19141-3099; phone: 215-456-9600; TDD: 215-456-9602).

Publications

Access Travel: A Guide to the Accessibility of Airport Terminals (Consumer Information Center, Dept. 578Z, Pueblo, CO 81009; phone: 719-948-3334).

Air Transportation of Handicapped Persons (publication #AC-120-32; US Department of Transportation, Distribution Unit, Publications Section, M-443-2, 400 7th St. SW, Washington, DC 20590).

The Diabetic Traveler (PO Box 8223 RW, Stamford, CT 06905; phone: 203-327-5832).

Directory of Travel Agencies for the Disabled and *Travel for the Disabled,* both by Helen Hecker (Twin Peaks Press, PO Box 129, Vancouver, WA 98666; phone: 800-637-CALM or 206-694-2462).

Guide to Traveling with Arthritis (Upjohn Company, PO Box 989, Dearborn, MI 48121).

The Handicapped Driver's Mobility Guide (American Automobile Association, 1000 AAA Dr., Heathrow, FL 32746; phone: 407-444-7000).

Handicapped Travel Newsletter (PO Box 269, Athens, TX 75751; phone: 903-677-1260).

Handi-Travel: A Resource Book for Disabled and Elderly Travellers, by Cinnie Noble (*Canadian Rehabilitation Council for the Disabled,* 45 Sheppard Ave. E., Suite 801, Toronto, Ontario M2N 5W9, Canada; phone: 416-250-7490, both voice and TDD).

Incapacitated Passengers Air Travel Guide (*International Air Transport Association,* Publications Sales Department, 2000 Peel St., Montreal, Quebec H3A 2R4, Canada; phone: 514-844-6311).

Ticket to Safe Travel (*American Diabetes Association,* 1660 Duke St., Alexandria, VA 22314; phone: 800-232-3472 or 703-549-1500).

Travel for the Patient with Chronic Obstructive Pulmonary Disease (Dr. Harold Silver, 1601 18th St. NW, Washington, DC 20009; phone: 202-667-0134).

Travel Tips for Hearing-Impaired People (*American Academy of Otolaryngology,* 1 Prince St., Alexandria, VA 22314; phone: 703-836-4444).

Travel Tips for People with Arthritis (*Arthritis Foundation,* 1314 Spring St. NW, Atlanta, GA 30309; phone: 800-283-7800 or 404-872-7100).

Traveling Like Everybody Else: A Practical Guide for Disabled Travel-

ers, by Jacqueline Freedman and Susan Gersten (Modan Publishing, PO Box 1202, Bellmore, NY 11710; phone: 516-679-1380).

The Wheelchair Traveler, by Douglass R. Annand (123 Ball Hill Rd., Milford, NH 03055; phone: 603-673-4539).

Package Tour Operators

Accessible Journeys (35 W. Sellers Ave., Ridley Park, PA 19078; phone: 215-521-0339).

Accessible Tours/Directions Unlimited (Lois Bonnani, 720 N. Bedford Rd., Bedford Hills, NY 10507; phone: 800-533-5343 or 914-241-1700).

Beehive Business and Leisure Travel (1130 W. Center St., N. Salt Lake, UT 84054; phone: 800-777-5727 or 801-292-4445).

Classic Travel Service (8 W. 40th St., New York, NY 10018; phone: 212-869-2560 in New York State; 800-247-0909 elsewhere in the US).

Evergreen Travel Service (4114 198th St. SW, Suite 13, Lynnwood, WA 98036-6742; phone: 800-435-2288 or 206-776-1184).

Flying Wheels Travel (143 W. Bridge St., PO Box 382, Owatonna, MN 55060; phone: 800-535-6790 or 507-451-5005).

Good Neighbor Travel Service (124 S. Main St., Viroqua, WI 54665; phone: 608-637-2128).

The Guided Tour (7900 Old York Rd., Suite 114B, Elkins Park, PA 19117-2339; phone: 800-783-5841 or 215-782-1370).

Hinsdale Travel (201 E. Ogden Ave., Hinsdale, IL 60521; phone: 708-325-1335 or 708-469-7349).

MedEscort International (ABE International Airport, PO Box 8766, Allentown, PA 18105; phone: 800-255-7182 or 215-791-3111).

Prestige World Travel (5710-X High Point Rd., Greensboro, NC 27407; phone: 800-476-7737 or 919-292-6690).

Sprout (893 Amsterdam Ave., New York, NY 10025; phone: 212-222-9575).

Weston Travel Agency (134 N. Cass Ave., PO Box 1050, Westmont, IL 60559; phone: 708-968-2513 in Illinois; 800-633-3725 elsewhere in the US).

Single Travelers

The travel industry is not very fair to people who vacation by themselves—they often end up paying more than those traveling in pairs. Services catering to singles match travel companions, offer travel arrangements with shared accommodations, and provide useful information and discounts. Also consult publications such as *Going Solo* (Doerfer Communications, PO Box 123, Apalachicola, FL 32329; phone: 904-653-8848) and *Traveling on Your Own,* by Eleanor Berman (Random House, Order Dept., 400 Hahn Rd., Westminster, MD 21157; phone: 800-733-3000).

Organizations and Companies

Gallivanting (515 E. 79th St., Suite 20F, New York, NY 10021; phone: 800-933-9699 or 212-988-0617).

Jane's International and Sophisticated Women Travelers (2603 Bath Ave., Brooklyn, NY 11214; phone: 718-266-2045).

Marion Smith Singles (611 Prescott Pl., N. Woodmere, NY 11581; phone: 516-791-4852, 516-791-4865, or 212-944-2112).

Partners-in-Travel (11660 Chenault St., Suite 119, Los Angeles, CA 90049; phone: 310-476-4869).

Singles in Motion (545 W. 236th St., Riverdale, NY 10463; phone: 718-884-4464).

Singleworld (401 Theodore Fremd Ave., Rye, NY 10580; phone: 800-223-6490 or 914-967-3334).

Solo Flights (63 High Noon Rd., Weston, CT 06883; phone: 203-226-9993).

Suddenly Singles Tours (161 Dreiser Loop, Bronx, NY 10475; phone: 718-379-8800 in New York City; 800-859-8396 elsewhere in the US).

Travel Companion Exchange (PO Box 833, Amityville, NY 11701; phone: 516-454-0880).

Travel Companions (Atrium Financial Center, 1515 N. Federal Hwy., Suite 300, Boca Raton, FL 33432; phone: 800-383-7211 or 407-393-6448).

Travel in Two's (239 N. Broadway, Suite 3, N. Tarrytown, NY 10591; phone: 914-631-8301 in New York State; 800-692-5252 elsewhere in the US).

Older Travelers

Special discounts and more free time are just two factors that have given older travelers a chance to see the world at affordable prices. Many travel suppliers offer senior discounts — sometimes only to members of certain senior citizen organizations, which offer other benefits. Prepare your itinerary with one eye on your own physical condition and the other on a map, and remember that it's easy to overdo when traveling.

Publications

The Mature Traveler (GEM Publishing Group, PO Box 50820, Reno, NV 89513-0820; phone: 702-786-7419).

The Senior Citizen's Guide to Budget Travel in the US and Canada, by Paige Palmer (Pilot Books, 103 Cooper St., Babylon, NY 11702; phone: 516-422-2225).

Take a Camel to Lunch and Other Adventures for Mature Travelers, by Nancy O'Connell (Bristol Publishing Enterprises, PO Box 1737, San

Leandro, CA 94577; phone: 510-895-4461 in California; 800-346-4889 elsewhere in the US).

Travel Tips for Older Americans (Publication #044-000-02270-2; Superintendent of Documents, US Government Printing Office, PO Box 371954, Pittsburgh, PA 15250-7954; phone: 202-783-3238).

Unbelievably Good Deals & Great Adventures That You Absolutely Can't Get Unless You're Over 50, by Joan Rattner Heilman (Contemporary Books, 180 N. Michigan Ave., Chicago, IL 60601; phone: 312-782-9181).

Organizations

American Association of Retired Persons (*AARP;* 601 E St. NW, Washington, DC 20049; phone: 202-434-2277).

Golden Companions (PO Box 754, Pullman, WA 99163-0754; phone: 208-858-2183).

Mature Outlook (Customer Service Center, 6001 N. Clark St., Chicago, IL 60660; phone: 800-336-6330).

National Council of Senior Citizens (1331 F St. NW, Washington, DC 20004; phone: 202-347-8800).

Package Tour Operators

Elderhostel (PO Box 1959, Wakefield, MA 01880-5959; phone: 617-426-7788).

Evergreen Travel Service (4114 198th St. SW, Suite 13, Lynnwood, WA 98036-6742; phone: 800-435-2288 or 206-776-1184).

Gadabout Tours (700 E. Tahquitz Canyon Way, Palm Springs, CA 92262; phone: 800-952-5068 or 619-325-5556).

Grand Circle Travel (347 Congress St., Boston, MA 02210; phone: 800-221-2610 or 617-350-7500).

Grandtravel (6900 Wisconsin Ave., Suite 706, Chevy Chase, MD 20815; phone: 800-247-7651 or 301-986-0790).

Interhostel (UNH Division of Continuing Education, 6 Garrison Ave., Durham, NH 03824; phone: 800-733-9753 or 603-862-1147).

OmniTours (104 Wilmont Rd., Deerfield, IL 60015; phone: 800-962-0060 or 708-374-0088).

Saga International Holidays (222 Berkeley St., Boston, MA 02116; phone: 800-343-0273 or 617-262-2262).

Money Matters

TRAVELER'S CHECKS AND CREDIT CARDS

It's wise to carry traveler's checks while on the road, since they are replaceable if stolen or lost. You can buy traveler's checks at banks and some are available by mail or phone. Although most major credit cards enjoy wide domestic and international acceptance, not every hotel, restaurant, or shop in Miami and Ft. Lauderdale accepts all (or in some cases any) credit cards. Keep a separate list of all traveler's checks (noting those that you have cashed) and the names and numbers of your credit cards. Both traveler's check and credit card companies have international numbers to call for information or in the event of loss or theft.

CASH MACHINES

Automated teller machines (ATMs) are increasingly common worldwide. Most banks participate in one of the international ATM networks; cardholders can withdraw cash from any machine in the same network using either a "bank" card or, in some cases, a credit card. At the time of this writing, most ATMs belong to the *CIRRUS* (phone: 800-4-CIRRUS) or *PLUS* (phone: 800-THE-PLUS) network. For further information, ask at your bank branch.

SENDING MONEY

Should the need arise, it is possible to have money sent to you via the services provided by *American Express* (*MoneyGram;* phone: 800-926-9400 or 800-666-3997 for information; 800-866-8800 for money transfers) or *Western Union Financial Services* (phone: 800-325-4176).

Time Zone

Miami and Ft. Lauderdale are in the eastern standard time zone. Daylight saving time is observed from the first Sunday in April until the last Sunday in October.

Business Hours

Miami and Ft. Lauderdale maintain business hours that are fairly standard throughout the US: 9 AM to 5 PM, Mondays through Fridays. Banks generally are open weekdays from 9 AM to 3 PM. Retail stores and department stores usually are open Mondays through Saturdays from 10 AM to 9 PM. Most larger stores and malls are open on Sundays from noon to 6 PM.

Mail

Miami's main post office (2200 NW 72 Ave.; phone: 305-470-0243) is open weekdays from 8:30 AM to 5 PM and Saturdays from 9:30 AM to 1:30 PM. The downtown office is located at 500 NW 2nd Ave. (phone: 371-2911);

the office in Miami Beach is located at 1300 Washington Ave. (phone: 531-3763).

In Ft. Lauderdale, the main post office (1900 W. Oakland Park Blvd.; phone: 305-735-3596 or 305-527-2074) is open weekdays from 7:30 AM to 7 PM and Saturdays from 8:30 AM to 2 PM. The downtown location is 330 SW 2nd St. (phone: 761-1172).

For other post office branches, call the main offices or check the yellow pages. Stamps also are available at most hotel desks and from public vending machines. For rapid, overnight delivery to other cities, use *Express Mail* (available at post offices), *Federal Express* (phone: 800-238-5355), or *DHL Worldwide Express* (phone: 800-225-5345).

You can have mail sent to you care of your hotel (marked "Guest Mail, Hold for Arrival") or to a post office ("c/o General Delivery, Hold for 30 Days"). *American Express* offices also will hold mail for customers ("c/o Client Letter Service"); information on this service is provided in their pamphlet *Travelers' Companion*. Members of the *American Automobile Association* (*AAA*; 1000 AAA Dr., Heathrow, FL 32746-5063; phone: 407-444-8544) also can have mail (marked "Hold for Arrival") held at *AAA* branches.

Telephone

The area code for both Miami and Ft. Lauderdale is 305. To make a long-distance call, dial 1 + the area code + the local number. The nationwide number for information is 555-1212; if you need a number in another area code, dial 1 + the area code + 555-1212. (If you don't know the area code, dial 0 for an operator.)

Although you can use a telephone company calling card number on any phone, pay phones that take major credit cards (*American Express, MasterCard, Visa,* and so on) are increasingly common. Also available are combined telephone calling cards/bank credit cards, such as *AT&T Universal* (phone: 800-662-7759), *Executive Telecard International* (phone: 800-950-3800), and *Sprint* (phone: 800-877-4646). *MCI VisaPhone* (phone: 800-866-0099) can add phone card privileges to your existing *Visa* card.

Long-distance telephone services that help you avoid the surcharges that hotels routinely add to phone bills are provided by *American Telephone and Telegraph* (*AT&T Communications,* International Information Service, 635 Grant St., Pittsburgh, PA 15219; phone: 800-874-4000), *MCI* (323 3rd St. SE, Cedar Rapids, IA 52401; phone: 800-444-3333), *Metromedia Communications Corp.* (1 International Center, 100 NE Loop 410, San Antonio, TX 78216; phone: 800-275-0200), and *Sprint* (offices throughout the US; phone: 800-877-4000). Some hotels still may charge a fee for line usage.

Also useful are the *AT&T 800 Travel Directory* (available at *AT&T*

Phone Centers or by calling 800-426-8686), the *Toll-Free Travel & Vacation Information Directory* (Pilot Books, 103 Cooper St., Babylon, NY 11702; phone: 516-422-2225), and *The Phone Booklet* (Scott American Corporation, PO Box 88, W. Redding, CT 06896; phone: 203-938-2955).

Medical Aid

In an emergency: Dial 911 for assistance, "0" for an operator, or go directly to the emergency room of the nearest hospital.

Hospitals

In Miami

Cedars Medical Center (1400 NW 12th Ave.; phone: 800-327-7386 or 305-325-5511).

Jackson Memorial Hospital (1611 NW 12th Ave.; phone: 305-325-7429).

Mercy Hospital (3663 S. Miami Ave.; phone: 305-854-4400).

Mt. Sinai Medical Center (4300 Alton Rd., Miami Beach; phone: 305-674-2200).

In Ft. Lauderdale

Hollywood Memorial Hospital (3501 Johnson St., Hollywood; phone: 305-987-2000).

Holy Cross Hospital (4725 N. Federal Hwy., phone: 305-771-8000).

North Beach Hospital (2835 N. Ocean Blvd.; phone: 305-568-1000).

Pharmacies

Eckerd: Open 24 hours daily. **In Miami:** 9031 SW 107 Ave. (phone: 305-274-6776); and 182 NE 1825 St., North Miami Beach (phone: 305-932-5740). **In Ft. Lauderdale:** 154 N. University Dr. (phone: 305-432-5510).

Walgreens: Open 24 hours daily; prescriptions available until 9 PM weekdays, until 6 PM weekends. **In Ft. Lauderdale:** 3101 N. Ocean Blvd. (phone: 305-563-3800).

Additional Resources

International Association of Medical Assistance to Travelers (IAMAT; 417 Center St., Lewiston, NY 14092; phone: 716-754-4883).

International Health Care Service (440 E. 69th St., New York, NY 10021; phone: 212-746-1601).

International SOS Assistance (PO Box 11568, Philadelphia, PA 19116; phone: 800-523-8930 or 215-244-1500).

Medic Alert Foundation (2323 Colorado Ave., Turlock, CA 95380; phone: 800-ID-ALERT or 209-668-3333).

TravMed (PO Box 10623, Baltimore, MD 21285-0623; phone: 800-732-5309 or 410-296-5225).

Legal Aid

If you don't have, or cannot reach, your own attorney, most cities offer legal referral services maintained by county bar associations. These services ensure that anyone in need of legal representation gets it and can match you with a local attorney. In Miami, contact the *Florida Bar Association* (phone: 800-342-8011 in Florida or 904-561-5600); in Ft. Lauderdale, contact the *Broward County Bar Association* (phone: 305-764-8040). If you must appear in court, you are entitled to court-appointed representation if you can't obtain a lawyer or can't afford one.

For Further Information

The **Greater Miami Convention and Visitors Bureau** is located at 701 Brickell Ave., Suite 2700, Miami, FL 33131 (phone: 305-539-3000). The **Greater Ft. Lauderdale Convention and Visitors Bureau** is located at 200 E. Las Olas Blvd., Suite 1500, Ft. Lauderdale, FL 33301 (phone: 305-765-4466). For other local tourist information, see *Sources and Resources* in THE CITY.

The Cities

Miami – Miami Beach

Difficult as it is to find adults over 30 who actually were born in Miami, practically all residents regard themselves — somehow — as natives. The year-round population of the greater Miami area is 1.8 million. Although visitors often consider Miami a haven for seniors, residents over age 65 constitute only 15% of the population in Dade County, and 20% in Broward County.

Newcomers escaping economic woes and harsh winters elsewhere arrive in droves daily. This figure swells tremendously during the winter months, when millions of "snowbirds" arrive. "Snowbird" is a tricky term as used in Miami. It refers primarily to tourists escaping the northeastern freeze, but just as easily could describe South Americans in town for a midsummer shopping spree. Some even distinguish between "snowbirds," who stay for the winter, and "snowflakes," who own homes here but fly back and forth to another home for short stays. Sprawling across 2,054 square miles of land (the metropolitan area also encompasses 354 square miles of water), Miami is a huge and cosmopolitan metropolis; however, it has managed to maintain a provincial quality in spite of commercialized efforts to identify it as a tropical New York City.

This is due in part to the way in which the metropolitan area is organized. Greater Miami — actually metropolitan Dade County — comprises almost 3 dozen municipalities and a scattering of totally unincorporated areas. This breeds something of a small-town attitude in residents who have a chauvinistic interest in their own enclaves. They identify with the whole city — it is, after all, all Miami. But their particular neighborhood is where they live.

In even larger part, this attitude is due to a deeply rooted tradition of hospitality and neighborliness that can only be described as somehow "Southern" — even while admitting that a large number of the residents who display it most openly are either recent arrivals or part-time snowbirds.

From an early, small settlement consisting primarily of Indians around the government's Fort Dallas, Miami's growth was slow until one Julia Tuttle tickled the fancy of a railroad tycoon with some orange blossoms. Tuttle was an early settler who was eager to see Miami become part of a railroad hookup with the rest of the state. She petitioned railroad magnate Henry M. Flagler to extend his *Florida East Coast Railroad* south from Palm Beach to Miami. He seemed in no great hurry to do so until the Big Freeze of 1894–95 devastated most of Florida's fruit and vegetable crops. Most, but not all. When he received a box of frost-free orange blossoms from Tuttle, he suddenly got her point. Soon enough Miami had rail access to the rest of the world.

Flagler's railroad didn't stop here. On January 22, 1912, he rode his own special car into Key West on a trackbed constructed at great hardship over 156 miles of water and marshy land from Miami. Hurricanes brought an end to Key West rail service in 1935, but 3 years later Flagler's trackbed was used to build the Overseas Highway, which still connects the mainland to Key West. Flagler always dreamed big. At his death in 1913, at age 83, he was still hoping to extend the line from Key West to Cuba.

It wasn't long until the rest of the world was glad of access to South Florida. Attracted by year-round warmth and sunshine, thousands of new residents began pouring into the area, only one step behind hundreds of shrewd (and even occasionally honest) entrepreneurs. Miami and Miami Beach became glittering wintertime destinations and later began drawing vacationers in summer, as well. While Miami Beach still remains tourist-oriented, the city of Miami has developed into a flourishing international business hub. Together they are an attractive combination that lures a wide variety of visitors.

Jolted into the realization that their fun-and-sun city had begun to lose its good reputation about 10 years ago, the local government began implementing a series of major programs dedicated to restoration and redevelopment. They began by renewing the beaches, sprucing up oceanfront hotels, and dressing up the historic hotel district in Miami Beach. The improvements weren't just for tourists. The Miami River was cleaned up and the city expanded its park system. Ecologists have pushed for strict enforcement of environmental laws to protect the delicate marine ecology, reflecting a determination to keep the good life good in South Florida. The result is truly a new Miami, attractive to residents and to visitors, clean, beautiful, and gleaming in the bright Florida sunlight.

In August 1992, a hurricane named Andrew dramatically changed the landscape. The country's third worst and most costly recorded hurricane, Andrew smashed through southern Florida with winds at 164 miles per hour. In its wake lay a 30-mile-wide swath of devastation resulting in $20 billion in damages, leaving 160,000 homeless. Amazingly, not many tourist attractions were affected and, except on Key Biscayne, virtually none of the hotels suffered long-lasting damage. And though some foliage is sparser than it used to be, Miami continues to flourish — thanks to a massive replanting effort and a benign climate.

That Miami still has the image of offering the good life is attested to by the waves of new residents who continue to settle in one or another of Miami's municipalities each year. Today, many of these new residents are Spanish-speaking, a large number of them coming from the steady flow of refugees from Cuba. Others have fled recent violence in Central America and poverty in the Caribbean; still others are affluent Venezuelans and Colombians who occupy their homes only part of the year. The current mayor of the city, Xavier Suarez, is of Cuban origin.

This Latin immigration has turned metropolitan Miami into a city where you can buy anything from fried bananas to Chilean wine, and where Spanish is the first language of more than 60% of the year-round residents. More recently, the Latin influence has been felt in Miami's art world, as an appreciation of and growing demand for the works of such renowned Latin American artists as Rufino Tamayo, Wilfredo Lam, Roberto Matta, and Armando Morales have made the city the undisputed center of Latin American art in the US. A group of recently opened galleries — most featuring the works of Latin American artists and sculptors — has had an extraordinary impact on the once-struggling Miami art community (see *Shopping*). Together with the higher-priced works of their famous colleagues, the affordably priced art of some up-and-coming Latins is drawing a loyal following of collectors and investors alike.

There also is an only slightly smaller tide of newcomers and regular visitors from the Caribbean, Britain, and Europe, bringing Miami an even more international aspect, with additions like Jamaican-Chinese restaurants, Haitian grocery stores, and elegant French cuisine. Miami today is a tropical melange of cultures, languages, ethnic eateries, and ambiences.

Coral Gables is Miami's prestigious planned community, conceived and built by entrepreneur George Merrick in the 1920s. Elegant gates to the city still are standing in various spots around the Gables, relics of Merrick's grand scheme to build "a place where castles in Spain are made real." Strict building codes prevail, and woe to the newcomer who tries to put a flat roof on his home. In a county where almost all the streets are laid out in a simple north-south-east-west numbered grid, Coral Gables sticks to its Spanish and Italian street names and layout; for those unfamiliar with its winding ways, it's easy to get lost here. Just 10 minutes from the airport, it also has become one of the favored locales for multinational corporations doing business in Latin America. For more information see *Tour 4: Cruising through Coral Gables* in DIRECTIONS.

South Miami, adjacent to the Gables, is reminiscent of an Anywhere, USA, crossroads town. Farther south, in an unincorporated part of Dade County called Kendall, lie expensive estates with pools and tennis courts, where not so long ago there were only extensive mango and avocado groves. Many of these properties are still recuperating from Hurricane Andrew's damage, which dealt its fiercest blow in the Homestead area.

Closer to downtown Miami is the area known as Coconut Grove, a base for wealthy year-round and winter residents and not so wealthy colonies of artists and writers. Here crafts shops stand next to expensive boutiques; health food stores sit alongside posh restaurants; and old Florida houses of coral rock nestle close to modern high-rises. Luxurious yachts and sailboats lie in Biscayne Bay, and the Grove's younger generation lies all over Peacock Park. (For more information, see *Tour 3: Coconut Grove* in DIRECTIONS.) The area known as Little Havana is part of the center city, but is really a small world unto itself, with its Latin culture intact. Increasingly, it dominates Miami's political and commercial life (see below and *Tour 5: Little Havana* in DIRECTIONS).

Also in a class by themselves are the communities of Miami Beach and Key Biscayne. Besides its glittering hotel row, the Beach and the small manmade islands between it and the mainland house some of the most luxurious waterfront homes in Greater Miami. The South Beach section has undergone a tremendous renaissance, with the rehabilitation of many classic Art Deco apartment buildings and hotels, as well as the construction of new high-rise condominiums. Key Biscayne, although badly hit by Hurricane Andrew, still has rows of luxury high-rises, expensive houses, and simple bungalows. Unfortunately it will take the area's once excellent parks and beaches many years to recover. But despite Andrew, Miami's Art Deco District has replaced New York's posh Hampton beach havens as the escape of choice for such luminaries as native Floridian Lauren Hutton, resident Floridian Gloria Estefan, Anne Bancroft and Mel Brooks, and John F. Kennedy, Jr. Attracted by the climate and good buys in real estate, celebrities, wanna-bes, and just plain folks have become the area's newest snowbirds.

With a mean annual temperature of 75F, 85,000-plus registered boats, miles of improved beaches, 61 marinas, 11,829 acres of parks, 354 square miles of protected waters, and 3,200 more of sheltered waters, Miami's vital statistics support its reputation as a sunny, water-oriented resort. Yet in recent years, the city has become a major urban area, with an economic diversity associated with cities of comparable size. To a large extent, this is a result of the Latin American–Caribbean connection. The population has grown by 54% since the early 1970s, and employment has doubled in local business and industry. Indeed, the export trade is expected soon to overtake tourism as the number one local industry.

Traditional tourist migration from the Northeast has slowed, due in great measure to the growing attractions of the Tampa–*Walt Disney World*–Orlando–Daytona axis; nevertheless, increased numbers of travelers from Europe and the Orient have taken up the slack. The drug problems and race-related flare-ups that have brought Miami unwanted national headlines in the past have largely been defused — though they remain very much alive in the public consciousness. With the city's new appearance and a calming of tensions, promoters anticipate encouraging increases in tourism.

Still, this area once was a small village stuck on the side of a swamp. In spite of its unappealing natural setting, Miami — and after it, other parts of South Florida — has evolved into America's single greatest tourist magnet. It's probably not true, as an old Florida legend claims, that a race of giants once lived here, but it surely is true that Miami today possesses a gigantic will that wants more than anything else to grow — and grow and grow and grow. Mother Nature's anger aside, it's hard to believe the new, revitalized — and resilient — Miami will not have its way.

Miami–Miami Beach At-a-Glance

SEEING THE CITY

The *Rusty Pelican* (3201 Rickenbacker Cswy., Key Biscayne) and the *Bayside Seafood* restaurant (3501 Rickenbacker Cswy., Key Biscayne) look across Biscayne Bay at the spectacular Miami skyline and have outdoor seating areas with good views; *Crawdaddy's* restaurant (1 Washington Ave.), on the southernmost tip of Miami Beach, affords spectacular views of Government Cut, the throughway for the dozens of cruise ships that dock at the Port of Miami.

Miami is largely a waterfront city, and one of the best ways to get to know it is by boat. Besides the *Island Queen,* which leaves from *Miamarina* (see *Special Places,* below), *Nikko's Gold Coast* cruises set sail out of *Haulover Marina* (10800 Collins Ave.; phone: 945-5461); the *Spirit* — with lunch, dinner, and "moonlight party" cruises at 2:30, 7, and 10:30 PM, respectively — departs from the *Fontainebleau Hilton* hotel (4441 Collins Ave.; phone: 458-4999); and *Harrah's Belle,* a replica of a paddle wheeler, offers sightseeing and dining cruises from the *Miami Beach Eden Roc* hotel (4525 Collins Ave.; phone: 672-5911). The *Heritage of Miami* is a dramatic tall ship that offers daily 2-hour tours of Biscayne Bay. It docks behind *Bayside Marketplace* (phone: 442-9697) and is available for charters.

Popular narrated sightseeing trips are offered by *Old Town Trolley* for $16; $7 for children under 12. The 90-minute tour provides on-and-off-again access at no extra charge for those wishing to spend time at different spots along the route. Tours leave every half hour, boarding at seven locations (phone: 374-TOUR).

Knowledgeable and folksy narrated walking tours are offered by Dr. Paul S. George, a local history professor. Itineraries include Little Havana, the Art Deco District, Coconut Grove, and Coral Gables (phone: 858-6021).

For a different view of the city, take *Miami Helicopter*'s flight over Miami Beach from Opa-Locka Airport; cost is $300 per hour for one passenger, $500 for four passengers. Available year-round (phone: 685-8223). On the south side of MacArthur Causeway, between downtown Miami and Miami Beach, try *Dade Helicopter Rides* (phone: 374-3737), flights are $49 per person for 10 minutes, $89 for 20 minutes, $119 for 30 minutes; half price for children under 12, who must be accompanied by two adults; or *Chalk's International Airlines* (phone: 371-8628 or 800-4-CHALKS), which charges $39.50 for adults, $29.50 for children 2 to 11 for half-hour flights.

Tropical Balloons (phone: 666-6645) offers an hour-long balloon tour of downtown Miami, Biscayne Bay, and the Everglades for $140 per person.

SPECIAL PLACES

The best way to see Greater Miami is by car.

> **NOTE** Bill Baggs Cape Florida State Park, a 406-acre spread of bike paths, woodlands, picnic areas, and a mile-long beach, was one of Hurricane Andrew's victims. As we went to press, work was underway to restore this area, a perennial favorite on our list of "Special Places." It's worth a call to see if the park is back in business at the time of your visit (1200 Crandon Blvd.; phone: 361-5811).

PORT OF MIAMI Every week thousands of people depart from here on Caribbean cruises, making Miami the world's busiest cruise port. About 3 million passengers embark annually; 18 cruise ships make it their home port, primarily offering 3- and 4-day Bahamas-bound trips and 1-week eastern or western Caribbean itineraries.

Cruises aren't free, but watching the tourist-laden ocean liners turn around in the narrow channel that leads to the open sea is. With the rise of terrorism a few years back, increased security measures were taken that now prevent non-cruising visitors from boarding ships. However, you can park your car on the MacArthur Causeway between downtown Miami and Miami Beach and watch the ships maneuver. Or have a cool drink at an outdoor café in the Art Deco District and watch the behemoths glide out to sea. Most ships leave Fridays, Saturdays, Sundays, and Mondays from 4 to 7 PM, but you'll spot the largest outbound fleets on Saturdays and Sundays around 4 to 5 PM.

Many vacationers will take a cruise before or after a Miami visit. Several day cruises also are offered (see *Day Cruises* in DIVERSIONS). Among the cruise lines serving the port are *Carnival Cruise Lines* (phone: 800-432-5424), *Chandris Fantasy Cruises* (phone: 800-437-3111), *Commodore Cruise Line* (phone: 800-832-1122), *Costa Cruises* (phone: 800-462-6782), *Dolphin Cruise Line* (phone: 800-222-1003), *Ivaran Line* (phone: 800-451-1639), *Majesty Cruise Line* (phone: 536-0000 or 800 532-7788), *Norwegian Cruise Line* (phone: 800 327-7030), *Royal Caribbean Cruise Line* (phone: 800-327-0271), *SeaEscape* (phone: 800-432-0900), and *Starlite Cruises* (phone: 800-354-5005). For port information, call 530-8847.

BASS MUSEUM OF ART The building itself is listed on the National Registry of Historic Places for its classic Art Deco, Key stone design, which means it was built of stone taken from the Florida Keys, and influenced by French Art Deco. The outside is adorned with carved nautical figures, and inside, the small museum counts several gems in its permanent collection, among them works by Botticelli, Ghirlandajo, Rembrandt, and Rubens. For more information see *Tour 1: South Beach — The Art Deco District* in DIRECTIONS. Changing exhibitions, lectures, concerts, readings and a classic film series complete the picture. Open 10 AM to 5 PM Tuesdays through Saturdays and 1 to 5 PM Sundays. Admission charge; no admission charge for children under 16. 2121 Park Ave. (off Collins Ave.), Miami Beach (phone: 673-7533).

ART DECO DISTRICT A drive or stroll through this area will convince you that you're in a decidedly different Miami, and will forever banish images of the city as a geriatric center. New and restored buildings, hotels, and cafés gleam with façades of shocking pink, bright turquoise, palpitating peach, and Day-Glo yellow. During the mid-1980s, local preservationists decided to upgrade the South Beach area, from Ocean Drive to Lenox Court, which was in a state of complete ruin. Over 800 buildings were rehabilitated and redecorated in a combination of Bauhaus and Art Moderne styles, which was dubbed — though not all architecturally authentic — "Art Deco." Española Way, between 14th and 15th Streets, from Drexel to Washington Avenues, has also undergone large-scale renovation. The Spanish Renaissance-style buildings — many have funky shops and art galleries on the ground floors — have been painted in warm coral tones with gaily striped awnings flapping in the breeze; gaslight lamps lend a romantic glow. For more information see *Quintessential Miami* in DIVERSIONS and *Tour 1: South Beach — The Art Deco District* in DIRECTIONS.

MIAMARINA Sightseeing and charter boats berth in this downtown marina adjacent to the *Bayside* complex (see below). Board the *Island Queen* (phone: 379-5119) for a daily 2-hour circle cruise of Biscayne Bay, viewing waterfront estates and residential islands. The marina is open daily from 7 AM to 11 PM. Admission charge. 400 SE 2nd Ave. (phone: 579-6955).

BAYSIDE MARKETPLACE On 20 acres of Biscayne Bay shoreline, this complex includes 160 shops and eating establishments, plus great views of the boats docking at the adjacent *Miamarina*. (Charter boats may be hired here, or you can catch a sightseeing ride aboard the *Nikko* to Biscayne Bay or sail to Ft. Lauderdale; phone: 945-5461 or 921-1193.) Stroll the 2-story peach-tinted buildings housing folk art displayed on pushcarts and at upscale boutiques. Among the jumping spots is *Dick Clark's American Bandstand Grill*, with TV sets showing old "American Bandstand" clips; the perennial teenager himself sometimes makes an appearance. Entertainment areas provide the setting for strolling jugglers and cartoon-costumed characters, and a life-size reproduction of the HMS *Bounty*. Built for the 1960 film *Mutiny on the Bounty*, the ship docks here from April to October (admission charge). *Bayside* is open Mondays through Saturdays from 10 AM to 10 PM and Sundays from noon to 8 PM; restaurants, other than those in the Food Arcade, often remain open later. Visitors may arrive by *Metrorail*'s PeopleMover, public bus, *Old Town Trolley*, car (parking available), or by boat. Entrance at NE 4th St. and Biscayne Blvd. (401 Biscayne Blvd.; phone: 577-3344).

LITTLE HAVANA, CALLE OCHO (8TH STREET) The real Latin flame burns in this community (see *Quintessential Miami* in DIVERSIONS, and *Tour 5: Little Havana* in DIRECTIONS), founded by Cubans who left the island after Castro's takeover. Shops feature handmade jewelry, dolls, and works of art. Fruit stands, bakeries, restaurants, and coffee stalls offer authentic Latin food. Try *Málaga* (740 SW 8th St.; phone: 858-4224) or *Versailles* (3555 SW 8th St.; phone: 445-7614) for lunch or dinner — roast pork with rice and black-bean sauce, then flan (a custard covered with caramel syrup) for dessert, followed by a cup of espresso at a sidewalk stall. Watch cigars being hand-rolled by Cuban experts in exile at *Padrón Cigars,* but never on Sunday (1566 W. Flagler St.; phone: 643-2117).

CARIBBEAN MARKETPLACE Designed by Haitian architect Charles Harrison Pawley, this vividly colored marketplace in Little Haiti — influenced by the tin roof and yellow-and-orange walls of the *Iron Marketplace* in Haiti's capital city of Port-au-Prince — recently received national recognition from the American Institute of Architects. Housed here are 2 dozen shops offering fresh produce, fish, Caribbean arts and crafts, records, and tapes. 59th St. and NE 2nd Ave. (phone: 751-4692).

METRO-DADE CULTURAL CENTER This huge, $25-million downtown complex, designed by Philip Johnson, provides a tranquil Spanish-style oasis in the midst of dingy commercial buildings. It houses the *Center for the Fine Arts* (open from 10 AM to 5 PM Tuesdays, Wednesdays, Fridays, and Saturdays, 10 AM to 9 PM on Thursdays, and noon to 5 PM on Sundays; admission charge; phone: 375-1700), which features traveling exhibitions. The *Historical Museum of South Florida* (open from 10 AM to 5 PM Mondays through Wednesdays, Fridays, and Saturdays, and Thursday and Sunday afternoons; admission charge; phone: 375-1492) has excellent exhibitions on Spanish exploration, Indian civilization, and maritime history. It's almost a microcosm of the groups that have settled here, with contributions by the Cubans, Jews, blacks, and others who make up Miami's unique ethnic tapestry. The Miami-Dade Public Library also is here (open 9 AM to 6 PM Mondays through Thursdays, and Sunday afternoons; phone: 375-BOOK). The cultural center is at 101 W. Flagler St. (phone: 375-1700).

METROZOO Miami's cageless zoo was extremely hard hit by Hurricane Andrew, with $15.5 million in damages. Particularly devastated was the free-flight aviary and its 300 exotic birds. But the Bengal tigers, elephants, chimpanzees, and other favorites roving through the 290-acre site still provide visitors with a full day's entertainment. Be aware that the monorail tracks were destroyed, so wear comfortable shoes. There's a restaurant on the premises. Open daily. Admission charge. 12400 SW 152nd St. (phone: 251-0401).

MIAMI SEAQUARIUM You can see the creatures who live in the oceans at South Florida's largest tropical marine aquarium. Among the 10,000 creatures swimming around the tide pools, jungle islands, and tanks (under a geodesic dome) are killer whales, sharks, sea lions, and performing seals and dolphins. The real stars, though, are Lolita, a killer whale, and Flipper, of TV fame (not the original dolphin, who starred in many episodes filmed here many years ago). Flipper performs in a stadium where audience members are often videotaped alongside the dolphins; tapes may be purchased as souvenirs. Established in 1955, the *Seaquarium* has been expanded, and is now better than ever. There are 18 all-new shows daily, including one with Salty, star of the TV film *Salty the Sea Lion*. There's a cafeteria on the premises. Open daily from 9:30 AM to 6 PM. Admission charge. 4400 Rickenbacker Cswy., Key Biscayne (phone: 361-5705).

MIAMI MARINE STADIUM This 6,500-seat roofed grandstand on Biscayne Bay hosts Miami's big shows, as well as powerboat races such as the *Budweiser Unlimited Hydroplane Regatta*, water shows, outdoor concerts, and fireworks displays. Check newspapers for details. 3601 Rickenbacker Cswy., Key Biscayne (phone: 361-6732 or 361-6730).

MICCOSUKEE INDIAN VILLAGE Just 25 miles west of Miami, descendants of Florida's original settlers are maintaining the lifestyle of their forebears. Among the attractions are alligator wrestling, crafts demonstrations, and airboat rides. Open daily from 9 AM to 5 PM. Admission charge. US 41 (Tamiami Trail) West (phone: 223-8380 weekdays or 223-8388 weekends).

VIZCAYA MUSEUM A palatial estate where James Deering, the International Harvester magnate, reaped his personal harvest. Built in 1916, the 70-room Venetian palazzo, with 34 rooms open to the public, is furnished with European antiques, precious china, and artworks from the 15th to the 19th centuries. The Roman sculpture, 17th-century Italian marble tables, and a Chinese snuff-bottle collection are very special. Not surprisingly, this is the site of Miami's annual *Italian Renaissance Festival*. The 10 acres of formal gardens, with fountains, grottoes, and statuary, as well as wonderful plant life, were badly damaged by Hurricane Andrew, and although they've been cleaned up, it will take years for the trees and shrubs to return to their former splendor. However the house alone is worth the trip. Guided tours available. Open from 9:30 AM to 4:30 PM daily except *Christmas Day*. Admission charge. 3251 S. Miami Ave., just off US 1 (phone: 579-2708 or 579-4626).

MUSEUM OF SCIENCE AND SPACE TRANSIT PLANETARIUM Exhibitions on a coral reef and the Everglades are enlightening, and there's a participatory science arcade, a wildlife center housing 180 live animals, and a history of cartography display. Kids love the hands-on exhibits and mini-shows on Florida natural life. The planetarium has several shows daily, and inspired visitors can search for the stars themselves, in the evenings, with the

Southern Cross Observatory telescope atop the building. Open daily from 10 AM to 6 PM; closed *Christmas Day* and *Thanksgiving*. Admission charge. 3280 S. Miami Ave. (phone: 854-4247 for general information; 854-2222 for the planetarium).

FAIRCHILD TROPICAL GARDEN Founded by a tax attorney with a touch of the poet in him, this might just be one of the most lyrical tax shelters imaginable — 83 acres of paradise with tropical and subtropical plants and trees (something's always blooming), and lakes. Hurricane damage in 1992 blew the roof off the rare plant house (it's been replaced); happily, its extensive collection of unusual tropical flora has been replanted. The gardens were not destroyed. A hurricane exhibit plot has been left in its storm-tossed natural state, so that students and scientists can observe the natural patterns of regrowth. Complimentary tram rides and walking tours are available through the grounds, complete with intelligent commentary. Open daily except *Christmas Day*. Admission charge. 10901 Old Cutler Rd. (phone: 667-1651).

PARROT JUNGLE More of the tropics, but this time, screaming, colorful, and talented. Not only do these parrots, macaws, and cockatoos fly, but they also ride bicycles, roller-skate, and solve math problems. If you don't believe it, just wait till you see the flamingos on parade — all amid a jungle of huge cypress and live oaks. Don't miss the photo opportunity to pose with brilliantly plumaged red, turquoise, and yellow parrots poised on your arms and head. The coffee shop here is a great breakfast stop. Open daily. Admission charge. Two miles south of US 1 at 11000 SW 57th Ave. (Red Rd.) and Killian Dr. (phone: 666-7834).

MONKEY JUNGLE The monkeys wander, run free, go swimming, and swing from trees while visitors watch from inside a wire cage. Naturally, some chimp stars perform (three shows daily), and there are also orangutans and gibbons. Open daily. Admission charge. 14805 SW 216th St. (phone: 235-1611).

FRUIT AND SPICE PARK Some 20 tropical acres feature over 500 species of fruit, nut, and spice trees and plants. Guided tours by Parks Department naturalists include samplings of seasonal fruits, and you're free to eat anything that's fallen to the ground. Appropriately, this also is the site of the *Summer Festival* each July. Tours are conducted Saturday and Sunday afternoons for a nominal charge. Open daily except *Thanksgiving, Christmas Day,* and *New Year's Day.* Admission charge. Thirty-five miles southwest of Miami, at 24801 SW 187th Ave., Homestead (phone: 247-5727).

MIAMI BEACH At one time, this 8-mile-long island east of the mainland was renowned for its glittering seaside resorts, until the beaches and hotels fell into decline. That old reputation, however, has been largely restored, along with the unique architecture. Recent efforts at renewal and redevelopment have brought tourists to the flashy *Fontainebleau Hilton* and the other big hotels that line Collins Avenue, the main drag. A $64-million beach renourishment program has created a 300-foot strand extending from Government Cut to Haulover Inlet, and a beach boardwalk runs 1.8 miles from 21st to 46th Streets (see *Quintessential Miami* in DIVERSIONS). The southern end of the island, between 5th and 20th Streets, known locally as South Beach, has been designated a National Historic District because of its many Art Deco buildings (see *Quintessential Miami* in DIVERSIONS and *Tour 1: South Beach — The Art Deco District* in DIRECTIONS). Ocean Drive has been widened and spruced up and is now lined with outdoor cafés, shops, galleries — and plenty of pedestrian traffic.

SPANISH MONASTERY The oldest building in the Western Hemisphere, this charming monastery, which today houses artworks, was first built in 1141 in Spain, dismantled, shipped, and rebuilt in Miami in 1954. Open daily 10 AM to 5 PM, Sundays noon to 5 PM. Admission charge. 16711 W. Dixie Hwy., North Miami (phone: 945-1461).

CORAL CASTLE This is testimony to lost love. Hand-built by a man who was jilted the day before his wedding, this unusual home required more than 1,000 tons of coral rock to be dug by hand and fashioned into a mansion that's a maze of rooms, complete with outdoor furniture and solar-heated bathtubs. Open daily 9 AM to 5 PM. Admission charge. 28655 US 1, Homestead (phone: 248-6344).

HOLOCAUST MEMORIAL A $3-million memorial park dedicated to the survivors of the Holocaust in Europe during World War II. At the center of the park is the sculpture *Love and Anguish,* a 42-foot bronze outstretched hand that seems to grow from the ground, symbolic of the concentration camp victims' struggle for survival. A walk surrounding the reflecting pool features touching photographs etched into a granite wall by a special chemical process. Open daily. No admission charge. Meridian Ave. and Dade Blvd., Miami Beach (phone: 538-1663).

VENETIAN POOL Once a rock quarry that provided material for many of the stately coral rock homes in Coral Gables, the Venetian Pool has undergone an extensive face-lift. A free-form lagoon with varying levels and waterfalls, it's a place for Esther Williams fantasies. It's crowded with camp children in summertime, but the rest of the year provides plenty of swimming space and the opportunity to view photographs of former swimming greats. Open daily from 11 AM to 7:30 PM June through August; limited hours other times. Admission charge. 2701 DeSoto Blvd., Coral Gables (phone: 442-6483).

Sources and Resources

TOURIST INFORMATION

The Greater Miami Convention and Visitors Bureau (701 Brickell Ave., Suite 2700, Miami, FL 33131; phone: 539-3000 or 800-283-2707; fax: 539-3113) is best for brochures, maps, and general tourist information. For information on fairs, art shows, and events in the area's parks, call the Parks and Recreation Department's information line (phone: 579-2568). Contact the Florida State Hotline (904-488-1234) for maps, calendars of events, health updates, and travel advisories. *Activity Line* (557-5600), a visitor information phone guide, offers updated schedules of events, plus dining, sports, and shopping tips.

LOCAL COVERAGE The *Miami Herald*, a morning daily, publishes its Weekend section on Fridays, full of a schedule of upcoming events; *South Florida* magazine, a monthly; *New Times,* an alternative weekly — Miami's answer to New York City's *Village Voice* — includes "The Wave," a listing of weekly happenings; and *New Miami,* a monthly business magazine. Spanish coverage includes the dailies *El Nuevo Herald* and *El Diario las Américas,* and monthly magazines *Miami Mensual* and *Selecta.*

TELEVISION STATIONS WPBT Channel 2–PBS; WTVJ Channel 4–NBC; WCIX Channel 6–CBS; WPLG Channel 10–ABC.

RADIO STATIONS AM: WIOD 610 (news); WEAT 850 (easy listening); WINZ 940 (news/talk). FM: WTMI 93.1 (classical music); WKIS 99.9 (country); WMXJ 102.7 (oldies); WJQY 106.7 (easy listening).

TELEPHONE

The area code for Miami is 305.

SALES TAX

There is a 6% statewide sales tax and a 12.5% hotel tax.

GETTING AROUND

BUS *Metrobus* serves downtown Miami, Collins Avenue in Miami Beach, Coral Gables, and Coconut Grove fairly well, but service to other areas tends to be slow and complicated. For information on routes, schedules, and fares, call 638-6700.

CAR RENTAL Miami is served by the large national firms; intensive competition makes rates here among the least expensive in the country, but if you want to drive a convertible during peak season, be sure to reserve one well in advance. For more information, see GETTING READY TO GO.

METRORAIL/METROMOVER *Metrorail,* an elevated rail system, operates from the *Dadeland* shopping mall in the Kendall area to downtown Miami, and beyond to the Civic Center and Hialeah; fare, $1.25. The *Metromover* rail system is a recently expanded 4.3-mile downtown loop; the fare is 25¢, free for those transferring from the *Metrorail*. For information, call 638-6700.

TAXI You sometimes can hail a cab in the street, but it's better to order one on the phone or pick one up in front of any of the big hotels. Major cab companies are *Central Cab* (phone: 532-5555), *Metro Taxi* (phone: 888-8888), *Super Yellow Cab* (phone: 888-7777), and *Yellow Cab* (phone: 444-4444).

TRI-RAIL The 67-mile commuter railroad system began operating in 1989, connecting Dade, Broward, and Palm Beach counties with increasingly frequent routes, Mondays through Saturdays. The fare is $3, $5 roundtrip, with discounts for seniors, students, and the disabled. Passengers board the double-decker trains at any of 14 stops, with free connecting passes to *Metrorail/Metromover* and to county and shuttle buses. The train provides access to major sights and to Miami, Ft. Lauderdale/Hollywood, and Palm Beach airports. Extra trains are scheduled for games at *Joe Robbie* and *Orange Bowl* stadiums, special events, and guided tours to *Bayside Marketplace* and other attractions. Accessible to disabled passengers (phone: 800-TRI-RAIL).

LOCAL SERVICES

AUDIOVISUAL EQUIPMENT *Spire Audio-Visual*, 24 NW 36th St., Miami (phone: 576-5736).

BABYSITTING *Lul-a-Bye Sitters Registry* (phone: 565-1222).

BUSINESS SERVICES *Ad Staff Temporary Service*, 273 Alhambra Circle, Coral Gables (phone: 443-2122).

CONVENTION FACILITIES *Miami Beach Convention Center* (1901 Convention Center Dr., Miami Beach; phone: 673-7311); *Miami Convention Center* (400 SE 2nd Ave., Miami; phone: 579-6341); and *Coconut Grove Convention Center* (2700 S. Bayshore Dr., Coconut Grove; phone: 579-3310).

COPIERS AND EQUIPMENT *Kinko's* makes standard and color copies, provides hourly rentals of typewriters and computers. Open 24 hours daily. Two locations: 1309 SW 107th Ave., Miami (phone: 220-8172) and 1212 S. Dixie Hwy., Coral Gables (phone: 662-6716).

DENTAL EMERGENCY *American Dental Association* maintains a 24-hour daily referral service (phone: 667-3647).

DRY CLEANER/TAILOR *La Salle Cleaners* (2341 LeJeune Rd., Coral Gables; phone: 444-7376); *Mark's* (1201 20th St., Miami Beach; phone: 538-6104).

LIMOUSINE *Red Top Sedan Service* (11077 NW 36th Ave.; phone: 688-7700); *Club Limousine Service* (11055 Biscayne Blvd.; phone: 893-9850).

LOCKSMITH *Master Key Locksmith* — a lifesaver if you've locked your keys in the car; open 24 hours daily (phone: 638-8078).

MECHANICS *Dave's Car Clinic* (5800 Commerce La.; phone: 661-7711); *Martino*, for foreign and American cars (7145 SW 8th St.; phone: 261-6071).

MEDICAL EMERGENCY For information on area hospitals and pharmacies, see GETTING READY TO GO.

MESSENGER SERVICES *Sunshine State Messenger Service*, open 24 hours daily (phone: 944-6363); *Metro Messenger Service* (phone: 757-7777).

PHOTOCOPIES *Sir Speedy* (locations include 1659 James Ave., Miami Beach; phone: 531-5858); *Ace Industries* (54 NW 11th St.; phone: 358-2571); see also *Kinko's*, above ("Copiers and Equipment").

PROFESSIONAL PHOTOGRAPHER *Convention Photographers International* (1630 Cleveland Rd., Miami Beach; phone: 865-5628); *Pelham Photographic* (665 Mokena Dr., Miami Springs; phone: 885-2006).

SECRETARY/STENOGRAPHER *Abacus Business Center*, English/Spanish (12000 Biscayne Blvd., Miami; phone: 892-8644); *Girl Friday* (25 SE 2nd Ave., Miami; phone: 379-3461).

TELECONFERENCE FACILITIES *Inter-Continental* hotel (100 Chopin Plaza, Miami; phone: 577-1000); *Miami Convention Center* (400 SE 2nd Ave., Miami; phone: 579-6341); *Omni International* (1601 Biscayne Blvd., Miami; phone: 374-0000); *Miami Beach Convention Center* (1901 Convention Center Dr., Miami Beach; phone: 673-7311).

TRANSLATOR *Berlitz* (phone: 371-3686 or 800-523-7548); *Professional Translating Services* (phone: 371-7887).

TYPEWRITER RENTAL *Beach Typewriter*, 1-week minimum (phone: 538-6272); *A-1 Etron*, 2-week minimum (phone: 264-4652); see also *Kinko's*, above ("Copiers and Equipment").

WESTERN UNION/TELEX Many offices are located around the city (phone: 223-8000 or 800-325-4045).

OTHER *ABC Office Equipment* (phone: 891-5090); *Florida Tent Rental*, tent pavilions for conferences or receptions, often set up at *Vizcaya Museum and Gardens* (phone: 633-0199); *Pearl's and Jessie's Catering* (20160 W. Dixie Hwy.; phone: 937-1511); *US Passport Agency*, open Mondays through Fridays 9 AM to 4PM; closed federal holidays (51 SW 1st Ave., Miami; phone: 536-5395).

SPECIAL EVENTS

Miami is the site of the annual *King Orange Jamboree Parade* (phone: 642-1515), nationally televised from Biscayne Boulevard each *New Year's*

Eve as a prelude to the *Orange Bowl* football classic (phone: 371-4600), which is played on *New Year's* night. (The *King Mango Strut* parade, held a few days earlier, pokes fun at the lavish *Orange Bowl* festivities.) *New Year's Day* also heralds the *Kwanzaa Festival,* a fairly new celebration for Miami, it recalls black African traditions, celebrated with food, music, and arts and crafts (phone: 576-1418). The third annual *International Fine Art Fair,* which showcases contemporary art, a good percentage of it Latin American, is at the *Miami Beach Convention Center* (this year from January 6 through 10). Two of the country's largest boat shows are held here each year, the *Boat Show in the Grove* (phone: 696-6100) at the *Coconut Grove Convention Center* in October, and the *International Boat Show* (phone: 531-8410) at the *Miami Beach Convention Center* in February. Miami Beach hosts the *Art Deco Weekend* every January on Ocean Drive, in the historic Art Deco District in South Beach (phone: 672-2014), as well as the *Festival of the Arts* each February (phone: 673-7733) and the *Coconut Grove Art Festival* (phone: 447-0401) during the same month. These festivals draw many folks away from the beach to stroll the shady lanes of this artists' haven. February also hosts the *Miami Film Festival,* 10 days of premieres of national and international films with visiting directors, producers, and stars (phone: 377-3456). In February there's also the *Toyota Grand Prix of Miami,* attracting top race drivers to the downtown "track" (Biscayne Blvd. between Flagler and NE 8th Sts.; phone: 665-RACE). In March, in Little Havana, natives and visitors alike head for Calle Ocho (8th St.) for *Carnaval Miami* (phone: 644-8888), a 9-day festival featuring a 23-block-long street party and the largest conga line in the world. In April, the *Greater Miami Billfish Tournament* attracts more than 500 anglers in pursuit of marlin and sailfish, vying for South Florida's richest fishing purse (phone: 598-8127 or 754-0710). *Taste of Miami* offers tidbits from area restaurants, cooking demonstrations, and wine tastings in May at Bayfront Park (phone: 375-8480). May also brings the *Haitian Festival* at Miami-Dade Community College (phone: 347-1320). Coconut Grove is the site of the *Miami/Bahamas Goombay Festival* in June, celebrating the area's Bahamian heritage and considered the country's largest black heritage festival, with *junkanoo* groups (local citizens who form bands and play calypso and reggae music on homemade instruments), continuous music, and lots of conch chowder and fritters (phone: 372-9966).

July brings the *Summer Festival* at the Fruit and Spice Park (phone: 247-5727) and the *Annual International Music and Crafts Festival* at the Miccosukee Indian Village in the Everglades (phone: 223-8388). Chocoholics won't want to miss the *Chocolate Festival* in September at the *Fontainebleau Hilton* (phone: 535-3240). The *Miami Mile,* a world class run, is held the third week of September. For sailboat enthusiasts, the 2-day *Columbus Day Regatta,* held in October, attracts more than 600 entrants. In November, the *Miami Book Fair International* welcomes authors, publishers, booksellers, and street vendors to one of the world's largest week-long celebrations of the printed word, considered the country's premier literary event by *The New York Times* and *Publisher's Weekly* (phone: 237-3258). The *Christmas* season gets off to an enchanting start in early December with the *Greater Miami Boat Parade*, when hundreds of brightly lighted and gaily decorated boats sail along the Intracoastal Waterway (phone: 935-9959). The Miccosukee tribe's annual *Arts Festival* in late December draws members from 40 tribes who exhibit song, dance, and other skills at the *Miccosukee Indian Village* (phone: 223-8380 weekdays or 223-8388 weekends). And the year ends as it begins with the *Blockbuster Bowl*, a top-ranked collegiate football classic, which takes place between *Christmas* and *New Year's Day* (phone: 564-5000).

MUSEUMS

In addition to those described in *Special Places*, other museums to see include the following.

AMERICAN POLICE HALL OF FAME AND MUSEUM A marble monument commemorates more than 3,400 slain officers. Exhibits in the 3-story building include law enforcement vehicles and equipment — such as a guillotine and an electric chair. At a mock crime scene, visitors are encouraged to solve a murder. Open daily from 10 AM to 5:30 PM. Admission charge; free to police officers and families of slain officers. 3801 Biscayne Blvd., Miami (phone: 573-0070).

ART MUSEUM AT FLORIDA INTERNATIONAL UNIVERSITY Collection of the works of contemporary North and South American artists. Open Mondays from 10 AM to 9 PM; Tuesdays through Fridays from 10 AM to 5 PM; Saturdays from noon to 4 PM; closed Sundays. University Park, SW 107th Ave. and 8th St. (phone: 348-2890).

CENTER FOR THE FINE ARTS Designed by Philip Johnson as part of the lovely complex at the *Metro-Dade Cultural Center*, it hosts major traveling exhibitions of artists such as Pablo Picasso and Jasper Johns. Signs are in English and Spanish. There is also a small gift shop. Open from 10 AM to 5 PM Tuesdays, Wednesdays, Fridays, and Saturdays, and until 9 PM on Thursdays; noon to 5 PM on Sundays. Admission charge; voluntary contributions on Tuesdays. 101 W. Flagler St. at 1st Ave., Miami (phone: 375-1700).

CUBAN MUSEUM OF ARTS AND CULTURE Changing exhibitions here promote the cultural heritage of Miami's growing Cuban community. Open Wednesdays through Sundays from 1 PM to 5 PM. No admission charge. 1300 SW 12th Ave. (phone: 858-8006).

HISTORICAL MUSEUM OF SOUTH FLORIDA Located on the graceful plaza at the *Metro-Dade Cultural Center*, it boasts excellent exhibitions on the histories of the various groups that have settled here. Numerous displays, including a *chickee* hut, depict Native American life, while the Spanish exploration period comes alive through 17th-century maps and a mock-up of a fort that kids can climb. Maritime history displays include artifacts from treasure fleets, such as a gold ear pick. There's also a full-size trolley car that was used in Miami in the 1920s. Ongoing contributions made by the settling Cubans, blacks, and Jews bring it up to date; a sign points out that only "30 years ago, Jews and blacks were barred from part of Dade County." Signs and recorded messages are in both English and Spanish. A fine gift shop sells books and colorful accessories. Open Mondays through Saturdays from 10 AM to 5 PM; Thursdays until 9PM; Sundays noon to 5 PM. Admission charge. 101 W. Flagler St. at 1st Ave., Miami (phone: 375-1492).

LOWE ART MUSEUM A permanent collection of Renaissance and baroque art, pre-Columbian, Asian and African art, and furniture and paintings from the Kress Collection of Renaissance and baroque art, plus visiting exhibits. Open Tuesdays through Saturdays from 10 AM to 5 PM; Sundays from noon to 5 PM; closed Mondays. Admission charge. 1301 Stanford Dr., on the University of Miami campus in Coral Gables (phone: 284-3535).

MIAMI YOUTH MUSEUM Hands-on exhibits, including "Kidscape," a miniature neighborhood with Dr. Smile's dental office, a fire station, and a supermarket, are fun for kids of all ages. New exhibits include a "Metro-Dade safe neighborhood" exhibit and a tent from "Tent City," established after Hurricane Andrew. Guided tours are in both English and Spanish. Open daily until 5 PM, from 10 AM Mondays and Fridays, from 1 PM Tuesdays, Wednesdays, and Thursdays, and from 11 AM Saturdays and Sundays; closed holidays. Admission charge. *Bakery Centre,* 5701 Sunset Dr., South Miami (phone: 661-3046).

MAJOR COLLEGES AND UNIVERSITIES

The University of Miami in Coral Gables, a 4-year college with highly regarded graduate schools, has an enrollment of 17,000 (1200 San Amaro Dr.; phone: 284-2211). Florida International University is a 4-year college with two separate campuses (SW 8th St. and 107th Ave., and NE 151st St. and Biscayne Blvd.; phone: 348-2000). Miami Dade Community College, with three campuses, is the largest junior college in the country (11380 NW 27th Ave., 11011 SW 104th St., and 300 NE 2nd Ave.; phone: 237-3135).

SHOPPING

In addition to sparkling blue waters and powdery white beaches, Miami also offers some sand-free sports, and the best of them is shopping. The places listed below carry a wide variety of items, and many have lovely restaurants and scenic views as well.

AVENTURA MALL One of South Florida's largest malls, with 200 shops and stores on 2 levels. Anchors are *Lord & Taylor, Macy's, JC Penney,* and *Sears.* A large food court offers a pause that refreshes. Open daily from 10 AM to 9:30 PM. 19501 Biscayne Blvd., North Miami Beach (phone: 935-1110).

BAL HARBOUR SHOPS Lovely open-air shopping amid gardens and fountains. The 100 upscale stores include *Saks Fifth Avenue, Neiman Marcus, Martha, Cartier, Gucci, Brooks Brothers,* and *F.A.O. Schwarz.* Good snack stops include *Ms. Grimble, American Way* and *Coco's.* Open Mondays, Thursdays, and Fridays from 10 AM to 9 PM, Tuesdays, Wednesdays, and Saturdays from 10 AM to 6 PM, and Sundays from noon to 5 PM. 9700 Collins Ave., Bal Harbour (phone: 866-0311).

BAYSIDE MARKETPLACE From the designers of Boston's *Faneuil Hall*, this open-air marketplace of 160 shops and restaurants, overlooking the water, offers a wide variety of shopping options, from *Victoria's Secret* and *The Gap* to *B. Dalton's, Brookstone*, and *Limited Express*. There are also pushcarts where you can buy arts and crafts items from South America, Central America, and the Caribbean. See also *Special Places* in this chapter. Open from 10 AM to 10 PM Mondays through Saturdays and noon to 8 PM on Sundays. 401 Biscayne Blvd. (phone: 577-3344).

BOOKS & BOOKS Two locations, one in Coral Gables and the other in Miami Beach. Both offer frequent readings by authors such as Carlos Fuentes and Susan Sontag. The Coral Gables store features a sizable selection of used and out-of-print books. The Coral Gables shop is open from 10 AM to 8 PM weekdays, 10 AM to 7 PM Saturdays, and noon to 5 PM Sundays; the Miami Beach store is open from 10 AM to 9 PM Mondays through Thursdays, 10 AM to midnight Fridays and Saturdays, and noon to 5 PM Sundays. 296 Aragon Ave., Coral Gables (phone: 442-4408); 933 Lincoln Rd., Miami Beach (phone: 532-3222).

COCOWALK An exciting open-air, Spanish-style shopping complex in the heart of Coconut Grove, it boasts 3 dozen shops, several eateries, and entertainment for the young and young-at-heart. Stores include *The Limited Express, The Gap, Banana Republic, Victoria's Secret,* and a *B. Dalton's* that remains open until 12:30 AM Fridays and Saturdays. There's also *Café Tu Tu Tango* and *Big City Fish* (see *Eating Out*). Stores are open from 11 AM to 10 PM daily except holidays. 3015 Grand Ave., Coconut Grove (phone: 444-0777).

DADELAND MALL This large mall in southern Miami claims Florida's largest *Burdine's,* along with *Saks Fifth Avenue, Lord & Taylor,* and 200 other shops. Open Mondays through Saturdays 10 AM to 9 PM, Sundays noon to 6 PM. 7535 N. Kendall Dr. (phone: 665-6226).

ELITE FINE ART Latin American art by masters and emerging artists. Includes paintings, drawings, and sculpture by artists such as the Brazilian Antonio Amaral, Cuban Mario Bencomo, and Panamanian Guillermo Trujillo.

Open Tuesdays through Saturdays 11 AM to 6 PM. 3140 Ponce de León Blvd., Coral Gables (phone: 448-3800; 800-USA-ELITE outside Florida).

EPICURE MARKET *The* place on the Beach for unusual grocery items and take-out goodies for sand or sea, including three types of smoked salmon, imported caviar, fresh-ground coffee, large cooked shrimp, and prepared meals. Open Mondays through Fridays from 9 AM to 7 PM and Saturdays and Sundays 9 AM to 6 PM. 1656 Alton Rd., Miami Beach (phone: 672-1861).

FALLS SHOPPING CENTER More than 60 upscale stores and restaurants set among splashing waterfalls. Open Mondays through Saturdays from 10 AM to 9 PM, Sundays noon to 5 PM. 8888 Howard Dr. (phone: 255-4570).

FASHION ROW Known as "Shmatte Row" (Yiddish for garments or rags), it offers discounts, discounts, and more discounts. One section of discount dress and handbag shops is located off Hallandale Beach Boulevard on NE 1st Avenue (dubbed "Fashion Row" on street signs); the other is on NE 2nd Avenue between NE 3rd and NE 4th Streets. Open daily 10 AM to 5 PM between December and March 30th, closed on Sundays other times. Stop at *Barnett's,* chock-full of everything for the home at discount prices; it stays open on Sundays year-round (100 E. Hallandale Beach Blvd., Hallandale; phone: 456-0566). Or, still in the home mode, try the *Dansk Factory Outlet* for discounts on seconds and overstocks of fine Danish designs. Open Mondays through Saturdays from 10 AM to 5:30 PM, Sundays noon to 5 PM (27 W. Hallandale Beach Blvd., Hallandale; phone: 454-3900).

A LIKELY STORY Children's books and imported educational toys, including easels, games, and specialized items. Open from 10 AM to 6 PM Mondays through Saturdays, and noon to 5 PM Sundays. 5740 Sunset Dr., S. Miami (phone: 667-3730).

MAYFAIR SHOPS IN THE GROVE High-fashion shops predominate, including *Polo/Ralph Lauren, Ann Taylor,* and *Benetton.* Open from 10 AM to 8 PM Mondays and Thursdays, 10 AM to 7 PM Tuesdays, Wednesdays, Fridays, and Saturdays, and noon to 5 PM Sundays. Grand Ave., Coconut Grove (phone: 448-1700).

SPY SHOPS INTERNATIONAL Fortunately, Miami is no longer at the top of every crime list. But just for protection, customers here may purchase high-tech security systems, anti-kidnapping devices, and electric surveillance gadgets, or arrange to have a vehicle armored. Open Mondays through Fridays 9:30 AM to 6 PM, Saturdays until 3 PM. 2900 Biscayne Blvd. (phone: 573-4779) and 350 Biscayne Blvd. (phone: 374-4779).

UNICORN VILLAGE MARKET This large, immaculate shop associated with the *Unicorn Village* restaurant features enormous displays of organically grown produce, prepared Pritikin Diet items, and wines produced without pesticides or added sulphites. Prepared takeout also available. Open Sundays through Thursdays 11:30 AM to 9:30 PM, Fridays and Saturdays until 10 PM. At *The Shops at the Waterways,* 3595 NE 207th St., North Miami Beach (phone: 933-8829).

VIRGINIA MILLER GALLERIES Features contemporary artworks by Latin Americans, including Carlos Loarca; European artists, including Karel Appel of the Netherlands; and US artists Larry Gerber, Tom Hopkins, and the late Alice Neel; plus Australian aboriginal paintings of the Turkey Creek art community. Open Mondays through Saturdays from 10 AM to 6 PM. 169 Madeira Ave., Coral Gables (phone: 444-4493).

> **MIAMI DUTY FREE** Travelers planning to leave the country, even for a short cruise, may buy items at duty-free prices right in Miami, in this clean, uncluttered shop. Drive into the highly secure parking lot and present either your cruise or flight ticket to the security guard. Select and pay for your goods. *MDF* will deliver your purchases to your plane or ship on the day of departure. Items include Givenchy and Calvin Klein scents, Absolut and Dewar's liquor, Fendi purses, Wedgwood china, Waterford crystal, Rolex watches, and Nina Ricci scarves. Salespeople speak seven languages. Prices are 20% to 40% below retail, and no Florida tax is levied. Open daily from 10 AM to 8 PM. 125 NE 8th St. (phone: 358-9774).

SPORTS AND FITNESS

BASEBALL The University of Miami *Hurricanes* play at *Mark Light Stadium* (on campus at 1 Hurricane Dr., corner of Ponce de León and San Amaro; phone: 284-2655). Miami's newest team, the National League's Florida *Marlins,* play at *Joe Robbie Stadium* (2269 NW 199th St.; phone: 620-2578 or 623-6100). Fans also can watch pre-season games of the Baltimore *Orioles,* whose spring training camp is in Miami; they often play the New York *Yankees,* who train in nearby Ft. Lauderdale.

BASKETBALL The *Heat,* Miami's NBA entry, burns up the court at the *Miami Arena* (721 NW 1st Ave.; phone: 577-HEAT for *Heat* tickets or 530-4400 for other information). The *Harlem Globetrotters* occasionally present their frantic antics here, too.

BICYCLING Almost every day, cyclists take to the more than 100 miles of bicycle paths in the Miami area. A self-guided bicycle tour of Key Biscayne originates in Crandon Park. The 3.5-mile path goes through the beach area, woods, and hammocks of trees and cane grass, ending at the park's marina. Dade County Parks & Recreation has more information (phone:

579-2676). Another favorite spot for cyclists and runners is Tropical Park. The 2-mile path winds through a wooded area, along 2 lakes, and sports facilities. Pick up a map at the park office, hours are Mondays through Fridays 9 AM to 5 PM (7900 40th Rd., Miami; phone: 553-3616); or the tennis center, open daily 9 AM to 9 PM (same address and phone as the park office).

Bicycle rentals are available throughout the Greater Miami area, and cost $3 per hour or $15 per day. A few to try: *Cycles on the Beach* (713 Fifth St., Miami Beach; phone: 673-2055); *Dade Cycle Shop* (3216 Grand Ave., Coconut Grove; phone: 443-6075); *Key Biscayne Rental* (260 Crandon Blvd., Key Biscayne; phone: 361-5555); *Miami Beach Bicycle Center* (923 W. 39th St., Miami Beach (phone: 531-4161).

BOATING Greater Miami is laced with navigable canals and has many private and public marinas with all kinds of boats for rent. Sailboats are available at *Dinner Key Marina* (3400 Pan American Dr., Coconut Grove; phone: 579-6980). Sailboats and powerboats, along with windsurfers and day sailers (some with free instruction), are available from *Easy Sailing* shops on Key Biscayne (3400 Pan American Dr.; phone: 858-4001 or 800-780-4001) or *Sailboats Miami* (phone: 361-SAIL or 361-3870). Rentals cost from $15 to $35. The *Pauhana,* a 49-passenger catamaran, is available for charter or sunset tours (401 NE. 4th St. at *Bayside Marketplace*; phone: 888-3002). For large and small sailboats, with or without captains, for long- or short-term rentals, try *Florida Yacht Charters* (1290 5th St., Miami Beach; phone: 532-8600). *Beach Boat Rentals* (2380 Collins Ave., Miami Beach; phone: 534-4307) has some nice 18-footers with or without captains. *Club Nautico,* good for powerboat rentals, has docks in Miami (phone: 371-4252 and 372-9931), Miami Beach (phone: 673-2502), Coconut Grove (phone: 858-6258), and North Miami Beach (phone: 945-3232). Charter boats for sport fishing are available at *Miami Beach Marina* (phone: 673-6000), and *Miami Marina* (downtown; phone: 374-6260). See also *Fishing,* below.

DOG RACING Greyhound racing is held at *Biscayne* (320 NW 115th St.; phone: 754-3484 or 800-432-0232). Check the racing dates before heading to the track.

FISHING Anglers of every ilk will find their special brand of fishing within reach here. Surf and offshore saltwater fishing is available year-round.

FIRST CLASS CATCHES

Charter boats offer a choice of half-day or full-day deep-sea fishing. Expect to pay about $400 for a half day for up to six anglers. There are dozens of party boats listed under "Fishing" in the Miami yellow pages. Our favorites are the following: *Castaways Dock,* which rents 60-foot and larger fishing boats with captain, mate, bait, and tackle (16485 Collins Ave., Miami Beach; phone: 945-1578). You will also find such old standbys here as the *Therapy IV* (phone: 954-1578) and the *Kelley Fleet* (phone: 945-3801 or 949-1173). *Crandon Park Marina* offers fishing boats, powerboats, and sailboats (4000 Crandon Blvd., Key Biscayne; phone: 361-1281). *Great Escape Yachts* charters fishing boats and dive cruises complete with captains and mates. Speedboats and overnight cruises are also available (300 Alton Rd., Miami Beach; phone: 936-0111). *Haulover Marina* includes rack storage facilities for boats (10800 Collins Ave., Miami Beach; phone: 945-3934).

Fishing seasons offshore vary by location, as do regulations on kinds and sizes of fish you're allowed to catch. The *Florida Fishing Handbook* is available at no charge by writing to the Florida Game and Fresh Water Fish Commission (620 S. Meridian St., Tallahassee, FL 32399-1600; phone: 904-488-1960). Licenses are required for both freshwater and saltwater fishing, and can be obtained from bait and tackle shops as well as *K-Mart* stores. A saltwater fishing license is $30 for non-residents, and $12 for residents. Long-term licenses also are available.

The boardwalks on the Rickenbacker, MacArthur, and Venetian causeways are popular fishing spots. The *Holiday Inn* Newport Pier, 16701 Collins Ave., Miami (phone: 949-1300), is open 24 hours daily and provides equipment rental (admission charge). There's also plenty of freshwater action in canals and backwaters, including the Everglades and Florida Bay.

Competitive fisherfolk may want to enter the *Greater Miami Billfish* tournament, for South Florida's richest fishing purse, in April (*Miami Beach Marina*, 300 Alton Rd., Miami Beach; phone: 754-0710).

FITNESS CENTERS Staying in shape is no problem in Dade County. Try the *YMCA* (at the downtown World Trade Center; phone: 577-3091); out-of-town visitors who are members of a *Y* back home (more than 50 miles away) are welcome without charge. The *Downtown Athletic Club* (atop the Southeast Bank Building; phone: 358-9988) and *Body and Soul* (355 Greco Ave., Coral Gables; phone: 443-8688) also are good places.

FOOTBALL The NFL *Dolphins* and *Dolphin*-mania infect the entire city during the pro football season, so for good seats call the *Joe Robbie Stadium* in North Dade in advance (2269 NW 199th St.; phone: 620-2578) The University of Miami *Hurricanes* play at *Orange Bowl Stadium;* for tickets, contact the University of Miami ticket office (1 Hurricane Dr., Coral Gables; phone: 284-2655), or go to the *Orange Bowl Stadium* (1501 NW 3rd St.).

GOLF Its almost constant sunshine, balmy breezes, and picturesque fairways make Greater Miami a golfer's dream — witness the preponderance of golf tournaments held here. Resorts and hotels without their own courses can usually provide access to other clubs.

TOP TEE-OFF SPOT

Doral At the moment, this 648-room resort stands like the grande golfing dame of the Miami–Miami Beach tourist axis. The *Doral*'s superb golf facilities (five 18-hole layouts, plus a par 3 executive course) thus far remain unassailed, and the fabled championship *Blue Monster* is still one of the most formidable challenges in the state, and the *Gold* course offers little diminution in challenge. Pro is Rob Brand; Jim McLean Learning Center is the pro workshop. 4400 NW 87th Ave. (phone: 592-2000, 800-327-6334, or 800-22DORAL; fax: 594-4682).

In addition, Miami has more first-rate courses open to the public than most places you can name. Among the better ones are *Kendale Lakes* (6401 Kendale Lakes Dr., Miami; phone: 382-3930), *Miami Springs* (650 Curtiss Pkwy., Miami Springs; phone: 888-2377), *Bayshore* (2301 Alton Rd., Miami Beach; phone: 532-3350), *Palmetto* (9300 SW 152nd St., Miami; phone: 238-2922), and *Key Biscayne* (6700 Crandon Blvd., Key Biscayne; phone: 361-9129). Cost is about $45 for 18 holes, including cart and greens fee. For more information in Miami, call the following Parks and Recreation Departments: Metro-Dade County (phone: 579-2968), City of Miami Beach (phone: 673-7730), or City of Miami (phone: 575-5256).

The *Honda Golf Classic* is one of the major US events on the PGA circuit, played in March at the private *Weston Hills Country Club* in Coral Springs. You might spot such pros as Nick Faldo, Tom Watson, or Greg Norman attempting a birdie here (phone: 384-4600). The $1.4-million *Doral-Ryder Open* is held annually on the championship *Blue Monster* course at the *Doral Resort & Country Club* in Miami in late February or early March. A Ladies PGA event is held each February at *Inverrary*, former home of the *Jackie Gleason Inverrary Golf Classic*.

HORSE RACING Betting is big in Miami. The *Hialeah Race Track* (2200 E. 4th Ave., Hialeah; phone: 885-8000 or 800-442-5324), listed on the National Registry of Historic Places, is worth a visit just to see the beautiful grounds and clubhouse and the famous flock of pink flamingos. Elegant equines are off and running daily except Mondays in April and May. Dining is available in the *Citation Room, Flamingo Terrace,* and *Turf Club*. There also is thoroughbred racing at *Calder Race Course*, the country's only all-weather race track, in North Miami, next to *Joe Robbie Stadium* (21001 NW 27th Ave.; phone: 625-1311 in Dade, 523-4324 in Broward). Open Tuesdays through Sundays from March to May and Saturdays through Thursdays from May to October. For kids of all ages, go to the stadium's Family Saturdays (from May to mid-December), with clowns, games, face painting, and a petting zoo. Recent additions to this track include dining at the *Turf Club*, two other dining rooms, and snack bars.

JAI ALAI From December through April, there's jai alai (a Basque game resembling a combination of lacrosse, handball, and tennis), and betting action nightly at the *Miami Jai-Alai Fronton,* the country's largest. You can pick up tickets at the gate or reserve them in advance. 3500 NW 37th Ave. (phone: 633-6400).

JET SKIING The latest craze in water fun, available at *Tony's Jet Ski Rentals* (3501 Rickenbacker Cswy., Key Biscayne; phone; 361-8280) and *Fun Watersports* (*Miami Airport Hilton and Marina*, 5101 Blue Lagoon Dr., Miami; phone: 261-7687). Cost averages $30 per half hour for two people.

JOGGING Run along South Bayshore Drive to David Kennedy Park, at 22nd Avenue, and jog the Vita Path; or jog in Bayfront Park, at Biscayne and NE 4th Street. On Miami Beach, run on a wooden boardwalk that extends along the ocean from 21st to 51st Street, or run toward the parcourse on the southern tip of South Beach. The *Miami Mile,* a world class event planned after New York's *Fifth Avenue Mile* and San Francisco's *California Mile,* is off and running the third week of January. For more information, contact Bob Rodriguez (phone: 756-8600).

NATURE WALKS There are nature walks at Fairchild Tropical Garden and the Fruit and Spice Park; the Parks & Recreation Department offers frequent guided tours through natural hammocks, tree forests, bird rookeries, and even through water (a marine walk, nature lesson, and dousing are at Bear Cut, Key Biscayne). For information contact the Parks Department office (phone: 662-4124).

SCUBA DIVING Endless diving opportunities abound along the coast, where the same three-banded basic reef system extends upward from the Florida Keys, past Miami and Ft. Lauderdale. Although it's broken up in spots, and some areas are polluted, plenty of opportunities exist for spotting elkhorn and brain coral — with bright red soft corals at deeper levels — and colorful tropical fish. The first reef is about 15 feet deep, the second about 40 feet deep, and the third is 60 to 100 feet deep. The practice of sinking freighters and other large objects in the sea to create artificial reefs lures oceans of finny friends at 100- and 200-foot depths (although some of these were disturbed by Hurricane Andrew). Miami boasts about 150 wrecks, and numerous dive shops operate in this area. Among them are *R.J. Diving Ventures* (15560 NE 5th Ave., North Miami Beach; phone: 364-3040), *Great Escape Yachts* (300 Alton Rd., Miami Beach, phone: 936-0111), and *Team Divers* (1290 Fifth St., Miami Beach; phone: 673-0101). Also look in the yellow pages. Expect to pay $30 for a half day.

SKATING Roller-skate to a computerized light show — 2 million lights, synchronized to music — at *Hot Wheels Roller Skating Center*, 12265 SW 112th St. (phone: 595-2958).

SKY DIVING *Skydive Miami* (Homestead General Airport; phone: 759-SKY-DIVE) will fly you up and let you sail down. Freefall costs run from $99 to $199, depending on the height of the dive; the company also will provide — for a charge — video or still shots of your dive.

SWIMMING With an average daily temperature of 75F, and miles of ocean beach on the Atlantic, Miami Beach and Key Biscayne offer some great places for swimming, all water sports, and another prime activity: sedentary sun worshiping. A 2-mile stretch of beach is open at Crandon Park, but the shade trees, picnic tables, and barbecue pits suffered Hurricane Andrew damage, and had not been repaired as we went to press. Open from 8 AM to sunset daily. Parking charge $3 per car. (Rickenbacker Cswy. to Key Biscayne; phone: 361-5421). Haulover Beach is a long stretch of beautiful beach, good for surfing and popular with families. Marina, sightseeing boats, charter fishing fleets, and restaurants. Open from 7 AM to 10 PM daily. No admission charge. (A1A north of Bal Harbour; phone: 947-3525). Miami Beach has several long stretches of public beach at various places, including South Beach for surfers (5th St. and Collins Ave.), Lummus Park with lots of shaded beaches (South Beach on Ocean Ave.), and North Shore Beach with landscaped dunes and an oceanfront walkway (71st St. and Collins Ave.). There are also small public beaches at the east ends of streets near major hotels.

TENNIS Mild and sunny weather make South Florida ideal for year-round tennis, as attested to by illustrious residents Gabriella Sabatini and Steffi Graf.

CHOICE COURTS

Doral Country Club A veritable metropolis of a resort, this 2,400-acre establishment offers 15 well-kept clay and hard-surface tennis courts, backboard and ball machines, court reservations, private lessons and group clinics. The late Arthur Ashe was director of tennis, which is currently managed by *Peter Burwash International Clinics.* 4400 N.W. 87th Ave. (phone: 592-2000, 800-327-6334, or 800-22DORAL; fax: 594-4862).

Inn at Fisher Island This exclusive resort's tennis program has 3 grass, 2 hard, and 14 clay courts, all lighted. You might bump into a well-known movie star or millionaire working on his or her serve. Private lessons, weekly clinics, and round robins help pick up your game. 1 Fisher Island Dr., Fisher Island (phone: 535-6000 or 800-624-3251 outside Florida; fax: 535-6003).

International Tennis Center The site of the annual *Lipton International Players Championship,* it is available for play year-round, offering 17 hard and 7 clay courts, a pro shop, racquet rentals, and lessons. 7200 Crandon Blvd., Key Biscayne (phone: 361-8633 or 361-9725).

Turnberry Isle Major Pro-Am tournaments, such as the *Sinatra Classic,* the *Fred Stolle Invitational,* and *Barry Gibb's Love and Hope* are held here.

There are 24 tennis courts (16 lighted), including 12 clay and 12 hard courts. Teaching staff is under the guidance of Fred Stolle, winner of *Wimbledon,* and the *French, US,* and *Australian Opens.* 19999 W. Country Club Dr., Aventura, Turnberry Isle (phone: 932-6200 or 800-327-7028; fax: 932-9096).

Most of Miami's major resort hotels have tennis courts for the use of their guests, and there are also public facilities throughout the county, including those at the *Abel Holtz Tennis Stadium* in Flamingo Park in Miami Beach with hard and clay courts (1200 12th St.; phone: 673-7761); *International Tennis Center* on Key Biscayne with 17 hard and clay courts, rentals and lessons (7200 Crandon Blvd.; phone: 361-8633); *Tamiami* (10901 Coral Way; phone: 223-7076); *North Shore Center* (350 73rd St., Miami Beach; phone: 993-2022); and *Tropical Park* (7900 SW 40th St., Miami; phone: 226-8315). In addition, there are over 550 courts in metropolitan Dade County (phone: 579-2676).

The 10-day *Lipton International Players Championships* is one of the world's largest tennis happenings, with such top players as Boris Becker and Ivan Lendl on hand in March. For information, contact the *International Tennis Center,* 2 Alhambra Plaza, Coral Gables, FL 33134 (phone: 446-2200); for tickets, 7300 Crandon Blvd., Key Biscayne, FL 33179 (phone: 361-5252).

WATER SKIING Those not staying at a beachfront resort can try the sport via *Fun Watersports, Miami Airport Hilton and Marina,* 5101 Blue Lagoon Dr., Miami (phone: 261-7687).

WINDSURFING Major beachfront hotels rent equipment, but the best spot is arguably Windsurfer Beach at Key Biscayne. Bring your own board or rent from *Sailboats Miami* (Rickenbacker Cswy; phone: 361-SAIL or 361-3870) at $15 an hour or $39 for a 2-hour lesson guaranteed to teach any novice.

THEATER

For current offerings, check the publications listed in *Sources and Resources* in this chapter. The *Coconut Grove Playhouse* (3500 Main Hwy.; phone: 442-4000) imports New York stars for its season of classics that runs from October to May. The *Jackie Gleason Theater of the Performing Arts,* referred to locally as *TOPA,* offers touring plays and musicals, including some pre- and post-Broadway shows (1700 Washington Ave., Miami Beach; phone: 673-7300). The *Gusman Cultural Center* (174 E. Flagler St., Miami; phone: 372-0925) and the *Dade County Auditorium* (2901 W. Flagler St., Miami; phone: 547-5414) book theatrical and cultural events year-round. The *Miami City Ballet* (905 Lincoln Rd., Miami Beach; phone: 532-7713), headed by Edward Villella, is one of the country's best young companies and performs a full season beginning each fall.

MUSIC

Visiting orchestras and artists perform in Miami at the *Gusman Cultural Center* (174 E. Flagler St.; phone: 372-0925) and at *Dade County Auditorium* (2901 W. Flagler St.; phone: 547-5414), or in Miami Beach at the *Theater of the Performing Arts* (1700 Washington Ave.; phone: 673-7300). The *Greater Miami Opera Association* (1200 Coral Way; phone: 854-7890) stages a full complement of major productions during the winter season, as does the *New World Symphony* (541 Lincoln Rd., Miami Beach; phone: 673-3331). Luminaries including *Gloria Estefan and the Miami Sound Machine,* Madonna, and Billy Joel often perform at the *Miami Arena* (721 NW 1st Ave.; phone: 530-4444), or the *Orange Bowl* (1501 NW 3rd St.; phone: 371-3351).

DANCE

The *Miami City Ballet* (905 Lincoln Rd., Miami Beach; phone: 532-7713), headed by Edward Villella, is one of the country's best young companies, and performs a full season beginning each fall. Touring companies such as the *American Ballet Theatre* often visit in season, and there are numerous performances of *The Nutcracker* throughout the region around *Christmastime*.

NIGHTCLUBS AND NIGHTLIFE

Miami's nightlife runs the gamut. The *Club Tropigala* show may make customers think they're watching a lavish "flesh and feathers" production in pre-Castro Havana at the *Fontainebleau Hilton* (4441 Collins Ave., Miami Beach; phone: 672-7469); *Les Violins* also presents a flashy show with a Cuban twist (1751 Biscayne Blvd.; phone: 371-8668). Shout *olé* to flamenco shows in Little Havana at *Málaga* (740 SW 8th St., Miami; phone: 858-4224) and *Centro Vasco* (2235 SW 8th St., Miami; phone: 643-9606). Las Vegas–style revues fill two stages at the *Holiday Inn Newport Pier* (16701 Collins Ave., Sunny Isles Beach; phone: 949-8701). For live blues and a bit of history, stop in at *Tobacco Road* (626 S. Miami Ave.; phone: 374-1198), Miami's oldest bar. If jazz is your bag, try *Greenstreet's* (2051 LeJeune Rd., Coral Gables; phone: 445-2131). For a gigantic nightclub experience complete with 10-piece band, enormous video, and 6 bars, head for *Facade* (3509 NE 163rd St., North Miami Beach; phone: 948-6868). Disco hot spots are the *Alcazaba* in the *Hyatt Regency Coral Gables* (50 Alhambra Plaza, Coral Gables; phone: 441-1234), the *English Pub* (320 Crandon Blvd., Key Biscayne; phone: 361-8877), and *Club Boomerang* (323 23rd St.; phone: 532-2002). The *Hungry Sailor* (3064 Grand Ave., Coconut Grove; phone: 444-9359) offers live reggae nightly. The south end of Miami Beach is the current "in" spot for nightlife. Head to the *Island Club* for hip-hop dancing (the latest rage in Miami) on Mondays, rock 'n' roll Fridays, and reggae Saturdays (701 Washington Ave.; phone: 538-

1213). Rock 'n' roll also reigns at *Penrod's* (1 Ocean Dr.; phone: 538-1111). *Egoist* (455 Ocean Dr.; phone: 534-7436), a late-night dance bistro, features reggae on Sundays. Clubs favored by gays include the *Paragon*, South Beach's largest gay club (1235 Washington Ave., Miami Beach; phone: 534-1235), *Warsaw Ballroom* (1450 Collins Ave.; phone: 531-4555), *Torpedo* (634 Collins Ave.; phone: 538-2500), and *Hombre* (925 Washington Ave.; phone: 538-7883). And, just for laughs, hit the *Improv,* where dinner is served at several shows nightly (*CocoWalk,* 3015 Grand Ave., Coconut Grove; phone: 441-8200). For authentic Haitian music, head for the *Chateau Club* (8267 NE 2nd Ave.; 751-0212) where Haitians, locals, and visitors listen and dance to the *compas* (pronounced *con*-pah), an ear-splitting mix of synthesizers, bongo drums, horns, and cowbells.

Best in Town

CHECKING IN

Winter is the busy season, and reservations should be made well in advance. In winter, a double room in the very expensive range will run $195 and up per night; $140 to $180 in expensive; $95 to $135 in moderate; and about $50 to $90 in inexpensive. Besides the hotels listed below, hundreds of others abound, including chains such as Howard Johnson or Holiday Inn; check the yellow pages or call the hotel toll-free 800 numbers. In summer, most hotels cut their rates, so shop around. For information about bed and breakfast accommodations, contact the Greater Miami Convention and Visitors Bureau (701 Brickell Ave., Miami FL 33131; phone: 539-3000; fax: 539-3113). As we went to press, the *Sonesta Beach* hotel, a 300-room property on Key Biscayne, was closed due to hurricane damage. Plans call for its reopening early this year. For information, call 361-2021 or 800-SONESTA. Most of Miami's major hotels have complete facilities for the business traveler. Those hotels listed below as having "Business services" usually offer such conveniences as meeting rooms, photocopiers, computers, translation services, and express checkout, among others. Call the hotel for additional information. All telephone and fax numbers are in the 305 area code unless otherwise indicated.

For an unforgettable Miami vacation experience, we begin with our favorites, followed by our recommendations of cost and quality choices of hotels, listed by price category.

GRAND HOTELS

Colonnade Built in the 1920s, this Coral Gables hostelry incorporates its original Spanish Renaissance façade and a 2-story, marble-floored rotunda with a late 19th-century decor and European elegance. Luxurious details in its 157 rooms and suites include carved mahogany furniture, king-size beds, armoires, marble vanities, and gold bathroom fixtures. No-smoking rooms are available. Upon arrival, guests are greeted with champagne and orange juice in the dark-paneled, intimate lobby with its overstuffed sofas and Oriental rugs; once settled in, visitors can expect complimentary coffee and the daily newspaper with wake-up calls. A room-service breakfast can be delivered to outdoor tables set among lovely gardens at the rooftop pool and Jacuzzi that overlook Coral Gables. The *Aragon Café* is one of Miami's best hotel restaurants (see "Incredible Edibles" in *Eating Out*). *Doc Dammers Bar & Grill* is a less formal eatery, with interesting early photos of the area, and live music nightly. There is a small health club, and guests also have free use of the *Scandinavian Health Club*, 3 blocks away. A concierge and 24-hour room service complete the picture. Business services. 180 Aragon Ave., Coral Gables (phone: 441-2600 or 800-533-1337; fax: 944-9706).

Doral Country Club It is well-nigh impossible to accurately pick the centerpiece here: the world class golf (5 championship courses and a par 3 practice course), 15 tennis courts, an equestrian center, virtually unlimited access (and free transportation) to its sister property, the *Doral Ocean Beach* resort, or the *Doral Saturnia International Spa* resort. *Saturnia* is the spa everyone's talking about (see *Sybaritic Spas* in DIVERSIONS), a luxurious $33-million facility modeled after the Terme di Saturnia in Italy. Guests live in posh spa suites, indulging in everything from *fango* (volcanic mud) treatments to workouts — all in European grandeur. Taking into account the availability of facilities at all the *Dorals,* virtually no physical or spiritual need is left unattended. 4400 NW 87th Ave. (phone: 592-2000 or 800-22-DORAL; fax: 594-4682).

Grand Bay Everything about this consistent winner of top Florida and US hotel awards is done in high style. Strains of Mozart and Mendelssohn fill the elegantly appointed, European-style lobby; lavish fresh flower arrangements are everywhere. All of its 181 spacious rooms (most have private balconies) overlook Biscayne Bay; suites are decorated in a theme — Italian terra cotta, French country, Japanese, and "Olde" English. Michael Jackson's suite — available when he's not in town — has its own dance floor and some suites have baby grand pianos. Attention to individual needs is paramount; details even extend to the placement of a mat beside your bed so your bare feet needn't touch the carpet. This also is home of the fashionable *Régine's* nightclub and 3 restaurants, including the famed *Grand Café* (see "Incredible Edibles" in *Eating Out*). 2669 S. Bayshore Dr., Coconut Grove (phone: 858-9600, 800-327-2788, or 800-341-0809in Florida; fax: 859-2026).

Turnberry Isle Set on a verdant, 300-acre island on the Intracoastal Waterway in North Miami, this complex of 3 hotels — each with its own distinct personality — offers a total of 340 rooms and suites, all with marble bathrooms with whirlpools. The *Country Club* is a stunner; its lobby/lounge is palatial; its *Veranda* restaurant, open only to registered guests and members, serves such innovative dishes as rum-glazed shrimp with passion-fruit sauce, plantain-crusted salmon filet, and fire-roasted ranch veal chops amid yet more flowers and French elegance. The hotel's exterior is Mediterranean, with barrel-tile roofs and fountains. The guestrooms are beautifully decorated, and even the meeting rooms are brighter and airier than most, with windows opening onto the golf course. Located on the marina, the *Yacht Club* attracts those who revel in things nautical — museum-quality ship models enhance the decor. Guests can charter *Miss Turnberry*, a 140-foot yacht, who makes this her home berth, for $12,000 per day. The marina facilities are superb, and can moor up to 117 150-foot boats. Add 5 pools, a beach reachable by free shuttle, 2 Robert Trent Jones, Sr. championship golf courses, and 24 tennis courts. The adjacent spa, features beauty and stress-management programs, a staff physician and nutritionist, steamrooms and saunas, plus the usual compliment of training machines. Beside the spa sits the *Marina* hotel, favored by such notables as Bill Cosby and Elton John for its no-lobby privacy. The design is Mediterranean. The complex, linked by complimentary shuttle, offers 9 restaurants and lounges, a disco, private beach club, 24-hour room service, and a concierge. Business services. 19999 W. Country Club Dr., Aventura, Turnberry Isle (phone: 932-6200 or 800-327-7028; fax: 932-9096).

VERY EXPENSIVE

Alexander An elegant, yet surprisingly homey place metamorphosed from former luxury apartments, with some units now selling as condominiums. A chandeliered portico, a grand lobby with a curving stairway and antiques from the Cornelius Vanderbilt mansion in New York, and 220 spacious, antiques-filled suites are all impressive, as is *Dominique's* restaurant, with a main dining room overlooking the ocean. Rack of lamb and *tarte tatin* are specialties. A $15-million expansion added a second restaurant and a ballroom. The grounds include an acre of tropical gardens, 2 lagoon swimming pools — 1 with its own waterfall — and 4 soothing whirlpools; a private marina and golf and tennis facilities are nearby. The cost is actually lower per person for a family staying in a suite here than in several rooms in other hotels. Business services. 5225 Collins Ave., Miami Beach (phone: 865-6500, 861-5252, or 800-327-6121; fax: 864-8525).

Doral Ocean Beach On the 18th floor of this 420-room high-rise is *Alfredo the Original of Rome* restaurant, known for its pasta dishes, but also heralded here for such entrées as veal stuffed with mushrooms. Not to be overlooked is the stunning view of the ocean, the Intracoastal Waterway, downtown Miami, and the cruise ships at the Port of Miami. The lobby's European-style gold mosaics, marble, and crystal chandelier have been retained, but other details have been spruced up. Other highlights include exclusive shops, an Olympic-size pool, water sports, 2 outdoor Jacuzzis, a disco, a lounge with live piano music, fitness center, day camp during holidays, a video gameroom, 2 lighted tennis courts, an 80-foot executive yacht available for meetings, and an FAA-licensed helipad. All meals are served indoors and out daily at the *Doral Café* in the hotel and the *Sandbar* at the ocean — more than just another beach bar. There's courtesy shuttle service to the country club (see above) and the spa (see below); *Doral* guests may use the facilities at these two locations at the normal guest rates. Relaxed elegance and friendly staff. Business services. 4833 Collins Ave., Miami Beach (phone: 532-3600 or 800-22DORAL; fax: 532-2334).

Doral Saturnia Spa Adjacent to the *Doral Country Club*, the spa evokes the feeling of its ancient namesake in Tuscany with its clay tile roofs and Roman arches, yet the equipment is thoroughly 20th century. Each of its 48 suites has its own whirlpool bath, but that's only the beginning. There's everything needed by those in search of enhanced fitness, health, and stress management (see *Sybaritic Spas* in DIVERSIONS). The Tuscan menu, based on the spa's Fat Point System of Nutrition, is served in the informal *Ristorante di Saturnia* or the luxurious *Villa Montepaldi*. All the facilities at the two previously mentioned Doral resorts are available to guests here. 8755 NW 36th St., Miami (phone: 593-6030, 800-331-7768, or 800-22DORAL; fax: 591-9266).

Fisher Island Just off the southern tip of Miami Beach, this exclusive 216-acre island was once the Spanish-style private winter playground of William Vanderbilt. Now a private club and elite residential resort refuge, the island has extravagantly furnished apartments, villas, and a couple of historic cottages surrounded by manicured gardens with strolling peacocks. Though the cost for transient rental is significant, it's worth it to many for the island's unique serenity and distance from "the outside world." A 40-person security force ensures that privacy. Facilities include a 9-hole golf course designed by P. B. Dye — plus clubhouse and complimentary golf cart — superb tennis courts (see *Tennis* in this chapter), croquet, basketball, an oceanfront beach, 2 marinas harboring enormous yachts, 7 restaurants (1 housed in the original Vanderbilt mansion, with marble floors and mahogany paneling), and several shops. The European-style *Spa Internazionale* (see *Sybaritic Spas* in DIVERSIONS) is a good place to unwind. Business services. Accessible only by helicopter, private boat, or private ferry; special treatment begins as drivers exit the ferry, when cars are hosed off to remove salt spray. 1 Fisher Island Dr., Fisher Island (phone: 535-6021 or 800-624-3251; fax: 535-6003).

Hyatt Regency Coral Gables A smaller property than its sister *Hyatt Regency* (on Second Ave.) and much more beautiful, this one has 242 rooms (half are nonsmoking) in Spanish-Mediterranean style influenced by the Alhambra Palace, an outdoor pool, a Jacuzzi, and health club. The *Two Sisters* restaurant features Spanish-Mediterranean cuisine, with a landscaped courtyard for outdoor dining (see *Eating Out*), and the *Alcazaba* disco swings. Business services. 50 Alhambra Plaza, Coral Gables (phone: 441-1234 or 800-233-1234; fax: 441-0520).

Mayfair House This all-suite hotel, part of the *Mayfair Mall* complex in the heart of Coconut Grove, has 182 suites, each with a Jacuzzi (in some cases on a terrace), and a small dining area where a complimentary continental breakfast (with lots of tropical fruit) is served each morning. Suites are beautifully decorated in dark woods and calming tones that accentuate eye-appealing angles of the architectural design; 50 have antique pianos and all include VCRs, marble bathrooms, and 2 phones. The lobby boasts two original Tiffany windows. Dining and/or drinking options include the highly regarded *Mayfair Grill* (see *Eating Out*), 2 lounges, and a bar at the rooftop pool with view of the bay. Business services. 3000 Florida Ave., Coconut Grove (phone: 441-0000, 800-433-4555, or 800-341-0809 in Florida; fax: 447-9173).

Sheraton Bal Harbour Located in the exclusive Bal Harbour area, this 666-room property sits within a lushly landscaped 10-acre garden leading directly to the ocean. Enticements include 2 outdoor pools, 2 tennis courts, a jogging path along the beach, a new health club with exercise equipment, volleyball, a Vita exercise course on the beach, water sports, and a gameroom. For sipping and supping, there are the *Bal Harbour Bar & Grille*, a steak and seafood restaurant with open-hearth kitchen; an enlarged coffee shop that's open all day; an oceanside snack and drink bar; 3 lounges; and the *Edible Express*, a 24-hour take-out deli. Business services. Directly across the street are the elegant *Bal Harbour Shops*, with tenants such as *Neiman Marcus*, *Saks Fifth Avenue*, and *Cartier*. 9701 Collins Ave., Bal Harbour (phone: 865-7511 or 800-325-3535; fax: 864-2601).

EXPENSIVE

Biltmore Originally opened in 1926, this gracious edifice was the creation of George Merrick, who built Coral Gables. Influenced by Seville's Giralda Tower, the 273-room property is Spanish Revival, with bits of Moorish and Italian influence. Now run by Westin hotels, the newly refurbished establishment boasts such elegant accents as carved wood-lined elevators, miles of travertine marble floors and columns, and antique furniture. High living types may choose the 2-bedroom, 3-bathroom Everglades Suite, known as the Al Capone Suite, after the mobster who lived here for 8 years. Standard guestrooms lack the opulence of the public areas. Amenities include a 17,000-square-foot U-shape pool (arguably the country's largest hotel pool), an 18-hole golf course, tennis on 10-lighted courts, and the extensive *Biltmore Club and Spa* (see *Sybaritic Spas* in DIVERSIONS). The hotel also has 2 restaurants. Business services. 1200 Anastasia Ave., Coral Gables (phone: 445-1926 or 800-727-1926; fax: 448-9976).

Fontainebleau Hilton This Miami Beach grande dame, with 1,206 guestrooms on 20 acres of beachfront real estate, is still glamorous. The lagoon-like pool has a grotto bar inside a cave; there also are 3 whirlpool baths. The 12 restaurants and lounges include *Ohba*, a new Japanese steakhouse and sushi bar, as well as a kosher kitchen. There's also a fully equipped *Spa Pavilion* (see *Sybaritic Spas* in DIVERSIONS) and 7 night-lit tennis courts with pro shop. Business services. 4441 Collins Ave., Miami Beach (phone: 538-2000, 800-HILTONS, or 800-548-8886 in Florida; fax: 534-7821).

Inter-Continental Miami Built in the grand old hotel tradition, this property is in the city center, near the Brickell Avenue financial district and *Bayside Marketplace*. The 644 rooms in the soaring 34-floor travertine triangle have marble baths and Oriental furniture, along with other luxurious appointments. Former President George Bush and actor Eddie Murphy have stayed in the 2-story Royal Suite. The lobby, with its 18-foot Henry Moore sculpture, is done in beige and bone travertine marble, accented with green rattan furniture and area rugs. Facilities include the highly regarded *Le Pavillon Grill* (see *Eating Out*) and 2 other restaurants, a lounge, and a swimming pool, plus a quarter-mile outdoor jogging trail that takes advantage of the stunning views of Biscayne Bay. Stores include a duty-free shop. There are 3 nonsmoking floors. Business services. Parking arrangements are less than ideal; guests have been known to wait as long as an hour for their cars to be tracked down in the garage and delivered to them. 100 Chopin Plaza, Miami (phone: 577-1000 or 800-327-0200; fax: 577-0384).

Marlin This Art Deco District hostelry combines 1930s architecture with 1990s amenities in 12 units, which include central air conditioning, TV sets with VCRs, and kitchens. Decor in the public rooms is "Jam-Deco," classic Deco with Jamaican hot colors. The hotel was developed by Chris Blackwell, founder of *Island Records*, who included a recording studio on the premises, attracting lots of show-biz types. The *Shabeen* restaurant serves West Indian food; the bar serves exotic drinks. 1200 Collins Ave., Miami Beach (phone: 673-8770).

Miami Airport Hilton Located on a lagoon at the airport (natch), the 500-room hostelry offers a pool, a Jacuzzi, a sauna, jet- and water-ski rentals, and 24-hour free use of 3 lighted tennis courts; they'll even lend you a racquet. There's also a concierge floor, café, nightclub, and a bar. 5101 Blue Lagoon Dr., Miami (phone: 262-1000 or 800-445-8667; fax: 267-0038).

Radisson Mart Plaza Convenient for business types, with a location next to the *Miami International Merchandise Mart*, it has 334 rooms and suites, a concierge level with complimentary continental breakfast and open bar for cocktails, 3 restaurants and lounges, a lushly planted outdoor pool, 2 lighted tennis courts, a health club with exercise room and racquetball courts. Business services. Rates include free parking and free airport transportation. 711 NW 72nd Ave., Miami (phone: 261-3800 or 800-333-3333; fax: 261-7665).

Sheraton Biscayne Bay This comfortable hostelry overlooks Biscayne Bay, with a view of the cruise ships docked at Port Miami. Located in the financial district, it has 612 newly renovated rooms and suites, and an outdoor pool. *Ashley's* restaurant serves moderately priced food (open daily for breakfast, lunch, and dinner), and the *Coco Loco* lounge features a DJ or live music on Friday nights. Business services. 495 Brickell Ave., Miami (phone: 373-6000 or 800-325-3535; fax: 374-2279).

MODERATE

Cavalier Built back in 1936, this 41-room property is decked out in tangerine, turquoise, and pink African-inspired decor; many rooms have canopy beds. Also offered are cable TV, VCRs, CD players, free parking, and complimentary continental breakfast; there's a restaurant at the nearby *Cardozo* hotel. 1320 Ocean Dr., Miami Beach (phone: 534-2135 or 800-338-9076; fax: 531-5543).

Leslie Another vintage 1930s hotel in South Beach. Newly redecorated in vivid island prints, the 43-room hostelry offers air conditioning, cable TV, VCRs, CD players, and complimentary continental breakfast. 1244 Ocean Dr., Miami Beach (phone: 534-2135 or 800-338-9076; fax: 531-5543.

Place St. Michel Charming, cozy, and elegant describe this small European-style bed and breakfast establishment built in 1926. In the heart of Coral Gables, it's favored by international architects who appreciate its Art Deco details and antique furnishings. On the premises is *Stuart's,* a jazz bar; *St. Michel,* an excellent dining spot (see *Eating Out*); and a charcuterie that's popular with the local lunch crowd. All 27 rooms are air conditioned and have TV sets. Continental breakfast is included; room service is available until 11 PM, and there's an obliging concierge desk. 162 Alcazar Ave., Coral Gables (phone: 444-1666 or 800-247-8526; fax: 529-0074).

Ritz Plaza This 1940s-style hostelry, with its much-photographed Art Deco squared finial, has been restored to its early splendor, with a soaring lobby featuring the original four-color terrazzo floor and a front desk made of coral — one of the few such pieces extant. (Protection of reefs now prohibits this kind of use.) The 132 redecorated rooms and suites feature central air conditioning, television sets, and modernized original cast-iron tubs. An Olympic-size pool overlooks the ocean, with water sports available a few feet away. The *Ritz Café,* a high-ceilinged dining room with a huge crystal chandelier and a round window wall facing the ocean, is open from 7 AM; meals also are served on the terrace. *Harry's Bar* has a 1940s–1950s look — with a glass brick bar, lots of chrome, and a jukebox playing 1950s music — and offers a light menu. Guests often include photography crews shooting fashion assignments nearby. 1701 Collins Ave. (near the Convention Center); Miami Beach (phone: 534-3500 or 800-522-6400; fax: 531-6928).

Sol Miami Beach Originally the *Cadillac* hotel, this 270-room, ocean-front property (ca. 1938) is now owned by the Spain-based Grupo Sol. The cool turquoise and blue deco exterior belies its glitzy interior: plum and yellow, with lots of neon. There are 5 restaurants and lounges, cable TV, air conditioning, and kitchenettes in some units. For action, a pool, volleyball and shuffleboard courts, and water sports are available. Business services. 3925 Collins Ave., Miami Beach (phone: 531-3534 or 800-336-3542; fax: 531-1765).

INEXPENSIVE

Miami River Inn Claiming to be the oldest continuously operating inn south of St. Augustine, this charming bed and breakfast establishment on the Miami River was built in 1908. Its 40 antiques-furnished rooms in 4 wooden buildings with lushly planted pool and whirlpool area make guests feel they're in another place and time. Close to Little Havana and downtown Miami, this inn offers 24-hour security. 118 SW South River Dr., entrance on SW 2nd St.; phone: 325-0045.

EATING OUT

Much of Miami's socializing centers around restaurant dining, so beware long lines during the winter season (December through April), when snowbirds swell the ranks of resident regulars. Residents always make reservations. Expect to pay $85 or more for a dinner for two at a place listed in the very expensive range; $70 to $80 at a place in the expensive category; $50 to $70 in the moderate range; and under $50 in the inexpensive range. Prices do not include drinks, wine, or tips. Many establishments in the very expensive and expensive categories require that men wear jackets; it's wise to call ahead to inquire. All telephone numbers are in the 305 area code unless otherwise indicated.

In a town where destination dining is a major league sport, separating the good from the great, the merely delicious from the unforgettable is part of the game. The range is broad — from sumptuous and sophisticated to homegrown and ethnic; don't be timid about trying it all. We begin with our culinary favorites, followed by our recommendations of cost and quality choices, listed by price category.

INCREDIBLE EDIBLES

Aragon Café The *Colonnade* hotel's outstanding dining room features Old World decor, with mahogany trim and crystal chandeliers. The menu includes a blue crab cake appetizer, an enormous veal chop, or exquisitely prepared

Muscovy duck with polenta. Delicious details include the sweet-potato mousse that accompanies entrées, and specialty dessert soufflés, which must be ordered at the beginning of dinner. (The pistachio soufflé with chocolate chips on a bed of vanilla sauce makes diners think they've gone to heaven.) Service is impeccable, without being condescending. Open for dinner Tuesdays through Saturdays from 6 to 11 PM. Closed Sundays and Mondays. Reservations advised. Major credit cards accepted. 180 Aragon Ave., Coral Gables (phone: 441-2600 or 800-533-1337).

Brasserie Le Coze On the theory that you can't have too much of a good thing, brother and sister Gilbert and Maguy Le Coze, owners of New York City's *Le Bernardin*, have brought their impressive culinary talents to the South. This star on the Miami dining scene had its roots in Paris (*Le Bernardin* was one of Paris's three-star restaurants) and the Le Cozes offer an appealing Gallic ambience in a setting of hand-painted Portuguese and French tiles, leather booths, and terrace doors that open onto sidewalk tables. The fare is first-rate and the menu is as diverse as the surroundings. Dining choices run the gamut from stone crab appetizers and grouper with aioli (garlic) sauce, to duck *confit* cassoulet or grilled Angus steak. Also try the shellfish, priced by-the-piece for oysters and clams. It's not the Faubourg St.-Honoré or West 51st Street, but it's close. Open Thursdays through Sundays, serving lunch from noon to 2:30 PM and dinner from 6 PM to midnight. Reservations advised. Major credit cards accepted. 2901 Florida Ave., Coconut Grove (phone: 444-9697).

Café Chauveron Transplanted many years ago from New York City to Bay Harbor without the slightest disturbance to its famous mile-high soufflés, this French dining place exudes elegance with its rich decor, dark wood paneling, and crystal chandelier. The dining area is divided into two levels, the lower one looking out onto Indian Creek. A good place for spotting Miami celebs. Everything is beautifully prepared, from *coquille de fruits de mer au champagne* (scallops in champagne), *pompano papillote* (local fish cooked in parchment paper), and stone-crab ravioli to Grand Marnier soufflé with raspberry *coulis* and *crème fraîche*. Docking space is provided if you arrive by boat. Open daily for dinner from 6 to 10:30 PM, but closed from June through early October. Reservations advised. Major credit cards accepted. 9561 E. Bay Harbor Dr., Bay Harbor Island, Miami Beach (phone: 866-8779).

Chef Allen's Chef/owner Allen Susser has won deserved national acclaim for his culinary achievements. (*Food & Wine* magazine voted him one of the country's Best New American Chefs.) Featured here is regional South Florida cooking, using local produce and fresh-caught yellowtail, tuna, and snapper (Norwegian salmon also is served here with its own caviar). The menu changes daily and may include whole-wheat linguini with lobster or Florida bay scallop ceviche with cilantro. Even the salad of field greens is beautifully presented, with tiny confetti-like squares of colorful peppers. Carrot *timbale* enhances the entrées, and the white chocolate bombe is as rewarding to the eyes as it is to the taste buds. For calorie and/or fat-gram counters, many creative "spa cuisine" dishes are also featured. The setting — highly lacquered furniture and bright, neon lights — is as upbeat, fresh and sophisticated as the food. Open daily for dinner from 6 to 10:30 PM, until 11 PM Fridays and Saturdays. Reservations advised. Major credit cards accepted. 19088 NE 29th Ave., North Miami Beach (phone: 935-2900).

Fish Market Far more elegant than its name implies, this is possibly South Florida's best seafood restaurant. In the *Omni International* hotel, the two-room dining area gleams with marble and mirrors. You can order just about any kind of fish grilled, with a broad choice of sauces, but the kitchen also performs magic with specialties like the colossal shrimp — Central American crustaceans as large as baby lobster tails, yet succulent and tender — or grilled snapper with buckwheat pasta. If ordered in advance, you can get superb sole filets stuffed with Florida lobster, mussels, and wild mushrooms, or the sumptuous scallops and medallions of lobster served with *risotto milanese* (Italian short-grain rice with saffron). And for a special treat, try the pâté of tropical fruits and berries with passion-fruit sauce for dessert. Businesspeople love the "executive service" lunch, when a 2-course meal is served in less than 30 minutes or there's no charge. Open weekdays for lunch 11:30 AM to 2:30 PM, Mondays through Saturdays from 6:30 to 11PM for dinner. Reservations advised. Major credit cards accepted. In the *Omni International Hotel,* 1601 Biscayne Blvd., Miami (phone: 374-4399).

Grand Café On Queen Elizabeth's 1991 visit to Miami, it was this eatery's Chef Suki who conferred with the royal chefs regarding local foods; moreover, *Grand Café* provided the hors d'oeuvres for her fete at the *Vizcaya* mansion (see *Special Places*). It has an elegantly European dining room, attentive service, and wonderful creations, including such international innovations as duck smoked over Texas pecan shells and topped with ginger-flavored passion-fruit sauce. Also try Suki's famous black linguine (made with squid ink), she-crab soup, or rack of lamb. Follow up with chocolate raspberry truffle cake. Jackets are recommended for men. Open daily for breakfast 7 to 11 AM, plus Sunday brunch 11:30 AM to 3 PM; Mondays through Saturdays for lunch 11:30 AM to 3 PM; daily for dinner 6 to 11 PM. Reservations necessary for dinner, advised for other meals. Major credit cards accepted. In the *Grand Bay Hotel,* 2669 S. Bayshore Dr., Coconut Grove (phone: 858-9600).

Joe's Stone Crab Our hands-down favorite for the ultimate Miami dining experience, this place has been selling tons of the best stone crabs around since 1913, along with scrumptious home fries, delectable coleslaw, and to-die-for Key lime pie. Diners often have to wait hours to be seated and service can be rushed and sporadic, but devoted fans — like us — say it's well worth the wait and inconvenience. Besides the crabs, lobster and fresh fish also are served. Picnickers can buy lunch from the restaurant's take-out section and avoid the lunacy in the dining room. It's big, noisy, and informal. A must meal. Open for lunch Tuesdays through Saturdays from 11:30 AM to 2 PM; dinner 5 to 10 PM Tuesdays to Thursdays, until 11 PM Fridays and Saturdays. Closed from mid-May to mid-October. No reservations. Major credit cards accepted. 227 Biscayne St., Miami Beach (phone: 673-0365 or 800-780-CRAB).

Mark's Place The modern interior — dramatized by vibrant contemporary Venetian glass sculptures — serves as an exciting backdrop for this Miami "in" spot. Chef Mark Militello whips up such imaginative dishes as grilled yellowtail snapper with Mediterranean salsa; West Indian pumpkin and hearts of palm; or salmon with couscous, fried onion strips, and nasturtiums. The rich desserts include a terrific pear tart. Open for lunch weekdays noon to 2:30 PM; for dinner Mondays through Thursdays 6:30 to 10:30 PM, Fridays and Saturdays 6 to 11 PM, and Sundays 6 PM to 10:30PM. Reservations necessary. Major credit cards accepted. 2286 NE 123 St., North Miami Beach (phone: 893-6888).

Le Pavillon For diners seeking creative cookery in elegant surroundings, here is top American food with a decidedly nouvelle bent: Everglade frogs' legs cakes with chilled vermouth mayonnaise, grilled venison medallions with cassis sauce, duck "in two acts" (sautéed breast and duck *confit*), tuna carpaccio, and grilled pompano with rosemary sauce. The *crème brûlée*, filled with fresh berries, is a visual and gustatory sensation. The setting is stylishly formal, with beveled mirrors and green granite; the food magnificently prepared, and the service faultless. Dinner only from 6 to 10 PM Mondays through Thursdays, until 11 PM Fridays and Saturdays; closed Sundays. Reservations necessary. Major credit cards accepted. In the *Inter-Continental Hotel,* 100 Chopin Plaza, Miami (phone: 577-1000).

VERY EXPENSIVE

Forge Once more famous for its 300,000-bottle wine collection (a recently purchased 1822 Lafitte Rothschild bottle went for $73,000!) and its elegance than for its complex dishes, the ornately decorated restaurant — filled with antique furnishings, stained glass, carved ceilings, and crystal chandeliers — has ditched its stodgy steaks and chops for more imaginative, continental fare, including roasted duck with black currant sauce and grilled salmon on a Mediterranean salad with citrus sauce. For dessert, regulars love the famed blacksmith pie — alternating layers of chocolate cake, French vanilla custard, and whipped cream — but don't bypass the chocolate cheesecake. Open for dinner nightly. Reservations necessary.

Major credit cards accepted. 432 Arthur Godfrey Rd., Miami Beach (phone: 538-8533).

A Mano The Art Deco section along Ocean Drive boasts numerous restaurants, running the gamut from good to fair, but this one, in the *Betsy Ross* hotel, rises far above the others. Award-winning chef Norman Van Aken bills his food as "New World Cooking," the style favored by South Florida's best chefs, who use contemporary American techniques married with local and Caribbean ingredients to create unique dishes. Outstanding examples are the tamarind-glazed grilled veal chop and fried crab cakes with Peruvian purple potato salad. Open for dinner Tuesdays through Sundays. Reservations advised. Major credit cards accepted. 1440 Ocean Dr., Miami Beach (phone: 531-6266).

EXPENSIVE

Cassis Bistro A stunning, contemporary South Beach bistro serving such elegant dishes as veal chops with shiitake mushroom sauce, polenta, and grilled tuna with couscous. For dessert try the *crème brûlée catalane* (flavored with anise) or *pot de mousse au chocolate*. Reservations suggested for parties of six or more and on weekends. Open daily for dinner. Major credit cards accepted. 764 Washington Ave., Miami Beach (phone: 531-7700).

Kaleidoscope Fine dining in the Grove, in a romantic enclosed garden, on a balcony, or in an air conditioned dining room. Favorites include Bahamian grilled seafood cakes, grilled swordfish, and fresh fruit tarts with almond pastry made on the premises. Open daily for lunch and dinner. Reservations advised. Major credit cards accepted. 3112 Commodore Plaza, Coconut Grove (phone: 446-5010).

Mayfair Grill Located in the *Mayfair House* hotel in Coconut Grove, the new menu has been created by chef Guy Schnaars, formerly of *Mark's Place*, using Florida cuisine, marrying classic techniques and local ingredients. Specialties include grilled veal chops with wild mushroom risotto, grilled grouper with black beans and fried plantains, veal medallions with stone crab sauce, and grilled baby chicken with corn pancakes. Open daily for breakfast, lunch, and dinner, plus Sunday brunch. Reservations advised. Major credit cards accepted. 3000 Florida Ave., Coconut Grove (phone: 441-0000).

Rusty Pelican For a dynamite view of downtown Miami across the bay, try the fare in this nautically decorated spot. Drinks are served on the waterside patio. Meals range from burgers and prime ribs of beef, to seafood and tropical fruits. Open for lunch Mondays through Saturdays, dinner daily, and Sunday brunch. Reservations suggested. Major credit cards accepted. 3201 Rickenbacker Cswy., Key Biscayne (phone: 361-3818).

Yuca The name derives from both a Miami acronym for Young Upscale Cuban-Americans and a starchy vegetable (actually spelled "yucca") that is a staple of Cuban cooking. The bilingual menu features nouvelle twists on Cuban standards: black-bean soup with rice cakes, excellent yellowtail filet in plantain leaves served with crab enchiladas — dishes savored by a sophisticated international clientele. A braille menu is available. Open for lunch Mondays through Saturdays, dinner daily. Reservations necessary. Major credit cards accepted. 177 Giralda Ave., Coral Gables (phone: 444-4448).

MODERATE

Big City Fish The Gulf Coast has been transported to South Florida in this seafood warehouse with an open kitchen serving such specialties as Florida stone crabs, "peel-and-eat-'em" shrimp broiled in cane sugar, and Apalachicola oysters — surprisingly good value for the money. The chef is imported from Mississippi, the beer from Louisiana, and the food from the whole region. We recommend the swordfish dip (smoked on the premises), seafood gumbo, and the oyster "po'boy." Open daily for lunch, dinner, and late-night snacks. No reservations, except for large groups. Major credit cards accepted. In *CocoWalk,* 3015 Grand Ave., Coconut Grove (phone: 445-CITY).

La Bussola Gleaming with mirrors and Italian Renaissance artwork, this Italian dining spot adds to the ambience with a pianist and a violinist. Selections include black linguine with calamari, and roasted peppers and yellowfin tuna with black olive sauce and fried capers. Open daily for lunch and dinner. Reservations advised. Major credit cards accepted. 270 Giralda Ave., Coral Gables (phone: 445-8788).

Casa Juancho Country hams hang over the bar and troubadours stroll and serenade at this lively Spanish spot, thought by many to offer the best Spanish food in Little Havana's *Calle Ocho* neighborhood. The *parrillada en marisco* (shrimp, scallops, squid, and lobster cooked on the big open grill) is a house specialty, as are the *tapas* (hors d'oeuvres), served straight from the bar. Open daily for lunch and dinner. Reservations advised on weekends, but not accepted for after 8 PM. Major credit cards accepted. 2436 SW 8th St., Miami (phone: 642-2452).

Crawdaddy's Primarily known for seafood including stone crabs, plus chicken and prime ribs, it is served among Victoriana in 9 dining rooms. The setting is in spectacular South Pointe Park on Government Cut where cruise ships sailing out to sea seem within touching distance of every table. Open for lunch Mondays through Saturdays, for Sunday brunch, and for dinner daily. Reservations advised. Major credit cards accepted. 1 Washington Ave., Miami Beach (phone: 673-1708).

Monty Trainer's A casual atmosphere pervades this bayside eatery in Coconut Grove. Guests can arrive either by car or boat (100 dock spaces are available for diners), then enjoy a seafood meal on a palm-fringed terrace or indoors in a more formal atmosphere with a view of the bay. Its inside, upstairs section — *Monty's Stone Crab* — serves those delectable crustaceans year-round (they're brought in from Virginia during the local off-season), as well as a wide array of fresh seafood, steaks, and pasta. Both open for lunch and dinner daily. Reservations advised. Major credit cards accepted. 2550 S. Bayshore Dr., Coconut Grove (phone: 858-1431).

SOBE Bar and Rotisserie This popular new eatery is fashioned after New York City's *Amsterdam* restaurant (*Amsterdam*'s owner, Ture Tufvesson, is also one of the owners here). The menu specializes in chicken broiled on a spit, as well as fresh seafood dishes. Diners can watch their meals being prepared in the open kitchen. Open daily; dinner only. Reservations advised. Major credit cards accepted. 560 Washington Ave., Miami Beach (phone: 531-7170).

Sundays on the Bay Steaks, pasta, fresh fish, and chicken head the bill at this bayside location for water watchers on Key Biscayne. Dining is inside or dockside, where lighter dishes are also available. Open daily for lunch and dinner, late snacks Sunday, and Sunday brunch. Reservations necessary for dinner. Major credit cards accepted. 5420 Crandon Blvd., Key Biscayne (phone: 361-6777).

Toni's Japanese standards and nouvelle Tokyo fare, such as grilled salmon, chicken, steaks, and shrimp teriyaki. Their sushi is the best on South Beach. Open daily for dinner. Reservations necessary on weekends. Major credit cards accepted. 1208 Washington Ave., Miami Beach (phone: 673-9368).

I Tre Merli An offshoot of a Manhattan eatery, it mimics its New York ancestry with a 20-foot ceiling, black slate floor, and exposed brick walls stacked with thousands of wine bottles. The Genoese fare includes *trenetto* (a linguini-like pasta) with pesto sauce, *vongole al salto* (clams in tomato sauce), and *scottata di salmone* (sliced salmon baked with lemon butter sauce and served with caviar). Open for dinner daily. Reservations advised on weekends. Major credit cards accepted. 1437 Washington Ave., Miami Beach (phone: 672-6702).

Unicorn Village Outstanding natural-food restaurant and marketplace, with tables inside and outside on a marina with dockage for diners arriving by boat. Creative salads, low-fat and low-sodium dishes, and Tongol tuna (which presents no threat to dolphins) are featured. A large selection of by-the-glass wines includes 7 organically produced choices (with no added sulfites). Open daily for lunch and dinner plus Sunday brunch. Reservations advised for parties of six or more. Major credit cards accepted. Note: This is a totally nonsmoking place. At *The Shops at the Waterways,* 3595 NE 207th St., North Miami Beach (phone: 933-8829).

INEXPENSIVE

Café Tu Tu Tango In Coconut Grove's *CocoWalk* complex, this jumping eatery decked out as an artist's loft touts its Italian and Spanish specialties as "food for the starving artist." It offers light, multi-ethnic dishes such as *fritattas* (Italian omelettes), pizza, smoked chicken quesadillas, and kebabs. Portions are appetizer-sized so patrons pick and choose. Don't miss the fabulous guava cheesecake. Open Tuesdays through Sundays for lunch, dinner, and late snacks. No reservations. Major credit cards accepted. 3015 Grand Ave., Coconut Grove (phone: 529-2222).

Centro Vasco Next to jai alai, this is Miami's favorite Basque import. The specialties are *filet madrilene de Centro Vasco,* seafood paella, and *arroz con mariscos* (shellfish and rice). A great sangria is made right at your table. Open daily for lunch and dinner. Flamenco shows Wednesday to Sunday nights in *Cacharrito's Place,* a separate entertainment lounge off the dining room. Reservations advised for dinner, but not accepted for the show. Major credit cards accepted. 2235 SW 8th St., Miami (phone: 643-9606).

Chez Moy For food in the Haitian tradition, try this small eatery. Favorite dishes include steamed fish with fried plantains or fresh conch served with rice and beans. The neighborhood is a bit rough; it's a good idea to come with a group if possible. Open daily for all 3 meals. Reservations advised. No credit cards accepted. 1 NW 54th St. (phone: 757-5056).

11th Street Diner This 1948 diner traveled from its home in Wilkes Barre, PA, to trendy South Beach. Good, old-fashioned dishes include meat loaf with mashed potatoes and gravy, and black cows (root beer floats), along with such modern items as Cobb salad and marinated dolphin. Open daily 24 hours. No reservations. Major credit cards accepted. 1065 Washington Ave. (phone: 534-6373).

Lazy Lizard On Lincoln Road Mall, this place serves some of the best Southwestern fare in town — from chicken or beef *fajitas* to Mexican-style "Aztec" pizza. Closed Mondays. No reservations. Major credit cards accepted. 646 Lincoln Rd., Miami Beach (phone: 532-2908).

Málaga This traditional Cuban eatery in Little Havana is a good place to get acquainted with the island basics. Best are standards like fried whole red snapper, spiced pork, or *arroz con pollo.* A must-try is the fried plantains. Terrific flamenco shows with a young female dancer and an aging male singer nightly except Tuesdays. Open daily for lunch and dinner. Reservations unnecessary. Major credit cards accepted. 740 SW 8th St., Miami (phone: 858-4224).

News Café An international newsstand-cum-bookstore-cum-sidewalk café that's an ideal spot for people watching or a pre-beach breakfast. The menu is light, with sandwiches, salads, and cheeses, and an emphasis on Middle Eastern fare. Located across from the ocean in the heart of South Beach. Open daily 24 hours. Reservations unnecessary. Major credit cards accepted. 800 Ocean Dr., Miami Beach (phone: 538-6397).

Palace Grill A popular Art Deco District eatery serving hamburgers and salads at indoor and outdoor tables. You can get a kosher hot dog or a serving of granola. Open daily for all 3 meals and late-night snacks. No reservations. Major credit cards accepted. 1200 Ocean Dr., Miami Beach (phone: 531-9077).

Rascal House One of only two Florida restaurants to make food guru Mimi Sheraton's list of the 50 best US restaurants (the other being *Mark's Place*). Long lines snaking into the parking lot attest to the restaurant's popularity for almost 40 years. Try the pastrami on rye or the *rugelach*. Open daily for all three meals and late snacks. No reservations or credit cards accepted. 17190 Collins Ave., Miami Beach. (phone: 947-4581).

Versailles Authentic Cuban food and a lively ambience characterize this Little Havana landmark. A favorite of Latins and knowledgeable gringos. They make wonderful Cuban sandwiches, and there are black beans and rice. Open daily for dinner until the wee hours. No reservations. Major credit cards accepted. 3555 SW 8th St., Miami (phone: 444-7614).

Wolfie's A Miami Beach institution since 1947, it might be described as an overgrown deli whose eclectic, 500-item menu carries everything from knishes to chicken parmesan and mountainous desserts. Open 24 hours daily. No reservations. Major credit cards accepted. 2038 Collins Ave., Miami Beach (phone: 538-6626).

Ft. Lauderdale

For many Americans, the mere mention of Ft. Lauderdale still conjures up images of the 1960 movie *Where the Boys Are* (or its 1980s remake), which immortalized the seasonal migration of the nation's college students to this sunny city during spring break. The annual migration has diminished, however; city leaders have discouraged that much-reported rite of spring in order to improve Ft. Lauderdale's overall appeal to adults and to expand family tourism.

It seems to have worked. Collegians now set their springtime compasses to Daytona Beach while Mom, Dad, and the kids — along with increasing numbers of visitors from Europe and Asia — populate Ft. Lauderdale's beaches. And with good reason: Ft. Lauderdale claims to receive 3,000 hours of sunshine a year — more than anywhere else in the continental US — and the year-round average temperature is in the mid-70s. And the city's public relations people would like it known that Ft. Lauderdale has never ever recorded a 100-degree temperature.

In addition to its benign climate, Ft. Lauderdale's proximity to the water has formed its character as a prime resort area. The city is virtually afloat. It (and surrounding Broward County) is bordered on the east by 23 miles of Atlantic Ocean coastline and beaches, on the west by that "river of grass," the Everglades. Between the two are 300 miles of the navigable Intracoastal Waterway and an intricate network of canals that have led to Ft. Lauderdale's nickname, the "Venice of America." Relaxed and informal, Ft. Lauderdale is best enjoyed in shorts and sandals, except at night, when things are a touch more formal.

While other resort areas count only their visitors, the Ft. Lauderdale area also counts boats. More than 40,000 are permanently registered, and 10,000 or so more join their ranks during the winter months, as the yachting crowd from as far away as Canada cruises down to the area's warm waters. (Author John D. MacDonald's readers will recognize the *Bahia Mar Yacht Basin* as the place where Travis McGee, the laid-back sleuth, moors his houseboat, the *Busted Flush*.) Moreover, thousands of smaller craft — sailboats and powerboats — knife through these waters throughout the year. Even the *Christmas* holiday is celebrated in special Ft. Lauderdale fashion. Hundreds of elaborately decorated and lighted boats and yachts take to the Intracoastal Waterway for the unusual *Winterfest Boat Parade* from Port Everglades to Pompano Beach. Every available waterfront viewing point is packed to watch waving Santas navigate their water-sleighs past crowded bridges, backyards, and hotel balconies.

The city is named after Major William Lauderdale, who arrived in 1838 to quell the Seminole Indians and build a fort on the New River amidst mosquito-infested, inhospitable mangrove swamps. The door for development first opened during the late 1890s, when the entrepreneur Henry Flagler began extending his *Florida East Coast Railroad* south from Palm Beach. (For more information on Palm Beach, see *Tour 7: Palm Beach* in DIRECTIONS.) A swamp drainage and reclamation project was undertaken in 1906, and canals were dug to create "finger islands," thus maximizing the city's waterside real estate. Ft. Lauderdale was incorporated in 1911, and has welcomed millions of visitors ever since.

Today, Ft. Lauderdale is the largest — and by far the best known — of the 28 municipalities that constitute Broward County, the second most populous of Florida's 67 counties. The permanent population of just over 1.2 million (in the county; Ft. Lauderdale itself has 150,000 residents) swells each winter season as 5 million tourists pour in. To these guests, Ft. Lauderdale and vicinity offer a wide choice of places to stay, from tiny motels to huge luxury hotels and sumptuous resorts; more than 30,000 rooms for visitors can be found in the five major oceanfront communities. Even the most demanding diner will find satisfaction in one of the area's more than 2,500 restaurants, while its many nightclubs, discos, and theaters provide diversion of an evening. And in the sun-splashed daytime, those who tire of frolicking on the beach may work out on the approximately 76 golf courses and 550 tennis courts.

But Ft. Lauderdale is not just sunshine and surf. It's also a bustling commercial city, and its pride, Port Everglades, is one of the nation's busiest cargo and passenger ports. Near Port Everglades on the Intracoastal Waterway, the nearly $50-million *Greater Ft. Lauderdale/Broward County Convention Center* opened in 1991.

City leaders also recently undertook a $670-million refurbishment and expansion of Ft. Lauderdale's downtown core, and a number of high-rise office buildings have sprung up, attracting new business. Near those structures, on the New River, sits the impressive $50-million *Broward Center for the Performing Arts*, which makes up the heart of the city's arts and science district. Across the street is the newest addition, the $30.6-million *Museum of Discovery and Science,* with everything from hands-on exhibits to a 5-story IMAX theater. *Riverwalk*, a lushly landscaped path along the New River, goes past the *Broward Center for the Performing Arts,* restaurants, and historic buildings.

Furthermore, the cities that make up the greater Ft. Lauderdale area are a diverse lot: Davie, whose residents prefer jeans and cowboy boots and hats, is one of the most "western" towns this side of the Pecos; it has dozens of farms, stables, saloons, country stores, and even a weekly rodeo. In Hollywood, there's a Seminole Indian Reservation, as well as a French-Canadian flavor on the Broadwalk. Hallandale is the home of the well-known *Gulfstream Race Track.* Dania, whose name reflects its early Danish settlers, is now called "the antiques center of the South." Stretching away to the west of Ft. Lauderdale are 3,700 fertile acres of fruit and vegetable farms, adding an agricultural side to the city's personality.

As more and more people discover its enviable lifestyle, the area continues to grow and evolve. "The Strip," made famous by spring break, has undergone a facelift. Installed along the beachside are a promenade, bicycle path, and a low white undulating sea wall, with a neon sculpture in ever-changing colors running along it. The wall has entryways from street to beach, flanked by spirals that look like sand castles. Though some of the original bars and T-shirt emporiums remain, hotels and shops are being remodeled and spruced up in sherbet colors.

Progress has its price, however, and ecologists already are sounding alarms as developers draw closer and closer to the last available land — the eastern fringe of the Everglades.

Ft. Lauderdale At-a-Glance

SEEING THE CITY

The most commanding view of this area is available from the *Pier Top Lounge* of the 17-story *Pier 66* hotel (2301 SE 17th St.; phone: 525-6666). As the lounge makes one complete revolution each 66 minutes, it affords sweeping vistas of the Atlantic Ocean and its beaches to the east; Port Everglades and Ft. Lauderdale International Airport to the south; the city's many canals, sprawling suburbs, and the Everglades to the west; and more canals and the Intracoastal Waterway, leading north to Palm Beach County.

WALKING TOURS The Ft. Lauderdale Historical Society conducts 3-hour walking tours of the historical district (between October and May), where participants learn about the Seminole Wars and early 19th-century farms and trading posts along the then-inhospitable New River (phone: 463-4431). Individual tours are also offered by history professor Dr. Paul S. George (phone: 858-6021).

BOAT TOURS Dubbed the "Venice of America," Ft. Lauderdale is best seen by boat. The *Jungle Queen* (at the *Bahia Mar Yacht Basin* on Rte. A1A; phone: 462-5596) offers 3-hour sightseeing tours three times daily; it also takes riders down to Miami twice weekly for shopping sprees. The *Paddlewheel Queen* (docked next to *Charley's Crab*; phone: 564-7659) runs a variety of sightseeing cruises up and down the Intracoastal Waterway. The *Carrie-B* (docked behind the *Woolley's* supermarket on Las Olas Blvd. and SE 5th Ave.; phone: 768-9920), runs daily 1½-hour trips on the New River down to Port Everglades. Boat cruises cost about $8 for daytime sightseeing trips without meals. Large families and small business groups can charter the 92-foot *Sir Winston* (formally the *Wrecking Krew;* on the New River dock; phone: 462-7411), which transports groups along the waterways past millionaires' homes.

The *Water Taxi* (1900 SE 15th St.; phone: 565-5507), in cooperation with the *Ft. Lauderdale Historical Society,* offers guided tours of the historic New River and the Intracoastal Waterway; 1-hour tour is $8.50; 2-hour, $13.50. *Water Taxi* also conducts 2-hour guided tours past the mansions and yachts of the area's more well-heeled residents; cost is $13. In addition to the tours, *Water Taxi* boats run from the 17th Street Causeway to the *Boca Raton Resort & Club* on demand daily from 10 AM until the wee hours, covering 80 landings. Some taxis are open-air boats; the newer vessels are larger and air conditioned. Fares are $5 one way; $13 all-day; $45 week-long passes also are available. Vessels are also available for charter; rates start at $80.

Two-hour glass-bottom boat tours are conducted on *Pro Diver II,* sailing from the *Bahia Mar Yacht Basin* (phone: 467-6030) daily except Mondays. Cost is $15.

TRAM TOURS Another wonderful way to sightsee is aboard the open-air *South Florida Trolley Tram Tour,* which winds its way through both the new and older sections of Ft. Lauderdale. Passengers can get on and off all day long, or stay put for the 1½-hour tour. There's a trolley booth on Route A1A, south of Las Olas Boulevard (832 Military Rd.; phone: 768-0700), where you can get tickets for the tram tours and other events as well. Also offered are visits to the *Swap Shop* and *Sawgrass Mills. Trolley World Tours* picks up cruise ship passengers at the pier in Port Everglades, offering shopping excursions and a 2½-hour city tour in conjunction with the *South Florida Trolley Tram* (phone: 463-8550).

HOT-AIR BALLOON *Rohr Balloons* literally gives passengers a bird's-eye view of Ft. Lauderdale. The balloons fly twice daily, with boarding at the Ft. Lauderdale Executive Airport, Hangar A-1. Cost for a 1-hour flight is $150 per adult, $125 per child ages 7 to 12. Reservations required. 6000 NW 28th Way (phone: 491-1774 or 371-9410 from Dade County).

SPECIAL PLACES

The best way to get around Ft. Lauderdale is by car. It's a sprawling city and there's a lot to see, in all directions.

PORT EVERGLADES Because it has the deepest water of any port between Norfolk, Virginia, and New Orleans, Port Everglades is a natural magnet for cargo ships and the marine outfitting business, as well as for luxury cruise ships. In fact, it's the world's second-largest cruise port, after Miami. It's also a convenient gateway to the Caribbean, the Gulf of Mexico, and the Panama Canal. Thanks to the remodeling of former warehouses and to new construction, the port today presents an attractive appearance, with some of its eight passenger terminals painted in a striking, bold design. The $50-million *Greater Ft. Lauderdale/Broward County Convention Center* occupies the northern end of the grounds, with major expansion planned. The port presently has one restaurant, *Burt & Jack's* (Berth 23, Port

Everglades; phone: 522-5225), co-owned by Burt Reynolds (see *Eating Out*). While there are no organized tours, visitors are free to roam around the port (except in the secured areas) from 8 AM to 6 PM. At times, naval vessels in port are open for free tours. State Rd. 84, east of US 1 (phone: 523-3404).

Business travelers and vacationers often combine an area visit with a cruise. A few ships make Port Everglades their home port, offering several options for day cruises (see *Day Cruises* in DIVERSIONS). Cruise lines offering ships with varied itineraries that sail from Port Everglades include *Celebrity Cruises* (phone: 800-437-3111), *Costa Cruises* (phone: 358-7330 or 800-462-6782), *Crystal Cruises* (phone: 800-446-6612), *Cunard Line* (phone: 800-221-4770), *Discovery Cruises* (phone: 525-7800 or 800-937-4477), *Holland America Line* (phone: 800-426-0327), *Kloster Cruise Line* (phone: 445-0866), *P & O Cruises* (phone: 415-382-9086), *Princess Cruises* (phone: 800-421-0522), *Seabourn Cruise Line* (phone: 800-351-9595), *Sea-Escape* (phone: 800-432-0900), *Starlite Cruises* (phone: 800-736-7827), *SunFest Cruises* (phone: 476-9900), *Premier's Big Red Boat* (phone: 800-473-3262), and *Sun Line* (phone: 800-468-6400).

MUSEUM OF DISCOVERY AND SCIENCE One lure of Ft. Lauderdale's 85,000 square-foot museum is its 5-story IMAX screen (the largest movie screen in the southeastern US), housed in a 300-seat theater. Among the delightful exhibits are walk-through simulated Florida habitats, a manned maneuvering unit space ride, a laser pinball, a human gyroscope, and a KidScience display — in which a giant bubble forms around kids. There are Saturday children's classes and a cafeteria and museum store on the premises. Tours also are offered of the *King-Cromartie House,* a restored turn-of-the-century residence replete with antiques and set on the New River. Open Mondays to Fridays from 10 AM to 5PM, Saturdays from 10 AM to 8:30 PM, and Sundays from noon to 5 PM. Admission charge (additional charges for theater which offers up to 11 shows daily). 401 SW 2nd St., across from the *Broward Center for the Performing Arts* (phone: 467-MODS OR 463-IMAX).

EVERGLADES HOLIDAY PARK Savor what the famed ecological area is all about by bird watching — you might even spot some American bald eagles — on a narrated airboat ride. You'll see the gold-colored sawgrass and nesting alligators, as well as some of the most beautiful birds Mother Nature has ever created. Your tour guide will give you a healthy respect for the power of alligator jaws, even those of the seemingly cute young ones. Alligators can live up to 100 years if they manage to come out on top of most of their battles. There are special tours offering insights into the lives of Seminole Indians, a group of Native Americans whose history is little known outside this region. If you're feeling adventurous, rent a boat or an RV for a closer experience with nature. There's also a campground here. Open daily 24 hours; airboat rides conducted daily. There's no admission charge to the park, but a fee is charged for airboat rides. 21940 Griffin Rd. (phone: 434-8111).

FLAMINGO GARDENS This 60-acre botanical garden has a flamingo exhibit (natch), a tropical plant house, a museum about the Everglades, orange groves, alligators, crocodiles, and river otters. A guided tram tour takes visitors through the groves, wetlands, and an indigenous hardwood hammock (a raised area of dense vegetation) with stands of oak, gumbo-limbo, and fig trees. A screened-in aviary re-creates several native settings — including a mangrove swamp and a sawgrass prairie — for those who can't get out to the Everglades; throughout the groves are free-flying local birds, including cormorants and ospreys. There's also a snack bar, a gift shop with nature books and crafts, and a produce stall for purchasing and shipping citrus fruit. Open daily 9 AM to 5 PM. Admission charge. 3750 Flamingo Rd., Davie (phone: 473-2955).

LOXAHATCHEE EVERGLADES TOURS Visitors to northern Broward County again can participate in an easy airboat trip through the Everglades without traveling great distances to the south. These airboats provide ramps for easy boarding of the handicapped and improved techniques for muffling the engine noises. Passengers skim over the "river of grass," spotting alligators and their babies in nests, plus myriad wild fowl such as gallinules. There's a small (and sparsely stocked) snack shop at the park. Park open daily 9 AM to 5 PM, with airboat tours between 9:30 AM and 4 PM. No admission charge to the park. Admission charge for airboat rides. From Rte. 441 take Lox Rd. (between Hillsboro Blvd. and Palmetto Park Rd.), then drive 6 miles west to the Everglades (phone: 800-683-5873).

SAWGRASS MILLS MALL This 2.2 million-square-foot complex features talking alligators and continuously running videos. Billed as the world's largest outlet mall, this discount shopping complex boasts such stores as *Saks Fifth Avenue, Macy's, Sears, Marshalls,* and *Spiegel's* — and 200 specialty shops. Among the temptations are an *AnnTaylor* clearance center and a *Joan & David* shoe outlet. Although some stores offer valid savings of 20 to 60%, others push products that are so old and shopworn it's hard to believe people would pay hundreds of dollars for them. This mall is for savvy shoppers: It's important to know what things sell for elsewhere. Several restaurants and two food courts provide respite. An 18-plex movie theater, billed as the largest east of the Mississippi, completes the picture. Open Mondays through Saturdays 10 AM to 9:30 PM, Sundays 11 AM to 6 PM. 12801 W. Sunrise Blvd., Sunrise (phone: 846-2350 or 800-FL-MILLS).

SWAP SHOP The largest flea market in the South, it claims to be Florida's second-largest tourist attractions after *Walt Disney World.* With 2,000 vendors, this is *the* place to find bargains on everything from electronic equipment to tomatoes. Free concerts by the likes of Marie Osmond and Loretta Lynn are presented; there's also a daily circus to amuse the children and help the mind clear between purchases. Open daily from 7:30 AM to 7:30 PM; Saturdays and Sundays to 7 PM; outdoor stalls close an hour earlier. 3291 W. Sunrise Blvd. (phone: 791-SWAP). A second branch with 625 booths is open Tuesdays, Saturdays, and Sundays from 4:30 AM to 2 PM. 1000 State Rd. 7, Margate (phone: 971-SWAP).

BUTTERFLY WORLD A refuge for butterflies where visitors can walk among the multicolored creatures fluttering freely in a re-created jungle atmosphere. These beauties are seen in all their stages of life, from larvae and pupae to cocoons and full adulthood. Certain species are attracted to light-colored clothing and certain scents; if you've spent a hot morning in traffic or sightseeing, you may find yourself converted into a temporary perch. This 3-acre habitat has butterflies from all over the world, and a spectacular museum of mounted insects. Open daily. Admission charge. 3600 W. Sample Rd., Coconut Creek (phone: 977-4400).

HUGH TAYLOR BIRCH STATE RECREATION AREA Just across the street from the beach is this lush, subtropical park, with 180 acres ideal for picnicking, playing ball, canoeing, biking, paddleboating, and hiking. The park is protected from development, so it will always remain a beautiful spot in the midst of the beach area hubbub. Open daily 8 AM to 5 PM. Admission charge. 3109 E. Sunrise Blvd. (phone: 564-4521).

JOHN U. LLOYD BEACH STATE RECREATION AREA Many Ft. Lauderdale residents consider this to be *the* place for picnicking, swimming, fishing, canoeing, and other recreation. There are 244 acres of beach, dunes, mangrove swamp, and hammock. Park rangers lead nature walks during winter months. Open daily. Admission charge. 6503 N. Ocean Dr., Dania (phone: 923-2833).

OCEAN WORLD All the requisite aquatic creatures — sharks, alligators, sea lions, turtles, and dolphins — are featured here in exhibits and water shows. Visitors enjoy watching the dolphins show off in Davy Jones's Locker, a 3-story circular tank, or the more than 40 sharks, sea turtles, and fish in the Shark Moat. Boat tours also are available. Open daily, with shows from 10 AM to 5:30 PM. Admission charge. 1701 SE 17th St. (phone: 525-6611).

HOLLYWOOD BROADWALK A 2.5-mile, 24-foot-wide concrete ocean promenade bordered by a bicycle path and lined with inexpensive outdoor cafés often featuring contemporary music. Bikes may be rented at various sites on the Broadwalk, and there's often free music and dancing (jitterbug and polka are favorites) at the bandstand on Monday nights. This area has a French Canadian flavor — a preponderance of snowbirds and vacationers hail from Quebec — and half the promenade signs are in French. Lifeguard stations are manned all year from 10 AM to 4 PM (phone: 985-4000 for information).

STRANAHAN HOUSE One of the area's oldest museums, this is the restored 1913 home and Indian trading post of early settler Frank Stranahan. It's hard to imagine the Ft. Lauderdale of those days, but a tour of this house provides some idea of the hardships early settlers had to endure against nature and the hostile Seminole. Open Wednesdays, Fridays, and Saturdays. Admission charge. 1 Stranahan Pl. at Las Olas Blvd. and the New River Tunnel (phone: 524-4736).

BONNET HOUSE Built in the 1920s as a family retreat, this 36-acre private estate is one of the few remaining oceanfront wildlife areas in South Florida. The 2-story house and grounds have been preserved. Tours are offered from May through November. Admission charge. 900 N. Birch Rd. (phone: 563-5393).

INTERNATIONAL SWIMMING HALL OF FAME Many of the world's top swimming and diving competitions are held here, but its Olympic-size pools are open to the public year-round when there's no meet scheduled. The entire complex recently underwent a $14-million renovation. The adjoining museum (multiple-gold-medal winner Greg Luganis was inducted into the *Hall of Fame* here last year) houses unusual aquatic memorabilia from more than 100 countries. Open daily. Admission charge. 1 Hall of Fame Dr., off Seabreeze Blvd (phone: 462-6536).

TOPEEKEEGEE YUGNEE PARK With 150 acres, this is one of the area's larger parks. Visitors can enjoy all kinds of activities — swimming, boating, canoeing, picnicking, barbecuing, hiking, biking, and water sliding. Open daily from 6:30 AM to 6 PM. Admission charge on weekends and holidays. 3300 N. Park Rd., just off I-95, Hollywood (phone: 985-1980).

SEMINOLE INDIAN RESERVATION The Native Village includes a museum, a gift shop with Indian arts and crafts, demonstrations of alligator wrestling, and snake and turtle shows. The museum gives an interesting glimpse into a little-known native group. The Seminole gave up their lands reluctantly and never did sign a treaty with the United States. Although bingo games for profit are not legal in Florida, they're allowed here on the reservation. The bingo hall holds up to 1,400 people, and often is full; winners have pocketed as much as $110,000 in a single game. There's an admission charge for the village and another for the bingo hall, which includes four bingo cards. Both are open daily. The village is at 3551 N. State Rd. 7, Hollywood (phone: 961-4519); the bingo hall is at 4150 N. State Rd. 7, Hollywood (phone: 961-3220). For more information, see *Tour 6: Cowboy and Indian Tour* in DIRECTIONS.

GOODYEAR BLIMP Though tourists may not go for a ride in the blimp (it's only for corporate clients), they can, however, visit the "Spirit of Akron" at its hangar in Pompano Beach and see the 205.5-foot-long blimp up close. Call to see when it's berthed here. Open at varied times November to May (call in advance for schedule). No admission charge. 1500 NE 5th Ave., Pompano Beach (phone: 946-8300).

> **EXTRA SPECIAL** To fully experience the subtropical beauty and laid-back ambience that is Ft. Lauderdale, drive east on Las Olas Boulevard past its chic boutiques and palm-lined streets. Continue through the Isles of Las Olas area, which is laced with canals and filled with fancy homes nestled among royal palm trees. Large, luxurious boats are docked outside many of the homes. Look up and you may spot some of the red and blue parrots that nest here; some claim they're native to the area; others say that they were visitors who liked the neighborhood and stayed. Proceed on past the sailboat cove, where towering masts grope for the blue sky, and cruise over the small bridge to Route A1A, along the Atlantic Ocean. Drive north, and around 4 PM, stop at one of the hotel patio bars facing the ocean for a cocktail with the "end of the day" beach people. In an hour or so, the beach will become nearly deserted, yet the ocean is filled with the multicolored sails of boats returning to safe harbor, and cruise and cargo ships steaming out to distant corners of the world. Take off your shoes, walk along the sand at the water's edge — and let the images soak in.

Sources and Resources

TOURIST INFORMATION

The *Greater Ft. Lauderdale Convention & Visitors Bureau* is in an easily accessible pink high-rise downtown (200 E. Las Olas Blvd.; Ft. Lauderdale, FL 33301; phone: 765-4466 or 800-356-1662). Stop in or call for information on accommodations, activities, attractions, sports, dining, shopping, touring, and special events. Or call in advance for a free, information-filled book (phone: 800-11SUNNY, ext. 711). The Broward County arts and entertainment hotline (phone: 357-5700) is updated weekly and provides recorded schedules of events and additional sources of information about visitor attractions. Contact the Florida state hotline (904-988-1234) for maps, calendars of events, health updates, and travel advisories.

LOCAL COVERAGE The *Fort Lauderdale Sun-Sentinel,* a morning daily, carries the following week's events in its Showtime section on Fridays; the monthly *South Florida* magazine lists cultural events and restaurants.

TELEVISION STATIONS WPBS Channel 2–public television; WTVJ Channel 4–NBC; WCIX Channel 6–CBS; WSVN Channel 7–Fox; WPLG Channel 10–ABC.

RADIO STATIONS AM: WEAT 850 (easy listening); WINZ 940 (news/talk). FM: WTMI 93.1 (classical music); WZTA 94.9 (classic rock); WFLC 97.3 (soft rock); WKIS 99.9 (country); WLYF 101.5 (easy listening); WSHE 103.5 (album rock); WJQY 106.7 (easy listening).

TELEPHONE
The area code for Ft. Lauderdale is 305.

SALES TAX
The city sales tax is 6½%; there also is a 3% Broward County hotel tax.

GETTING AROUND

BUS *Broward County Transit* serves most of the area. Weekly passes are available at hotels. For information, call 357-8400.

CAR RENTAL Ft. Lauderdale is served by all the major national firms, two of which have their corporate headquarters in the city: *Alamo* (110 SE 6th St.; phone: 522-0000 or 800-327-0400) and *General Rent-A-Car* (2741 N. 29th Ave.; Hollywood, phone: 926-1700 or 800-327-7607). There also are several regional agencies; check the yellow pages. Rates are about $30 a day or $175 a week for a mid-size car with unlimited mileage. For more information, see GETTING READY TO GO.

TAXI While you can hail a cab on the street, it's best to pick one up at a major hotel or restaurant, or to call for one. The major cab company is *Checker/Yellow Cab* (phone: 565-5400). For information on cabs that accommodate wheelchairs, phone: 565-2800.

TRI-RAIL A double-decker train runs from West Palm Beach south through Ft. Lauderdale to Miami, and connects with Miami's *Metrorail/Metromover* and county and shuttle bus lines to deliver visitors to most of each city's major attractions. The train also travels to the airport in Broward (with a short shuttle ride), as well as the ones in Dade and Palm Beach counties, and schedules extra trains for games at *Joe Robbie* and *Orange Bowl* stadiums, the *Swap Shop, Bayside Marketplace,* and special events. At times, they schedule special sightseeing package tours. This is a convenient way to see a large part of South Florida and its attractions. Call for assistance in locating the stops nearest to the places you want to visit. Accessible to the disabled (phone: 728-8445, 800-TRI-RAIL or 800-874-7245).

LOCAL SERVICES

AUDIOVISUAL EQUIPMENT *Central Audio Visual,* 1212 S. Andrews Ave. (phone: 522-3796).

BABY-SITTING *Lul-A-Bye Sitters Registry*, PO Box 24945, Oakland Park (phone: 565-1222).

BUSINESS SERVICES *Professional Office Service, Inc.*, 4520 NE 18th Ave. (phone: 772-6520).

DENTAL EMERGENCY The *American Dental Association* maintains a 24-hour referral service (phone: 944-5668).

DRY CLEANER/TAILOR *Fashion Cleaners* (2427 W. Broward Blvd.; phone: 583-8225); *Lauderdale-by-the-Sea Cleaners* (4329 N. Ocean Dr., Lauderdale-by-the-Sea; phone: 776-0055).

EQUIPMENT RENTAL *Kinko's*, at two locations, provides typewriters and computers for hourly rentals (6318 NW 9th Ave., Ft. Lauderdale; phone: 492-0006 and 3775 Hollywood Blvd., Hollywood; phone: 985-0411).

LIMOUSINE *Airport Express* (phone: 527-8690); *Club Limousine Service* (phone: 522-0277).

LOCKSMITH Locked your keys in the car? Try *A Lock & Safe*, offering 24-hour service (phone: 763-7479).

MECHANICS *Ocean Exxon* (3001 N. Ocean Blvd.; phone: 561-3120), for American and foreign makes.

MEDICAL EMERGENCY For infomration on area hospitals and pharmacies, see GETTING READY TO GO.

MESSENGER SERVICE *All Florida Messenger & Delivery*, open 24 hours (6822 NW 20th Ave.; phone: 973-3278); *Sunshine State Messenger Service*, open 24 hours (6775 NW 15th Ave.; phone: 975-8100).

PHOTOCOPIES *Copyright* (969 W. Commercial Blvd.; phone: 491-2679 and 1135 S. Federal Hwy.; phone: 779-2649) and *Kinko's* for standard and color copies (6318 NW 9th Ave., Ft. Lauderdale; phone: 492-0006 and 3775 Hollywood Blvd., Hollywood; phone: 985-0411).

PROFESSIONAL PHOTOGRAPHERS *University Studios* (phone: 772-6644); *Woodbury & Associates* (phone: 977-9000).

SECRETARY/STENOGRAPHERS *Alpha Temporary Services*, 1001 W. Cypress Creek Rd. (phone: 776-6030).

TELECONFERENCE FACILITIES *Marriott's Harbor Beach* (3030 Holiday Dr., phone: 525-4000); *Ft. Lauderdale Marina Marriott* hotel (1881 SE 17th St.; phone: 463-4000). See *Checking In*, below, for more information on both.

TRANSLATORS *Berlitz Translation Services* (2455 E. Sunrise Blvd.; phone: 563-6303 or 800-523-7548) or *Master Translating Services* (1881 NE 26th St., Wilton Manors; phone: 563-2899).

TYPEWRITER RENTAL *A & J Business Machines* (phone: 563-0438), 1-week minimum.

WESTERN UNION/TELEX Many offices located around town (phone: 800-325-6000).

SPECIAL EVENTS

The *Seminole Indian Tribal Fair* at Flamingo Gardens, normally held during the first 2 weeks in February, is a showcase of Indian crafts, entertainment, and food. In March, the *Florida Derby Festival* hits town; activities include a beauty pageant, the *Derby Ball,* and parades, culminating in a thoroughbred race with a purse of about $500,000. The last week of February, the annual *Las Olas Art Festival,* hosted by the *Museum of Art,* attracts 205 juried artists, who display their work in Bubier Park; many of these artists don't exhibit elsewhere. Out in Davie, cowboys kick up their heels at the March *Orange Blossom Festival and Rodeo.* The *Honda Golf Classic,* one of the biggest PGA tournaments, is held in late February or early March at the *Weston Hills Country Club;* it attracts the PGA's top players. In April, seafood is king at the *Ft. Lauderdale Seafood Festival* at Bubier Park, where over 30 leading restaurants offer visitors samples of their house specialties. Also in April, the annual *Sun-Sentinel New River Jazz Festival* brings 3 days of jazz to the *Broward Center for the Performing Arts,* with free outdoor concerts along the New River's *Riverwalk.* Anglers get to test their skills in May during the *Pompano Beach Fishing Rodeo and Seafood Festival,* where more than $250,000 in cash is awarded for the largest catches. Of special interest this year is the *Whitbred Round the World Sailing Race,* a 9-month event in which a group of multi-million-dollar sailing yachts circle the globe. Though the race begins and ends at Southampton, England, it will stop in Ft. Lauderdale from mid-April to May 21, during which time the classy craft will be on view to the public. A flotilla of 500 boats is scheduled to meet the arriving yachts. *July 4* sees the *Sun-Sentinel SandBlast,* where contestants sandsculpt on the beach for prizes; kids' sandsculpting lessons and nighttime fireworks add to the fun. *Oktoberfest* falls (naturally) in October and features lots of German food, drink, and music. The *Ft. Lauderdale Boat Show,* at the *Bahia Mar Yachting Center,* is the world's largest in-water display of all types and sizes of watercraft, held in late October. In November, there's the *Promenade in the Park,* which showcases artwork, arts and crafts, food, and entertainment at Holiday Park; plus the *Greater Ft. Lauderdale Film Festival,* which shows more than 50 independent films; and the *Broward County Fair,* in Hallandale. The year's activities are capped by the month-long *Winterfest,* culminating in the Ft. Lauderdale and Pompano Beach boat parades, with processions of about 100 boats, festooned with colored lights and *Christmas* decorations, plying the Intracoastal Waterway, and a "Light up Lauderdale" laser show downtown on *New Year's Eve.*

MUSEUMS

In addition to those described in *Special Places,* other museums include the following:

FT. LAUDERDALE HISTORICAL SOCIETY Located in the historic district, the society conducts tours and hosts exhibits such as "South Florida's Mediterranean Revival Architecture." Open Tuesdays through Saturdays 10 AM to 4 PM and Sundays 1 to 4 PM. Admission charge. 219 SW 2nd Ave. (phone: 463-4431).

MUSEUM OF ART Housed in a building designed by Edward Larabee Barnes, this 63,800-square-foot museum features 19th- and 20th-century American and European art. The collection includes more than 2,000 paintings, 5,000 prints, and West African, pre-Columbian, and American Indian art. Traveling exhibits, such as Audubon's watercolors of birds, are housed in three galleries, and there's a sculpture garden and auditorium. Open Tuesdays from 11 AM to 9 PM, Wednesdays through Saturdays from 10 AM to 5 PM, and Sundays from noon to 5 PM. Admission charge; tours are included on Tuesdays, Thursdays, and Fridays at 1 PM. 1 E. Las Olas Blvd. (phone: 525-5500).

YOUNG AT ART CHILDREN'S MUSEUM Primarily a hands-on museum, where young artists can develop their skills. Open Tuesdays through Saturdays 11 AM to 5 PM and Sundays noon to 5 PM. Admission charge, except for children under 2. 801 S. University Dr., Plantation (phone: 424-0085).

MAJOR COLLEGES AND UNIVERSITIES

Broward Community College has three campuses (central, 3501 SW Davie Rd., Davie; north, 1000 Coconut Creek Blvd., Coconut Creek; and south, 7200 Hollywood Pines Blvd., Pembroke Pines; phone for all: 475-6500). Nova University is at 3301 College Ave., in Ft. Lauderdale (phone 800-541-NOVA). The University Tower (220 SE 2nd Ave.; phone: 355-5200) is a facility for graduate classes shared by Broward Community College, Florida Atlantic University, and Florida International University, whose main campuses are in Broward, Palm Beach, and Dade counties, respectively.

SHOPPING

For a break from the beach (believe it or not, people do need that once in a while), visit one of the many shopping malls in the Ft. Lauderdale area. Here you can find anything your heart desires — malls are great for browsing and people watching as well.

BROWARD MALL One of the South's largest shopping malls, with 130 specialty shops, the ultramodern mart's mainstay stores are *Burdine's, Sears, Mer-*

vyn's, and *JC Penney.* Open Mondays through Saturdays 10 AM to 9 PM, Sundays noon to 6 PM. Broward Blvd. and University Dr., Plantation (phone: 473-8100).

DANSK FACTORY OUTLET For discounted Danish-designed housewares, featuring seconds and overstocks on stainless flatware, wood serving pieces, and well-designed Scandinavian tableware. Open Mondays through Saturdays 10 AM to 5:30 PM and Sundays noon to 5 PM. At two locations: 27 W. Hallandale Beach Blvd., Hallandale (phone: 454-3900) and 2401 W. Atlantic Blvd., Pompano Beach (phone: 973-7527).

FESTIVAL FLEA MARKET A 400,000-square-foot indoor flea-market-type mall in western Ft. Lauderdale, where 650 vendors offer brand-new merchandise as well as antiques and collectibles. There also are 8 movie theaters, an amusement arcade, and an international food court. Many items are discounted. Open Wednesdays through Sundays from 9:30 AM to 5 PM. 2900 W. Sample Rd., Coconut Creek (phone: 979-4555).

GALLERIA High-fashion clothes and home furnishings are sold at this 3-story mall, featuring *Neiman Marcus, Saks, Lord & Taylor,* and *Burdine's.* Smaller shops include *Bally of Switzerland, Laura Ashley, The Sharper Image, Brooks Brothers* and *Godiva Chocolates.* Valet parking available. Open Mondays through Saturdays, Sundays noon to 5 PM. 2414 E. Sunrise Blvd. (phone: 564-1015).

LORD & TAYLOR CLEARANCE CENTER Clothing discounted 50% initially, with further reductions for special sales. Open Mondays through Saturdays, Sundays noon to 5 PM. 7067 W. Broward Blvd., Plantation (phone: 581-8205).

MAUS & HOFFMAN Upscale men's clothing. Closed Sundays. 800 E. Las Olas Blvd. (phone: 463-1472).

SAWGRASS MILLS MALL This gigantic, alligator-shape, 2.2 million-square-foot shopping center is billed as the world's largest outlet mall (for more information, see *Special Places*). Open Mondays through Saturdays, Sundays noon to 5 PM. 12801 W. Sunrise Blvd., Sunrise (phone: 846-2350 or 800-FL-MILLS).

SOPHY CURSON Open only from late October through May, this store has high-fashion women's clothing. Closed Sundays. 1508 Las Olas Blvd. (phone: 462-7770).

SWAP SHOP Indoor and outdoor booths beckon at this massive flea market — the largest in the South and a true bargain-hunter's heaven. For more information, see *Special Places*. Open daily. There are two Broward locations: 3291 W. Sunrise Blvd. (phone: 791-SWAP) and 1000 N. State Rd. 7, Margate (phone: 971-SWAP).

WHISPERS Designer clothes at a discount. Closed Sundays. 1507 Las Olas Blvd. (phone: 767-4606).

ZOLA KELLER Upscale fashions for women. Closed Sundays. 818 Las Olas Blvd. (phone: 462-3222).

SPORTS

BASEBALL Fans can watch spring training and pre-season games during February and March. The New York *Yankees* play at *Yankee Stadium* (5301 NW 12th Ave.; phone: 776-1921). A bit farther afield, West Palm Beach is the springtime home of the Atlanta *Braves* and Montreal *Expos*. *Yankee Stadium* also hosts the *Mickey Mantle/Whitey Ford Fantasy Baseball Camp* in April, October, and November. Mantle, Ford, Hank Bauer, Mike Ferraro, and other former diamond biggies teach the over-thirtysomething crowd who wanted to be pros how to hit home runs. Contact Wanda Greer (PO Box 68, Grayson, KY 41143; phone: 606-474-6976; 212-382-1660 in New York).

FISHING As in Miami, there's just about every kind of angling you can think of. For deep-sea adventure, charter boats are available. Half-day charters cost from $350 to $550 for up to six anglers. There are plenty of listings under "Fishing" in the Ft. Lauderdale yellow pages.

FIRST CLASS CATCHES

We recommend the *Bahia Mar Yacht Basin* across A1A from the beach (801 Seabreeze Blvd.; phone: 523-5400) and *Club Nautico,* which charters power boats by the hour, half-day, or full-day, with docks in Dania (at the *Seafair* shopping complex, 801 NE 3rd St.; phone: 960-2796), and Ft. Lauderdale (2301 SE 17th Cswy., Slip A19; phone: 523-0033). *Ft. Lauderdale Yacht Charters*, at *Pier 66*, charters power and sailboats from 2 hours to 2 months (2301 SE 17th St. Cswy.; phone: 522-6666).

Landlubbers fish 24 hours a day from the 1,080-foot Pompano Beach Fishing Pier (2 blocks north of East Atlantic Blvd.; phone: 943-1488), and Anglin's Fishing Pier (2 Commercial Blvd.; phone: 491-9403) for an admission charge.

For more information see "Fishing" in *Miami,* THE CITIES.

FITNESS CENTERS *Nautilus Fitness Center,* with certified instructors, offers all the standard Nautilus exercise equipment, plus saunas. Cost is $10 per day or about $30 per week. 1624 N. Federal Hwy. (phone: 566-2222).

GOLF Not surprisingly, Ft. Lauderdale boasts some great greens. Several resorts have excellent golf courses, and many that lack their own links provide access to other clubs. It's usually necessary to call ahead for reservations, especially during the winter season.

TOP TEE-OFF SPOTS

Bonaventure Two championship 18-hole courses lure golfers to this 504-room resort. The east course is considered one of Florida's top ten, and the waterfall hole is certainly challenging. There's also a driving range, putting green, and pro shop. Moonlight golf (for groups of 20 or more) adds to the standard tee-off times. Special plans combine spa and golf vacations (see *Sybaritic Spas* in DIVERSIONS). Pro is Rick Weber. 250 Racquet Club Rd. (phone: 389-2100 or 800-327-8090; fax: 389-2124).

Palm-Aire Courses here have hosted the *Florida Open, US Open* qualifying matches, and the *Florida PGA* tournament. The resort is part of a 1,500-acre hotel and residential development, with two 18-hole championship golf courses (the *Palms* and the *Pines*) and an 18-hole executive course (the *Sabals*). The *Pines* is considered one of Florida's toughest 20. Instruction available, combination spa and golf packages possible. Golf director at the *Palms* is Tom Malone (phone: 968-2775). 2601 Palm-Aire Dr. N., Pompano Beach (phone: 972-3300 or 800-272-5624; fax: 968-2744).

PGA National Resort Headquarters for the Professional Golfers Association of America, and hosts of the annual *PGA Seniors Championships* and other major national and international tournaments, it has five 18-hole tournament courses, designed by such pros as George and Tom Fazio, Arnold Palmer, and Jack Nicklaus. It's also the only East Coast facility to offer the Nicklaus/Flick Golf School. Daily clinics, pro shop, and equipment rental are available. There are also such full-resort amenities as 19 tennis courts, 5 indoor racquetball courts, and a fully-equipped spa (see *Sybaritic Spas* in DIVERSIONS). 400 Avenue of the Champions, Palm Beach (phone: 407-627-2000 or 800-633-9150; fax: 407-622-0261).

Other good greens open to the public include *American Golfers Club* (3850 N. Federal Hwy.; phone: 564-8760); *Rolling Hills* (3501 W. Rolling Hills Cir., Davie; phone: 475-3010); *Grand Palms* (110 Grand Palm Dr., Pembroke Pines; phone: 431-8800); *Weston Hills* (2603 Country Club Way; phone: 384-9422); and *Jacaranda* (9200 W. Broward Blvd., Plantation; phone: 472-5836). Cost is about $50 for 9 holes, including cart and greens fees. For additional information, call the Parks and Recreation Division of Broward County (phone: 357-8100).

HORSE AND DOG RACING There's thoroughbred horse racing at *Gulfstream Park* daily except Wednesdays from mid-January through March (on Hallandale Beach Blvd. and US 1, Hallandale; phone: 454-7000), and harness racing at *Pompano Harness Track* from October through July (1800 SW 3rd St., Pompano Beach; phone: 972-2000). You can "go to the dogs" at *Hollywood Greyhound Track* from December through April (831 N. Federal Hwy., Hallandale; phone: 454-9400). Phone for racing dates.

HORSEBACK RIDING Most people don't think of southern Florida as the Wild, Wild West, but horse country is within closer range than you would think. Out west (western Ft. Lauderdale, that is), cowboy country awaits in Davie (see *Tour 6: Cowboy and Indian Tour* in DIRECTIONS), with many stables in the area offering trail rides and horse rentals. Among the larger ones are *Bar-B Ranch* for horse rentals (4601 SW 128th Ave., Davie; phone: 434-6175) and *Stride-Rite Training Center* for supervised rides (5550 SW 73rd Ave., Davie; phone: 587-2285). Both are open daily, and charge about $15.50 for half-hour lessons. Broward County also operates stables at *Tradewinds Park* on Saturdays and Sundays (3600 W. Sample Rd., Coconut Creek; phone: 968-3880).

JAI ALAI This Basque import is the area's most action-packed sport, with pari-mutuel betting adding spice. The season is year-round, except for 10 days in April and May. Closed Sundays and Mondays. At *Dania Jai-Alai,* 301 E. Dania Beach Blvd., Dania (phone: 927-2841 or 920-1511 for reservations).

NATURE HIKES The Broward Parks & Recreation Department sponsors a different nature walk each Friday and Saturday, October through May. Call for a schedule (phone: 357-8100 or 536-PARK).

PARASAILING Soar like a bird over Ft. Lauderdale with *Watersports Unlimited* (301 Seabreeze Blvd.; phone: 467-1316 or 941-4044) or *Sunrise Watersports* (2025 E. Sunrise Blvd.; phone: 462-8962). Ten-minute flights cost about $40. Open daily.

RODEO The "Wild West" can be found at the *Rodeo Arena* in Davie, where cowboys compete in bronco riding, calf roping, and other activities. Admission charge (4201 SW 65th Way; phone: 797-1166 or 437-8800). For more information see *Tour 6: Cowboy and Indian Tour* in DIRECTIONS.

SAILING After the sunshine, the water is one of South Florida's greatest draws. The US Corps of Engineers has eliminated most of the shoal areas and maintains navigational aids. Private and public marinas provide virtually every type of boat for rent. For large charters, power, or sailboats, see *Fishing* in this section. Jet skis and mini–Cigarette boats may be rented from *Sunrise Watersports* (2025 E. Sunrise Blvd.; phone: 462-8962). Average cost is about $50 per person, depending on size of party.

SCUBA DIVING Stretching north from the Keys past Ft. Lauderdale, Florida's natural coral reef has suffered an environmental impact: Broken reef in some places, and pollution in others threaten to reduce both living spaces for sea life and an interest in scuba diving. But diving is making a strong comeback in this part of Florida, due in large part to the practice of sinking freighters and other large objects into the sea to create artificial reefs.

BEST DEPTHS

The most famous sinking in recent years was the tanker *Mercedes*, which somehow landed on socialite Mollie Wilmot's terrace before being "dumped" in Ft. Lauderdale, but lots of other sunken wrecks (50 is the official count here) also lure fish and coral to depths of 200 feet. While many people say these manmade reefs can't replace nature's delicate work, colorful fish certainly congregate around the sunken ships off the beaches in Pompano and Ft. Lauderdale. Three tiers of coral reefs — one at 15 feet deep, the second at 40 feet, and the third at 60 — provide beautiful, more natural sights.

Dozens of dive shops such as *Lauderdale Diver* (1334 SE 17th St. Cswy.; phone: 467-2822 or 800-654-2073) and *Pro Dive* (*Bahia Mar Yachting Center,* 801 Seabreeze Blvd.; phone: 761-3413 or 800-772-DIVE outside Florida) operate in Broward for about $35 a trip; check the yellow pages or go directly to the boats that depart from Hillsboro Inlet in the northern part of the county, and from Port Everglades. Many operators offer package deals with hotels.

SNORKELING The 60-foot glass-bottom boat *Pro Diver II* offers snorkeling daily except Mondays from *Bahia Mar Yachting Center* (801 Seabreeze Blvd.; phone: 467-6030); 2-hour trip costs $20, including equipment.

SWIMMING The most crowded beach is along "The Strip," from Sunrise Boulevard to Bahia Mar. The Galt Ocean Mile is quieter, with an older crowd. Perhaps the quietest strand is the stretch between Galt Ocean Mile and NE 22nd Street, and if you search you may find small pockets of peace in John U. Lloyd Beach State Recreation Area (6503 N. Ocean Dr., Hollywood; phone: 923-2833) or North Beach Park (Sheridan Rd. and Rte. A1A, Hollywood; phone: 926-2444). Deerfield Beach is a favorite of locals, from the border of Broward and Palm Beach counties south to SE 10th Street. This beach area has some of the best shower facilities around, and its huge boulders in the water create intriguing coves that invite exploration.

TENNIS Although most major hotels here have tennis courts, one is a true ace.

CHOICE COURTS

Bonaventure The best tennis facilities in Ft. Lauderdale are likely to be found at this elegant resort, with its 24 tennis courts — most nightlit, and 7 clay. There also are 5 indoor air conditioned racquetball and squash courts, and a pro shop. Combination tennis and spa packages are available. 250 Racquet Club Rd. (phone: 389-8667 or 800-327-8090; fax: 384-0563).

There also are numerous courts open to the public. Among them are *Holiday Park Tennis Center* (701 NE 12th Ave.; phone: 761-5378); *Dillon Tennis Courts* (4091 NE 5th Ave., Oakland Park; phone: 561-6180); *Pompano Beach Tennis Center* (900 NE 18th Ave.; phone: 786-4115); and *George W. English Park* (110 Bayview Dr.; phone: 566-0622). For more information, contact the Broward County Parks and Recreation Division (phone: 357-8100). Court time runs about $5 per hour, with private lessons available for $18 a half hour.

THEATER

The area's major theaters are the *Parker Playhouse* (707 NE 8th St.; phone: 764-0700), which stars name actors in touring companies of Broadway productions, and *Sunrise Musical Theater* (5555 NW 95th Ave.; phone: 741-7300), which features touring Broadway musicals and individual stars in concert. Opened in 1991, the $50-million regional *Broward Center for the Performing Arts* (201 SW 5th Ave.; phone: 522-5334 or 462-0222 for tickets) stages opera, theatrical, ballet, and philharmonic productions. Theatrical and cultural events also are staged at the *War Memorial Auditorium* (800 NE 8th St.; phone: 761-5381) and *Bailey Hall* at Broward Community College, which also presents children's productions (3501 SW Davie Rd.; phone: 475-6880). Local youngsters also perform in the *Ft. Lauderdale Children's Theatre* (phone: 763-6901). The playwright Vinnette Carroll, who wrote *Your Arms Too Short to Box with God,* opened a multi-cultural theater in a converted church, the *Vinnette Carroll Theater* (503 SE 6th St.; phone: 462-2424). For current offerings, check the newspapers.

MUSIC

The *Philharmonic Orchestra of Florida* usually plays at the *Broward Center for the Performing Arts* (phone: 561-2997 or 800-226-1812 for *Philharmonic* tickets); the center is also the site for performances by the *Sinfonia Virtuosi* (phone: 561-5882) and the *Opera Guild* (phone: 462-0222) during winter months; the latter often features visiting artists from New York and from the *Greater Miami Opera Company.* The *Gold Coast Symphony Orchestra* (1323 NE 17th St., Suite 668; phone: 475-6840) stages several major productions at various sites. Student and guest chamber music, jazz, opera, and symphonic performances are staged throughout the year at Broward Community College (phone: 475-6884).

NIGHTCLUBS AND NIGHTLIFE

Most hotels and larger motels offer music and/or comedy acts nightly. Growing in popularity are such comedy clubs as *The Comic Strip* (1432 N. Federal Hwy.; phone: 565-8887) and *The Comedy Stop* (3001 E. Commercial Blvd,; phone: 938-9033), which showcase New York and Los Angeles comics. The *Musician's Exchange Café* (729 W. Sunrise Blvd.; phone:

764-1912) is the place to go for jazz, blues, and rock. For dance music, try *Riverwatch Lounge* in the *Ft. Lauderdale Marina Marriott* hotel (1881 SE 17th St.; phone: 463-4000); *Confetti's* (2660 E. Commercial Blvd.; phone: 776-4080); *Café 66* and the *Pier Top Lounge* (2301 SE 17th St. Cswy.; phone: 525-6666); *Squeeze* (2 S. New River Dr.; phone: 522-2151); and *Yesterdays* (3001 E. Oakland Park; phone: 561-4400). There's dancing and dinner for an older crowd at *Stan's* (3300 E. Commercial Blvd.; phone: 772-3777). A live band plays weekends at *Riverwalk Brewery* (111 SW 2nd Ave.; phone: 463-2337). *Chardee's* (2209 Wilton Dr., Wilton Manors; phone: 563-1800) attracts a gay crowd.

Best in Town

CHECKING IN

Ft. Lauderdale's busiest period is winter, when reservations should be made as far in advance as possible. In addition to the major hotels listed here, Ft. Lauderdale has hundreds of smaller chains (check the phone book for their toll-free 800 numbers) and family-operated hotels and motels. During high season, a double room listed in the very expensive range could run $180 to $300 per night; a room in the expensive range will cost $140 to $180; in moderate, $95 to $135; and $50 to $90 in inexpensive. In the summer, occupancy (and room) rates drop. Note that a 3% county tourist development tax and a 6½% state sales tax are added to all hotel bills. Most of Ft. Lauderdale's major hotels have complete facilities for the business traveler. Those hotels listed below as having "Business services" usually offer such conveniences as meeting rooms, photocopiers, computers, translation services, and express checkout, among others. Call the hotel for additional information. All telephone numbers are in the 305 area code unless otherwise indicated.

For an unforgettable Ft. Lauderdale vacation experience, we begin with our favorite, followed by our recommendations of cost and quality choices of hotels, listed by price category.

A REGAL RESORT

Marriott Harbor Beach Ft. Lauderdale's premier resort offers 16 acres of beachfront elegance. Guests think they're in a posh Caribbean retreat, what with 5 restaurants (including the outstanding *Sheffield's;* see *Eating Out*), 2 lounges, a pool bar, 5 tennis courts, and exercise facilities. There's also a tropically landscaped free-form pool with a waterfall and 50 cabañas. The 589 rooms are standard for the price; the 35 suites, however, are super. Free transport to the *Bonaventure Country Club* for golfers. Business services. 3030 Holiday Dr. (phone: 525-4000 or 800-327-8874; fax: 766-6152).

VERY EXPENSIVE

Bonaventure One of the most popular spas in town, this 1,250-acre resort, complete with waterfalls, offers some of the best golfing facilities in town (see *Golf*), plus 5 swimming pools, 24 tennis courts, 5 racquetball courts, a squash court, horseback riding, indoor roller skating, and bowling. The spa also has a full range of health and nutrition programs in separate facilities for men and women, complete with resident nurse (see *Sybaritic Spas* in DIVERSIONS). The 504 rooms and suites are all divided into 4-story structures, along with 4 restaurants and 2 lounges. Business services. 250 Racquet Club Rd. (phone: 389-3300 or 800-327-8090; fax: 984-6157).

Ft. Lauderdale Marina Marriott Located on the Intracoastal Waterway at the 17th Street Causeway, there are great views north and south from the 14-story tower and 2 low-rise sections. Most of the 580 rooms have balconies and all have in-room safes and two telephones. The focal points of the property are a free-form pool with adjacent bar, and the marina, with slips for up to 35 yachts. There are 4 tennis courts, a health club, sauna, outdoor Jacuzzi, gift shop, restaurants, and lounges. Business services. 1881 SE 17th St. (phone: 463-4000 or 800-228-9290; fax: 527-6705).

Palm-Aire This is Ft. Lauderdale's original spa — over 1,500 acres with 191 rooms, 37 tennis courts, 1 executive and 4 championship golf courses, 3 pools, a jogging track, 2 racquetball courts, 1 squash court, and 4 dining rooms. Special 3- and 7-day packages may be booked at the spa, where health programs prevail, or just enjoy the hotel or sports facilities. (See *Golf*, above, and *Sybaritic Spas* in DIVERSIONS.) Business services. 2501 Palm-Aire Dr. N., Pompano Beach (phone: 968-2705 or 800-272-5624; fax: 968-2744).

EXPENSIVE

Crown Sterling Suites Formerly *Embassy Suites,* the chain's largest property in Florida offers 359 suites at prices equivalent to a standard hotel room. Facilities include a restaurant and lounge, pool, sauna, steamroom, and Jacuzzi. Breakfast and happy hour cocktails are free. Saluted by *Consumer Reports* magazine, the accommodations also feature a wet bar with refrigerator, microwave oven, coffee maker, and dining table. Complimentary beach shuttle service, parking, and 24-hour airport transportation are also available. Business services. 1100 SE 17th St. Cswy. (phone: 527-2700 or 800-433-4600; fax: 760-7202).

Guest Quarters Next to the *Galleria* shopping mall and situated on the Intracoastal Waterway, its 230 suites offer fully equipped kitchens, cable TV, 24-hour room service, a complimentary 1-hour cruise on a 110-foot yacht, a pool, a Jacuzzi, a health club, a restaurant, and a lounge, plus a gameroom. Business services. Access is by water taxi. 2670 E. Sunrise Blvd. (phone: 565-3800 or 800-424-2900; fax: 561-0387).

Westin Cypress Creek The Westin group's first foray into Florida, this 15-story, 293-room, luxury property overlooks a 5-acre lagoon that's spectacularly lighted at *Christmastime*. It features a health club, a large outdoor pool, and a lakeside pavilion; tennis and golf are a 5-minute drive away. There are 2 restaurants — one for fine dining, a second for casual food — and a bar complex. Free parking. Business services. 400 Corporate Dr., in the Radice Corporate Center (phone: 772-1331 or 800-228-3000; fax: 491-9087).

MODERATE

Bahia Mar This nautically oriented hotel and marina, at the *Bahia Mar Yacht Basin* at the southern end of "The Strip," has 298 rooms, 2 restaurants, the *Schooner's Lounge,* and 4 lighted tennis courts. There are 350 slips for fishing boats and pleasure yachts, and it is the home of the country's largest in-water boat show (in November). Business services. 801 Seabreeze Blvd. (phone: 764-2233 or 800-327-8154; fax: 524-6912).

Ramada Beach All of its 220 rooms have balconies that overlook either the Atlantic or the Galt Ocean Mile, and some are beautifully decorated in soothing rose and mauve tones. Its *Ocean Café* offers a mostly continental menu, and the lounge features live music and dancing on weekends during the winter months. On the beach, it has a heated pool, a tiki bar for hors d'oeuvres and cocktails, and sailboat rentals. Business services. 4060 Galt Ocean Dr. (phone: 565-6611 or 800-272-6232; fax: 564-7730).

Sheraton Yankee Clipper "Moored" across the street from the beach, the oldest building in this landmark complex looks like — what else? — a clipper ship. The 4-building complex boasts 450 recently refurbished rooms. There are 2 heated swimming pools, a restaurant, and 2 lounges which provide entertainment. Business services. 1140 Seabreeze Blvd. (phone: 524-5551 or 800-325-3535; fax: 523-5376).

INEXPENSIVE

Bahia Cabana Small and unpretentious, nestled by the *Bahia Mar Yacht Basin,* this is an informal place and very Floridian. There are 116 rooms and apartments with kitchenettes, 3 swimming pools, a 36-person Jacuzzi, saunas, a dining room, and an outdoor patio bar/restaurant — a popular gathering spot for locals — overlooking the marina. Business services. 3001 Harbor Dr. (phone: 524-1555 or 800-BEACHES; 800-922-3008 in Florida; fax: 764-5951).

Riverside Some 116 rooms and suites in one of the city's oldest structures, located on fashionable Las Olas Boulevard. Built in 1936, this European-style hostelry has a sedate ambience and cozy lobby, with chandeliers, armchairs, touches of wicker, and fireplaces. There's a restaurant, plus an intimate restaurant/lounge decorated with etched glass — and a swimming pool set amid tropical landscaping on the New River. Business services. 620 E. Las Olas Blvd. (phone: 467-0671 or 800-325-3280; fax: 462-2148).

> **WORTH A SHORT DETOUR** Just 30 minutes north of Ft. Lauderdale, the elegant (and pricey) *Boca Raton Resort & Club* is definitely worth a visit. Old-world elegance permeates the *Cloister*, the original 1926 Mizner-built hotel. The best rooms in the house, however, are those on the *Boca Beach Club*'s ground floor. The rooms are large and well furnished, and the club's site on a spit of land between the Intracoastal Waterway and the Atlantic guarantees a watery vista no matter where your room is. They offer lanais for lounging and direct access to the beach on the Atlantic side. There also are 2 large pools, and guests have access to the 34 tennis courts, 2 golf courses, 3 fitness centers, meeting space, a concierge level, and the considerable other amenities of the sprawling 963-room resort, including 19 restaurants and lounges. *Boca Raton Resort and Club,* 501 E. Camino Real, Boca Raton (phone: 407-395-3000 or 800-327-0101).

EATING OUT

There are nearly 2,500 restaurants in Broward County. Many of these are well known, and most get quite crowded during the winter season, so it's always a good idea to make reservations. In fact, restaurant dining is such a part of the lifestyle that a recent *Restaurants & Institutions* magazine survey found Ft. Lauderdale restaurants second only to New York City as the country's busiest eating establishments. Casual dress is accepted at most restaurants, though a few of the more expensive ones prefer gentlemen to wear jackets. Expect to pay $75 or more for dinner for two in a restaurant listed in the very expensive range; $60 to $70 in the expensive range; $35 to $50 in the moderate range; and $25 or less for inexpensive. Prices do not include wine, drinks, or tips. All telephone numbers are in the 305 area code unless otherwise indicated and are in Ft. Lauderdale unless noted.

We begin with our culinary favorites, followed by our recommendations of cost and quality choices, listed by price category.

INCREDIBLE EDIBLES

By Word of Mouth This European café–style spot in the heart of Ft. Lauderdale's industrial district serves some of the finest continental fare in the area. The owner has not advertised since opening the restaurant 11 years ago, but folks flock here to order the abundant salads, hand-size portobello mushrooms stuffed with brie, duckling soaked in apricot brandy, Acapulco shrimp salad, outrageous sun-dried tomato and pesto pie — and the pastries! — a half-dozen chocolate choices, with brownie decadence followed closely by white chocolate mousse with raspberry sauce — the best. Menu changes daily. Open for lunch Mondays through Fridays ll AM to 3 PM; and for dinner Wednesdays and Thursdays 5 to 9 PM; Fridays Saturdays 5 to 10 PM. Reservations advised. Major credit cards accepted. 3200 NE 12th Ave. (phone: 564-3663).

Darrel & Oliver's Café Maxx The decor is simple, the focus is on great food. And though it's not an elegantly styled room, the dishes created here are on the cutting edge of "new" American cooking; many have been recipients of much praise and their recipes written up in well-known food magazines. Created by restaurateur Dennis Max and chef Mark Militello (who now owns *Mark's Place;* see below), owners now are Darrel Broek, and Oliver Saucy, who is also the executive chef. Each presentation is a visual masterpiece: Oysters are dipped in ground pistachios and fried, then replaced in their shells atop a bed of corn and tomato salsa and surrounded by a mound of red and green curly lettuce, enoki mushrooms, lemon grass, and a nasturtium blossom. The Peking pork with honey-sesame glaze, and white chocolate mousse pie with raspberry sauce and a white chocolate truffle attest to the chef's melting-pot inventiveness. Open daily for dinner 6 to 11 PM. Reservations advised. Major credit cards accepted. 2601 E. Atlantic Blvd., Pompano Beach (phone: 782-0606).

Plum Room One of South Florida's most romantic, intimate dining rooms, featuring beautifully prepared and presented continental food as a harpist plays in the background. There are classic dishes, including sole Veronique and beef Wellington; don't miss the cream of mushroom soup, made with shiitake, enoki, and white mushrooms — or such exotica as ostrich and elk. There's also an extensive — and impressive — wine list. Open from 6:30 to 11 PM Sundays through Thursdays, until midnight Fridays and Saturdays. Reservations advised. Major credit cards accepted. 3001 E. Oakland Park Blvd. (phone: 563-4168).

VERY EXPENSIVE

Carambola A chic modern dining room on chic Las Olas Boulevard. The wood-burning Tuscan oven at the bar is used to prepare many specials. Their rack of venison is among the finest nationwide; chicken Fantasia translates to chicken breast stuffed with lobster medallions and precious black truffles. *Tiramasù* (Italian charlotte) hits a peak in elegance. Open for lunch Mondays through Fridays, dinner Mondays through Saturdays; closed Sundays. Reservations advised. Major credit cards accepted. 1032 E. Las Olas Blvd. (phone: 522-4952).

Casa Vecchia Fine northern Italian and Mediterranean food is served inside this lovely old house (built in the 1930s by the Ponds cold-cream family), tastefully decorated with plants, ceramics, antiques, and wrought iron. Famed South Florida restaurateurs Leonce Picot and Al Kocab provide elegant atmosphere and excellent service, with a view of the Intracoastal Waterway from the *Greenhouse* dining room. New California chef, Emile Labrousse, has raised the culinary level to match the surroundings. The osso buco is a favorite, but the wild mushroom cappuccino soup and grilled pork medallions are hard to beat. Can be reached by water taxi. Open nightly. Reservations advised. Major credit cards accepted. 209 N. Birch Rd. (phone: 463-7575).

Sheffield's Located in *Marriott's Harbor Beach*, this posh hotel dining room offers superb gravlax, lobster bisque, rack of lamb and chicken forestiere with a mountain of wild mushrooms. Dinner ends with arguably the best *tiramisù* on the coast. Open nightly. Reservations advised. Major credit cards accepted. 3030 Holiday Dr. (phone: 525-4000).

EXPENSIVE

Armadillo Café Serves Florida foods in a Southwest tradition, in the land of Florida's own cowboys. The café's black-and-white soup (contrasting semicircles of black-bean and Jack-cheese-with-jalapeño soups) is excellent. Favorites include Florida lobster quesadillas and grilled chicken with tomato and avocado salsas. Open for dinner only; closed Mondays. Reservations necessary. Major credit cards accepted. 4630 SW 64th Ave., Davie (phone: 791-4866).

Burt & Jack's Owned by actor Burt Reynolds and partner Jack Jackson, this beautiful Spanish-style villa offers first-rate seafood and steaks and chops. Try for a window table so you can watch the cruise and cargo ships pass by. Open for dinner only; closed Mondays. Reservations advised; jackets required for men. Major credit cards accepted. Berth 23, Port Everglades (phone: 522-5225).

Mai-Kai For more than 35 years, this place has been a Ft. Lauderdale landmark, with its huge entranceway torches flanking a rattling plank-bridge entrance. Choose from the main dining room, where you can watch Polynesian dancing, smaller lavishly decorated dining rooms, or outdoor seating by a waterfall. The gardens are lush, with authentic South Seas statuary. The food is even better than the ambience, with exotic drinks, such as the famous Mystery Drink — a show in itself — and Polynesian, American, and Cantonese dishes (a specialty is Peking duck). The *Molokai Bar* is filled with old-time nautical memorabilia. The nightly Polynesian show (cover charge) is professional and highly entertaining. Open nightly. Reservations advised. Major credit cards accepted. 3599 N. Federal Hwy. (phone: 563-3272).

Martha's Located on the Intracoastal Waterway, where the passing boat scene provides its own entertainment. The restaurant has a split personality —

the glitzy downstairs serves dress-up types, while the second-floor deck is less formal, more tropical in flavor. The same courteous service and outstanding menu apply to both. Steaks, chops, and seafood are well prepared; fresh Florida snapper is offered eight different ways — the blackened version is perfectly cooked. Chicken gorgonzola with walnuts is also first-rate. Boat dockage available. Open daily for lunch and dinner, plus Sunday brunch. Reservations necessary Saturday nights, advised otherwise. Major credit cards accepted. 6024 N. Ocean Dr., Hollywood (phone: 923-5444).

Silverado Café A bit of the Napa Valley has been transplanted to the *University Park Plaza* shopping center, where good cooking and California wines prevail. Dine amid Victorian decor or in a small room designed to look like the gondola of a hot-air balloon. Appetizers include an outstanding black bean soup and lobster ravioli; fresh grilled fish or cashew chicken l'orange are tops for main courses. Open for lunch Tuesdays through Saturdays, and dinner Tuesdays through Sundays; closed Mondays. Reservations advised. Major credit cards accepted. 3528 S. University Dr., Davie (phone: 474-9992).

MODERATE

Chart House This branch of the chain offers the standard steaks and seafood with unlimited salad, and fantastic mud pie for dessert. Its downtown Ft. Lauderdale location is a knockout. Housed in two homes (ca. 1904) on the New River, the window tables offer a passing show of pleasure craft and working vessels. Before or after dining, stroll along the 2 miles of the lushly landscaped Riverwalk to the *Broward Center for the Performing Arts*. Or take a water taxi back to your hotel. Open nightly. Reservations advised. Major credit cards accepted. 301 SW 3rd Ave. (phone: 523-0177).

L'Ile De France A bistro that serves outstanding French fare prepared by chef Remi Coulon, who worked aboard the Aga Khan's yacht, and his wife Sandra. The ever-changing menu may include chicken breast stuffed with goat cheese and sun-dried tomatoes, or honey-smoked duck with sun-dried fruit relish. Leave room for the white chocolate mousse cake with praline ganache filling and molasses sauce — mmm. Open for dinner only; closed Mondays. Reservations advised. Major credit cards accepted. 3025 N. Ocean Blvd. (phone: 565-9006).

Rainbow Palace Not your ordinary Chinese eatery, this sophisticated spot offers leisurely dining amid tasteful surroundings. Shrimp with ginger sauce starts the meal off right, followed by pan-fried angel hair noodles dressed with a fisherman's catch of shrimp, calamari, lobster, and scallops. Desserts are decidedly non-Oriental, yet wonderful — especially the Key lime curd cheesecake and White Russian mousse cake. Open for lunch Mondays through Fridays, dinner Mondays through Saturdays; closed Sundays. Reservations advised. Major credit cards accepted. 2787 E. Oakland Park Blvd. (phone: 565-5652).

MODERATE

Bimini Boatyard Bahamian decor and a view of the marina — plus good food at reasonable prices and lots of singles action at the bar. Specialties include conch fritters, grilled swordfish with black bean sauce, and jerk ribs — along with the wonderful Bimini bread. Open daily for lunch, dinner, and snacks. Reservations accepted only for parties of eight or more. Major credit cards accepted. 1555 SW 17th St. (phone: 525-7400).

Brasserie Max Noted restaurateur Dennis Max created this affordable spot (though he no longer owns it) where the young and young-at-heart eat in a casual atmosphere. Creative pizza and pasta dishes are favorites, but the restaurant hits its peak with oak-grilled specialties such as salmon with candied walnut vinaigrette. Open daily for lunch and dinner. Reservations for five or more advised. Major credit cards accepted. 321 N. University Dr. (in *The Fashion Mall*), Plantation (phone: 424-8000).

Charley's Crab One of the best of Chuck Muer's six South Florida restaurants, it has a wonderful location on the Intracoastal Waterway, with tables inside and out. The passing water show ranges from a 110-foot Italian-designed yacht to a Labrador retriever, wearing life vest and sunglasses, skimming along in a Seadoo. Specialties include an excellent Martha's Vineyard salad, a wide range of fresh fish prepared almost every way imaginable, and a terrific apple tart with homemade cinnamon ice cream. Can be reached by water taxi. Open daily for lunch and dinner; plus Sunday brunch. Reservations advised. Major credit cards accepted. 3000 NE 32nd Ave. (phone: 561-4800).

La Ferme Marie-Paul Terrier welcomes guests with a smile, and closely watches over their well-being while husband Henri tends to the kitchen, whipping up traditional and nouvelle delights, including snapper *peolé Bretonne* (sautéed with a sauce made from veal stock) and grilled chicken with Dijon mustard. The dining room is small and cozy, with French-inspired dishes and decor set off by lace tablecloths. Open for dinner only; closed Mondays. Reservations advised. Major credit cards accepted. 1601 E. Sunrise Blvd. (phone: 764-0987).

Gibby's An enormous eatery offering good value in a pretty setting, divided into several dining rooms aglow with twinkling lights. A humongous salad is included with basic steaks and fish dishes and veal parmesan. Among the country's busiest restaurants, it serves about 1,500 dinners nightly in season. In the summer, the lobster specials are unbeatable. Open daily for dinner; weekends for lunch. Reservations advised. Major credit cards accepted. 2900 NE 12th Ter. (phone: 565-2929).

Marco's A small, 13-table place in a strip mall, it dishes out surprisingly good food. The Marco brothers, from Peru, offer an eclectic mix: mussels with white sauce, shrimp a la Marco (with a marinara/champagne sauce), and Wiener schnitzel. Save room for the apple strudel. Closed Saturdays for lunch and Mondays. Reservations advised. Major credit cards accepted. 11262 Pines Blvd., Pembroke Pines (phone: 433-3969).

Pelican Pub Downstairs, the casual, open-air eatery uses paper plates to serve food freshly plucked from the sea. Upstairs, the decor gets a bit fancier, but the food is just as fresh, with chicken and steaks added to the menu. Specialties of the house include a smoked fish spread, Maine lobster, and swordfish parmesan. Open daily for lunch and dinner, plus Sunday brunch. Reservations advised for parties of more than six. Major credit cards accepted. 2635 N. Riverside Dr. (phone: 785-8550).

La Perla Good southern Italian cooking lures the dressy crowd. Regulars rave over pasta made fresh daily on the premises. Try the homemade pasta or gnocchi, and the osso buco or fresh fish. Open nightly. Reservations advised. Major credit cards accepted. 1818 E. Sunrise Blvd. (phone: 765-1950).

Ronieri's Fine continental fare is featured in this western Broward County eatery tucked away in a shopping center. Specialties include raspberry chicken wings and veal *crustada* (a scaloppine stuffed with eggplant, mushrooms, mozzarella cheese, and pine nuts). The *tiramisù* is among the best in Florida. Calorie counters will appreciate the selection of freshly made Weight Watcher specials. Open for dinner only; closed Mondays. Reservations advised. Most major credit cards accepted. 207 N. University Dr., Pembroke Pines (phone: 966-2233).

Sea Watch One of the few South Florida dining spots set on the Atlantic Ocean beach, this woodsy eatery has been here for almost 21 years. The fare is mostly fresh fish, including those famous stone crabs; oysters Rockefeller and Gulf garlic shrimp are also favorites. Open daily for lunch and dinner. No reservations for under five people. Major credit cards accepted. 6002 N. Ocean Blvd. (phone: 781-2200).

Victoria Park Set on an unlikely looking street, this tiny gem (only 10 tables) produces outstanding French cookery with Caribbean overtones. Shrimp wrapped in bacon and grilled with a caramelized shallot dressing is only excelled by the grilled chicken with honey-chili glaze. Open for dinner only; closed Sundays. Reservations advised. Major credit cards accepted. 900 NE 20th Ave. (phone: 764-6868).

INEXPENSIVE

Brother's This popular place offers bagels and lox and corned beef on rye, as well as roasted chicken dinners and the like, to droves of locals. Save room for the 7-layer cake. Open daily for breakfast, lunch, and dinner. No reservations. Major credit cards accepted. 1325 S. Powerline Rd., Pompano Beach (phone: 968-5881).

Cap's Place Marilyn Monroe, John F. Kennedy, and Winston Churchill (not together!) ate in this wonderful old Florida island dining place. Founded during the 1920s, this fishing shack once held many wild gambling parties and was the base for a thriving rum-running operation. Now it's strictly a seafood eatery. Diners are picked up by boat at NE 28th Court and taken for a 5-minute ride to Cap's Island, off Lighthouse Point. Open nightly. Reservations advised. Major credit cards accepted. 2765 NE 28th Ct. (phone: 941-0418).

Carlos & Pepe's The clientele at this popular hangout is eager and hungry; the setting is crowded, but pleasant (light wood, green plants, and tile tables); and the menu is lighthearted Mexican (*fajitas, chimichangas,* and *chiles rellenos*). Open daily for lunch, dinner, and snacks. No reservations. Major credit cards accepted. 1302 SE 17th St. (phone: 467-7192).

Ernie's Bar B Que A local institution for 30-plus years, the ribs, chicken, pork, and beef are prepared in a special barbecue sauce that's famous throughout the area. For something different, try the fiery conch chowder. The decor has a rustic Key West style. Open daily for lunch, dinner, and snacks. Reservations unnecessary. Major credit cards accepted. 1843 S. Federal Hwy. (phone: 523-8636).

Flamingo Diner Besides hamburgers and salads, the nostalgic may indulge in the *Flamingo*'s old-fashioned meat loaf, cabbage soup, or a black cow — a root beer with ice cream. On Friday nights, members of the Florida Gold Coast Classics car club meet, many arriving in their 1950s wheels. No reservations. No credit cards accepted. 7750 Peters Rd., Plantation (phone: 424-7464).

Pumpernik's For 15 years, this enormous place has been supplying locals with corned beef on rye or blintzes with sour cream. They serve plenty of broiled fish and burgers, too. The restaurant boasts that it uses 4,000 eggs per week in season (definitely not for cholesterol watchers). Open daily from 7:30 AM until midnight. Reservations accepted for groups of ten or more. Major credit cards accepted. 917 E. Hallandale Beach Blvd., Hallandale (phone: 454-6773).

Diversions

Exceptional Experiences for the Mind and Body

Quintessential Miami

When people think of Miami, it's most often Don Johnson and "Miami Vice" that come to mind — a land of sun, fun, and guns, pastel coated and complete with bronzed bodies tooling around in racy convertibles. But there's more to Miami than meets the television-viewing eye. It is a town of varied cultures — Cubans, Caribbeans, Seminole Indians, and retired Northerners are all here; colorful neighborhoods; great seafood; Art Deco design; the popular NFL *Dolphins* — and the beach. There are nightclubs for night owls, the nearby Everglades for those who are into gators and grasslands, and the Florida Keys for those looking for some respite from the mobs and some hints of Hemingway and Tennessee Williams. Below are some of the musts to put you in a Miami state of mind.

THE BEACH *The* reason most vacationers choose Miami. Back in the 1920s, developer Carl Fisher raised the land that's now Miami Beach 5 feet above sea level by loading it with sand that he then secured with rows of large palm trees. Ever since, visitors have been flocking to Dade County's 15.5 miles of beaches to enjoy the mild air, plentiful sun, and warm, aqua-colored sea. Numerous restoration projects replenishing the sands (the latest in 1988) have made the beach even more beautiful than it was when Betty Grable and Robert Cummings romped here in the 1941 movie *Moon Over Miami*. Over the years, the beach has retained its glamour; oceans of movies — including *Goldfinger,* starring Sean Connery as James Bond — have been filmed on its glistening white sands. The most recent on-screen incarnation of Miami Beach was TV's "Miami Vice," whose shots of the beach, the Art Deco District, and the posh hotels introduced the city to a new generation of sun worshipers. The beach continues to attract film-makers, and others who just come here to catch some rays are still apt to catch a glimpse of a celebrity or two.

The water, especially in the summer, is comfortably warm and inviting; in winter, diehard surfers can pit themselves against some respectable waves. At most points, the beach is a 300-foot-wide swath of clean white sand reached by boardwalks; the approach is fringed with a 65-foot-wide band of beach grass and sea grapes that protects the dunes and the beach from erosion (thanks to the Dade County Beach Vegetation Project). Those not staying at beachfront hotels can enjoy the sand and surf at numerous public beaches. (All Dade County beaches are open to the public; parking, however, may be difficult.) Perhaps the best spot at which to capture a vintage Florida tan while sampling the true flavor of a Miami beach is at the North Shore Recreation Area, a 40-acre state park that runs from 79th to 86th Streets in Miami Beach. For a nominal charge (50¢ for Florida residents, $1 for non-residents), beach lovers can sun and swim at a well-maintained, policed beach (entrances at 81st and 85th Sts., at Collins Ave.). Features include boardwalks, picnic tables and barbecue pits under palm trees, bicycle paths and bike rentals, bathrooms with lockers, outdoor showers, a playground area for tots, access ramps for the disabled, a concession stand (at 83rd St.), and metered parking. There's also a Vita Course — a trail with marked stops with workout equipment and instructions for specific exercises. Open year-round, it's definitely earned its place in the sun.

THE ART DECO DISTRICT This unique square-mile district, listed on the National Registry of Historic Places, boasts the largest concentration of Art Deco resort architecture in the world. There are about 650 individual buildings in the area — better known by locals as South Beach — designated by the National Registry as 5th to 22nd Streets, from Ocean Drive to Alton Road. Besides its historical value, the Art Deco District has become Greater Miami's hot, "in" place. Throughout are pastel delights — it's as if a mad Miamian had scattered Necco wafers all over! Tropical Deco combines buildings painted warm peach and turquoise or lavender teamed with pink with stylized nautical motifs (mermaids, waves, and flying porpoises). Quintessential expressions of Miami, these buildings abound with features such as porthole windows and metal railings, juxtaposed against palm trees from the coconut plantation that once stood on the white strand across the street.

The "art" in Art Deco extends far beyond the architecture, however; the human street scene is an artwork in its own right. With a backdrop of wonderfully, whimsically restored buildings built between the 1920s and 1940s, a young man wearing bike shorts and sporting a live snake draped around his neck roller-blades by; beautiful blonde fashion models from Germany drape themselves in front of archways as cameras click away; tables chockablock with patrons line the wide sidewalks; an old woman shuffles along, wearing three sweaters and gloves in the 80F heat; and a Japanese tourist looks perplexed. The photogenic potential of such contrasts appealed to "Miami Vice" producer Michael Mann, who opted for the realism of shooting here rather than on a Hollywood set; today the area is so much in demand for photo shoots for fashion magazines and catalogues that ten modeling agencies have sprung up here.

The popularity of this district has undergone some changes over the decades. In the 1920s and 1930s, hotel guests and residents here were largely Jews, who were restricted to living south of 15th Street and east of Washington Avenue; beyond those boundaries, developer Carl Fisher enforced the "Caucasian Clause" of his predecessors' real-estate contracts, and denied Jews and blacks the opportunity to stay in his hotels or to buy real estate. This area, also known as South Beach, was then developed by the Lummus brothers, who admitted Jews but prohibited blacks. Over the years, the area fell into decline, and the former hotels became homes for the elderly living on Social Security; in a few instances, they still can be seen sitting on their porches in rocking chairs.

In 1980, many émigrés from Cuba's famous Mariel boatlift settled here. Some of the hotels that remain have small rooms and unit air conditioners, but provide very inexpensive accommodations. A few, like the *Leslie* and *Beach Paradise* hotels, stand out (see "Checking In" in *Miami,* THE CITIES); it's a good base for exploring the region. A 90-minute guided tour, led by a historian who regales visitors with fascinating anecdotes, leaves the *Miami Design Preservation League* office (*Leslie Hotel*, 1244 Ocean Dr.; phone: 305-672-2014) every Saturday at 10:30 AM; admission charge. Reservations unnecessary. Another historian-led tour, a 2-hour trip on bicycle, leaves from *Cycles on the Beach* (713 Fifth St.; phone: 305-672-2014 or 305-673-2055) Sundays at 10:30 AM; admission charge. Reservations advised. Additional tours are available during *Art Deco Weekend* in January, with juried artists, culinary booths, stage concerts, and the *Moon Over Miami* ball. Those driving will find inexpensive, safe parking at Lincoln Road Mall Parking near the *Theater of the Performing Arts (TOPA)* and the *Miami Beach Convention Center* or the municipal lot on 13th Street between Ocean Drive and Collins Avenue; the major Ocean Drive restaurants offer valet parking as well. For more information see *Tour 1: South Beach — The Art Deco District* in DIRECTIONS.

LITTLE HAVANA With Cuba off-limits to most of us, this enclave of Cuban and Nicaraguan immigrants is the next best thing to experiencing a slice of Havana life firsthand. The neighborhood now called Little Havana was primarily a Jewish community until about 35 years ago. Cuban immigrants then began arriving in droves, especially once Castro took power. Now a stroll down Calle Ocho can evoke images of the Havana many remember from the classic film versions of Hemingway's *The Old Man and the Sea* and Graham Greene's *Our Man in Havana.* The sounds of samba and rumba music can be heard wafting out of apartment windows and bars; the smells of *plátanos* (plantains), chicken and rice, black beans, and grilled pork strips comingle in the air, while street vendors sell vegetables and other wares. Mothers and their children attired in brightly colored, ruffled dresses sit together on steps and watch the tourists watching them. Men in *guayaberas* (tieless, embroidered shirts often worn in Latin American countries) gather in doorways or in Máximo Gomez Park (SW 8th St.

and SW 15th Ave.) to play dominoes or chess and smoke cigars (no cursing, gambling, or women allowed!). The air is alive with activity accented with the vibrant colors of the Latin world — oranges, reds, and yellows.

Eateries with grill-fronted windows that open onto the street dispense strong *café con leche* and guava *pasteles;* stores sport signs in Spanish and, if you can't speak any, you may have problems communicating; vendors in open-air markets hawk sugarcane stalks and green coconuts complete with straws for drinking the coconut milk. For a taste of Cuba, try a Cuban sandwich (ham, cheese, pickles, and mustard on crispy Cuban bread) at *El Pub* (SW 16th Ave.). For a complete Latin meal, try *Málaga* (740 SW 8th St.) or *Versailles* (3535 SW 8th St.) for roast pork with rice and black-bean sauce, then flan (a custard covered with caramel syrup) for dessert. Cuban products even can be seen being made at various spots in the neighborhood. At *El Crédito* (1106 SW 8th St.), watch cigars being made at Miami's largest hand-rolled cigar factory, a business that was launched here in 1969, but began in Havana in 1907. Peek in at the *Botánica la Abuela* (1122 SW 8th St.); besides the handmade dolls and a few *piñatas,* shelves bear such items as leaves and roots used for *santería* rituals, an Afro-Cuban mixture of voodoo and Catholicism. A few blocks away, *Casa de Guayaberas* (5840 SW 8th St.; phone: 305-266-9683; closed Sundays) carries a fine selection of *guayaberas*. Shirts come in every size, fabric, and color; prices range from $15 to $150. Nearby, *La Casa de las Piñatas* (1756 SW 8th St.) sells wonderful *piñatas*. The standard paper donkeys (stuffed with toys and surprises) from Mexico are moderately priced (about $25), but prices go up for the fantastic creations suspended from the ceiling, such as a 4-foot-high Big Bird, which sells for $179; others are priced as high as $500 (squawk!). A more somber note prevails at the Brigade 2506 Memorial (at SW 13th Ave.), built to commemorate those who fell in the ill-fated Bay of Pigs invasion. But the Hispanic fervor really erupts each year for *Carnaval Miami,* a 10-day-long celebration in early March featuring a *paseo,* an 8-km run, and folkloric entertainment; it culminates in *Calle Ocho: Open House,* the country's largest street festival. Begun in 1978 as a block party, this event now includes 23 blocks of 50 stages featuring 200 musical groups and 500 vendors selling everything from hot dogs to paella — with plenty of samples. More than 1 million people participate. For information, contact the *Kiwanis Club of Little Havana* (phone: 305 644-8888). For those who really want to sample the flavor of Little Havana, *Miami River Inn* (see "Checking In" in *Miami,* THE CITIES) is a charming bed and breakfast establishment in the heart of the area. But if it's the sultry sensuality of a Latin night that you seek, pick a dimly lit table for two at one of the local restaurants, order up some Cuban chow, make sure the salsa music is well within earshot, and then close your eyes — you might almost forget for a moment that you're in Miami!

FOOTBALL FEVER From September to January, both Miami and Ft. Lauderdale go nuts over football — collegiate and professional. Frequent NFL-division champions, the Miami *Dolphins* play at *Joe Robbie Stadium* in Greater Miami North (2269 NW 199th St.; phone: 305-620-2578; fax: 305-620-6596). Dan Marino — *Dolphins* quarterback and *Pro Bowl* choice — has raised local football fanaticism to new heights. The competitive national college football power, the University of Miami *Hurricanes*, toss the pigskin at *Orange Bowl Stadium* (1501 NW 3rd St.; phone: 305-358-5885 for tickets, 305-643-7100 for other *Orange Bowl* information; fax: 305-643-7115). Or contact the University of Miami ticket office (1 Hurricane Dr., Coral Gables; phone: 305-284-2655). The world-famous Federal Express *Orange Bowl Football Classic,* pitting the Big Eight collegiate conference champion against another nationally ranked team, is played at *Orange Bowl Stadium* on *New Year*'s night (phone: 305-642-5211). It's preceded by the *King Orange Jamboree Parade,* a lavish procession downtown on Biscayne Boulevard on *New Year's Eve* (phone: 305-642-1515). In response to this craziness, the *King Mango Strut* parade developed a few years back; it winds its way through Coconut Grove a few days in advance — a socially satirical poke at much that is considered "holy" these days (phone: 305-441-0944). Top-ranked collegiate teams go head-to-head in the *Blockbuster Bowl* at *Joe Robbie Stadium* during the last weekend in December (phone: 305-620-2578; fax: 305-620-6596).

EARLY-BIRD DINNERS The classic joke is that Florida's state tree is the sabal palm and the state bird is the "early bird." Early-bird dinners are a regular topic of conversation around pools, on golf courses, and in lines at the supermarket; dining out is a favorite South Florida activity and early-bird specials afford a full dinner at less money than the same meal will cost later in the evening. To spread business over a longer dinnertime (especially in season, when long lines are frequently the norm), restaurateurs provide incentives to dine early by lowering prices before peak hours (sometimes people have their evening meal as early as 4 PM). Some eateries, though, offer their early-bird hours as late as 6 PM or so. Experienced early birds know what is the latest possible time to get in line and still qualify for an early-bird dinner. For the rest of us, it's best to check the local papers for times. That way, you too can enjoy the same tropical decor, attentive service, scenic views, and first-rate fare that will be served a few hours later at up to twice the price. An example is *Charley's Crab* (see "Eating Out" in *Ft. Lauderdale,* THE CITIES), where diners from 5 to 5:45 PM daily can choose from a menu that is limited but still features fresh fish and the noteworthy Martha's Vineyard salad — all for about $10 — while enjoying the same waterfront entertainment as later diners. Or try a restaurant as elegant as *Dominique's* (see "Eating Out" in *Miami,* THE CITIES), where you can savor the wonderful terrine of duck or beef medallions with merlot glaze. An elegantly served three-course dinner costs $17 from 5 to 6:30 PM.

Be aware that early-bird meals sometimes masquerade as "sunset specials," "twilight dinners," or the like. If you don't mind eating early, be sure to ask restaurants if they offer such a deal. A better-kept secret is the summertime bargain. Since business falls off drastically when the "season" ends — usually about April or May — some restaurateurs have trouble retaining and paying their staffs over the summer. To drum up business, they provide specials such as two meals for the price of one. *Gibby's* (see "Eating Out" in *Ft. Lauderdale,* THE CITIES) features dinners with two Maine lobsters and other accoutrements for the cost of a chicken meal during season — $17. The outdoor *Pelican Bar* at *Pier 66* has a lobster dinner with salad and a drink for $10. Never mind the worm; here it's definitely the early bird that catches the inexpensive lobster.

Antiquing

Not everybody in Greater Miami lives among glass and lucite. Many traditionalists prefer antiques, and lots of estate sales keep the suppliers going and customers coming.

Those who love to prowl among things old may find a bonanza at the *Coconut Grove Antique and Jewelry Show* in August at the *Coconut Grove Convention Center* (phone: 305-579-3312).

"Antique Row" runs along the 100 block of Federal Highway (US 1) between North First Street and Dania Beach Boulevard in Dania, and spills into several of the side streets. The 150 stores and stalls deal in old china, furniture, books, jewelry, and assorted "chatchkes." Most are open Mondays through Saturdays 10 AM to 5 PM. The following are worth a look:

English Accent Antiques: 57 N. Federal Hwy., Dania (phone: 305-923-8383).

House of Hirsch Antiques: 75 N. Federal Hwy., Dania (phone: 305-925-0818).

Kleinman Antiques: 60 N. Federal Hwy., Dania (phone: 305-920-2801).

Maxine's Antiques: 8 N. Federal Hwy., Dania (phone: 305-920-0588).

Rose Antiques: 17 N. Federal Hwy., Dania (phone: 305-921-0474).

RULES OF THE ROAD FOR AN ODYSSEY OF THE OLD

Buy for sheer pleasure, not for investment. Forget about the carrot of supposed retail values that dealers habitually dangle in front of amateur clients. If you love something, it will probably grace your home long after the moon over Miami stops shining.

Buy the finest example you can afford of any item, in as close to mint condition as possible. Chipped or broken "bargains" will haunt you later with their shabbiness. They also don't increase in value the way the mint stuff does.

Train your eye in museums and/or collections of things in the period that interests you. (Remember, Miami is practically the mother of Art Deco.) These are the best schools for the acquisitive senses, particularly as you begin to develop special passions.

Get advice from specialists when contemplating major acquisitions. Much antique and collectible furniture and many paintings have been restored several times. If you want to be absolutely certain that what you're buying is what you've been told it is, stick with the larger dealers. Some auction houses and even small museums have an evaluation office whose experts will make appraisals for a fee.

Don't be afraid to haggle — a little. Most dealers don't have fixed prices, so sharpen your negotiating skills and make an offer they can't refuse. A word of warning: While most larger dealers take credit cards, smaller shops do not.

When pricing an object, don't forget to figure the cost of shipping. Shipping home a large piece — furniture, sculpture, antique garden paraphernalia — can be considerable. Be sure to figure this into the cost of your purchase.

Historic Churches

Although Miami's history only goes as far back as the late 1800s (the city was incorporated in 1896, when the railroad came to town), there are a few historical churches of note. The oldest dates from the 12th century and was brought here from Spain. Most of the other noteworthy houses of worship fall into one of two basic architectural categories, either bearing the Spanish mark, with capped steeples, hand-carved wooden doors, and stone exteriors, or the Art Deco influence, with stucco exteriors, rounded corners, and spires. All welcome worshipers and wanderers alike.

CORAL GABLES CONGREGATIONAL CHURCH Dating from 1923, its Spanish design has a barrel-tile roof, pews carved from native cypress, and 16th-century furnishings. The bell tower is based on Spain's Giralda Tower. Guided tours are offered at 11:15 AM. Information: *Coral Gables Congregational Church,* 3010 DeSoto Blvd., Coral Gables (phone: 305-448-7421).

PLYMOUTH CONGREGATIONAL CHURCH This 1917 Spanish-style limestone church boasts a 375-year-old hand-carved walnut door from a Spanish monastery. Call to arrange a visit and guided tour. Information: *Plymouth Congregational Church,* 3400 Devon Rd., Coconut Grove (phone: 305-444-6521).

SPANISH MONASTERY The Western Hemisphere's oldest building was not erected in Florida, but built in 1141 in Segovia, Spain. Publishing magnate William Randolph Hearst had it shipped in pieces to America in the 1920s. Twenty-five years later, Miami developers put it back together on this site.

It is a functioning Episcopal church, and it's worth visiting for its small collection of ancient art and furnishings. Open daily 10 AM to 5 PM, Sundays noon to 5 PM. Admission charge. Information: *Ancient Spanish Monastery,* 16711 W. Dixie Hwy., North Miami Beach (phone: 305-945-1461).

TEMPLE BETH JACOB Miami's oldest synagogue, its two cream-colored stucco buildings, both on the National Register of Historic Places, house an Orthodox congregation. The older building (311 Washington Ave.), dating from 1922, is Mediterranean-looking and features the original wooden front doors; the copper-domed building with stained glass windows (301 Washington Ave.) dates from 1936. Information: *Temple Beth Jacob,* 311 Washington Ave., Miami (phone: 305-672-6150).

TEMPLE EMANU-EL Built in 1946 (although the congregation dates from 1938), the temple is important for its size and its cultural activities (guest performers and lecturers have included the late Isaac Bashevis Singer, Norman Schwarzkopf, Henry Kissinger, and Itzhak Perlman). Of white stucco with a silver dome over the sanctuary, and seating 1,800, the Conservative synagogue is the place of worship for 1,200 families. Information: *Temple Emanu-El,* 1701 Washington Ave., Miami Beach, near the Art Deco District and the Miami Beach Convention Center (phone: 305-538-2503). For synagogue tours featuring colorful stories of Jewish heritage, contact Dr. Sam Brown, Newport S, Apt. 4086, Deerfield Beach 33441 (phone: 305-421-8431).

TRINITY EPISCOPAL CATHEDRAL Home of Miami's oldest congregation, the white neo-Romanesque church, known for its beautiful rose window, is now the seat of the South Florida Episcopal Archdiocese. Information: *Trinity Episcopal Cathedral,* 464 NE 16th St., Miami (phone: 305-374-3372).

Miami from Another Angle: From the Farm to the Keys

For a very different look at Miami, drive south along US 27 through miles of what used to be its little-known farmland. Now the area is known worldwide because of Hurricane Andrew, but you can still stock up on fresh fruit and vegetables such as strawberries and tomatoes at numerous stands, or go right out into the U-Pic fields and choose your own. Many mango, avocado, and lime trees were lost to Andrew, and it will take several years until they're replaced and bear crops. Destruction of farm equipment and movement of farm laborers out of the area reduced production temporarily. But much of the rural, sleepy little orchards remain, reminders perhaps, of what Miami once was.

Forty miles south of Miami (turn off on US 1) is Everglades National

Park, a unique and extremely diverse subtropical wilderness with some of the best naturalist-oriented activities anywhere in the world. This 1½-million-acre preserve features alligators, raccoons, manatees, mangroves, and thousands of rare birds, all in their natural habitats. (For more information see *Tour 9: Everglades National Park* in DIRECTIONS.) Farther south along US 1 stretch the Florida Keys, a chain of islands connected by the Overseas Highway. Key Largo is the site of the only living coral reef in the continental United States, which you can see in all its glory only by skin diving or snorkeling, or in a glass-bottom boat at John Pennekamp Coral Reef State Park, the only underwater park in this country. As you drive down the highway, you'll pass great fishing possibilities and even better food and drink: conch chowder, Key lime pie, and colorful tropical concoctions with romantic names to enjoy, appropriately, in a tropical sunset. The 7-mile bridge is a spectacular part of the drive, and you'll pass through a series of little islands, or keys, with intriguing names like Little Torch and Big Coppitt. The road finally reaches Marathon and Key West, where you'll find reminders of Ernest Hemingway, a museum displaying the bounty from local treasure hunter Mel Fisher's Spanish galleon, and a hotel built by Henry M. Flagler that's still operating. There's lots to do in Key West, most of it involving the sun and the water, and keeping your body full of good things to eat and drink. For more information see *Tour 8: Florida Keys and John Pennekamp Coral Reef State Park* in DIRECTIONS.

Sybaritic Spas

With several resorts featuring health and fitness spas, there is an abundance of opportunities to be pampered and pummeled throughout Miami and Ft. Lauderdale. Although sun worshiping with abandon is no longer in vogue, these spots provide new ways to care for your health and appearance. In addition to skin-care programs, massages, and facials, diet and stress-management plans help visitors to care better for their bodies — and their minds.

Many clients of these spas are show-business and *Fortune* 500-executive–types who slip down to Florida for stays lasting from a day to a few months. Many facilities are at the high end of the scale — and can make a major dent in the pocketbook. But remember, even the more costly spas include all meals and most activities in their rates, and we are talking sybaritic. So relax. It's time to do something nice for yourself — you've earned it.

BILTMORE Located in the hotel of the same name, its facilities include an aerobics room, plus 2,800 square feet of Nautilus, Stairmaster, and free-weight equipment. There are deep- and shallow-water aerobics, yoga, facials, and massages, and a complimentary computerized body analysis. Spa selections appear on the regular menu. Information: *Biltmore,* 1200 Anastasia Ave., Coral Gables, FL 33134 (phone: 305-445-1926 or 800-727-1926; fax: 305-448-9976).

BONAVENTURE Frequently judged among the country's best, attractions are hot and cold plunge pools, aerobic and water aerobic exercise classes, massage options (Swedish, shiatsu, and reflexology), aromatherapy, herbal and sea kelp body wraps, thermal back treatments, and nutrition consultation. There is an executive wellness program in conjunction with the Miami Heart Institute. The resort's beautiful grounds feature 5 swimming pools, 24 tennis courts, two 18-hole championship golf courses, racquetball, and squash courts. The spa dining room has a varied menu; smoking is prohibited. Information: *Bonaventure,* 250 Racquet Club Rd., Ft. Lauderdale, FL 33326 (phone: 305-389-3300 or 800-327-8090; fax: 305-384-0563).

DORAL SATURNIA Based on the *Terme di Saturnia* in Tuscany, Italy, where restorative volcanic waters have supposedly helped sojourners for thousands of years, this complex lures those interested in health and fitness, diet control, and stress management. Recently judged the top North American spa by "Lifestyles of the Rich and Famous," its international guests consider it the country's most beautiful and luxurious. Fabulous facilities include 4 exercise studios (with 30 daily exercise classes), a weight room with cardiovascular equipment, large outdoor pool with hot tub, outdoor lap pool, indoor exercise pool, hydrotherapy tubs, saunas, indoor track for walking and jogging, and an outdoor quarter-mile par-course and exercise stations. There are personalized assessments, cholesterol- and blood pressure–reduction programs, dance classes, cellulite-reduction programs, collagen-repair facials, personal trainers, a beauty salon, cooking demonstrations, and take-home programs. Meals are elegantly served in 2 restaurants, with surprisingly sumptuous choices — even a glass of wine. Guests also may use facilities at the adjoining *Doral Resort and Country Club* and the beachfront *Doral Ocean Beach* (see "Checking In" in *Miami,* THE CITIES). Information: *Doral Saturnia,* 8755 NW 36th St., Miami, FL 33178 (phone: 305-593-6030, 800-331-7768, or 800-22DORAL; fax: 305-591-9266).

FONTAINEBLEAU HILTON The hotel's *Spa Pavilion* enticements include massage therapy, mineral baths, whirlpool baths, Nautilus machines, free weights, aerobics classes, cellulite treatment, and a cardiovascular room supervised by the Mount Sinai Sports Institute. More than 100 classes are conducted weekly, including water aerobics and special programs for children. There are some spa items on hotel menus. Information: *Fontainebleau Hilton,* 4441 Collins Ave., Miami Beach, FL 33140 (phone: 305:538-2000 or 800-HILTONS; fax: 305-534-7821).

INN & SPA AT FISHER ISLAND With its Spanish-style architecture, the *Spa Internazionale* on fabulous Fisher Island offers several programs for beauty, fitness, and relaxation treatment: thalassotherapy, aromatherapy, hydromassage, Swedish massage, Vichy Shower body polish, herbal wraps, facials, computerized fitness assessment, and personal training. Other novelties include an indoor lap pool with retractable roof, a Jacuzzi with cold plunge pool, an outdoor Roman waterfall, aerobics classes, and a beauty salon. The ultimate experience is "The Perfect Day," renting the luxurious marble and tile VIP Private Suite for a half- or full-day program of customized fitness and/or beauty treatment. The resort has 19 tennis courts and a 9-hole golf course. Information: *Inn at Fisher Island,* One Fisher Island Dr., Fisher Island, FL 33109 (phone: 305-535-6030 or 800-624-3251; fax: 305-535-6008).

PALM-AIRE Stars such as Elizabeth Taylor, Billy Joel, and Liza Minnelli often shape up at this 20-year-old spa and resort (see "Checking In" in *Ft. Lauderdale,* THE CITIES). Spa facilities include aerobics and water exercise classes, outdoor and private indoor whirlpool baths, saunas, massage choices (Swedish, shiatsu, and reflexology), aromatherapy, thalassotherapy, facials, herbal wraps, and a solarium. The spa dining room features delicious calorie-controlled meals, plus take-home books and instruction. Information: *Palm-Aire,* 2601 Palm-Aire Dr. N., Pompano Beach, FL 33069 (phone: 305-972-3300 or 800-272-5624; fax: 305-968-2744).

PIER HOUSE CARIBBEAN SPA Located in a separate section of the *Pier House Resort,* with 22 guest rooms and a small gym, it's worth a visit just to rejuvenate with a massage from Dominic Fabis, recipient of the Best Massage of the Year award by the Florida Massage Association. Other inducements include aromatherapy facials and massages, reflexology, loofah salt treatment, free weights, Stairmaster, and fitness classes. Healthful buffet breakfasts; spa dishes available for lunch and dinner in the dining rooms. Information: *Pier House Resort,* One Duval St., Key West, FL 33040 (phone: 305-296-4600 or 800-327-8340; fax: 305-296-7569).

PIER 66 The full-service *Spa LXVI* at this Intracoastal resort offers Nautilus machines, sauna and steamroom, loofah and Swedish-Esalen massage, herbal wraps, a beauty salon and more. There are 2 swimming pools, indoor and outdoor Jacuzzis, and 2 lighted tennis courts. Information: *Pier 66 Resort & Marina,* 2301 SE 17th St., Ft. Lauderdale, FL 33316 (phone: 305-525-6666 or 800-432-1956; fax: 305-728-3541).

SPA AT PGA The renowned Professional Golfers Association of America (PGA) facility, with 5 championship 18-hole golf courses, 19 tennis courts, and 3 indoor racquetball courts, has added a state-of-the-art spa. The 26,900-square-foot *Health & Racquet Center* offers 22 private spa treatment rooms, Swedish and shiatsu massage, hydrotherapy, Jacuzzis, and salon treatments. Highlight is the "Relaxing Waters of the World," a complex of 6 outdoor therapy pools, including 3 with imported mineral salts. Spa guests also have access to the Nautilus center, aerobics classes, 5-lane lap pool, and Health Bar at the *Health & Racquet Club*. Accommodations are in the main hotel. Information: *Spa at PGA National Resort*, 400 Avenue of the Champions, Palm Beach Gardens, FL 33418 (phone: 407-627-2000 or 800-633-9150; fax: 407-622-0261).

TURNBERRY ISLE This marina/golf/tennis complex also offers a health- and beauty-oriented spa with Finnish sauna, Turkish steamrooms, cold plunge pool, indoor and outdoor whirlpool baths, Nautilus equipment, 8 Cybex training machines, racquetball courts, aerobics classes, and more. Diet plans are supervised by a staff physician and a nutritionist; spa dishes are available on both dining room menus, including "Cuisine Salu" at the highly regarded *Veranda* restaurant. Resort options include 2 championship Robert Trent Jones, Jr. golf courses, and 24 tennis courts. Information: *Turnberry Isle,* 19999 W. Country Club Dr., Aventura, FL 33180 (phone 305-932-6200 or 800-327-7028; fax: 305-937-0528).

Day Cruises

A favorite activity of vacationers and Floridians alike is the 10-day cruise. This provides an introduction to the sea for novices, but also is popular among many frequent cruisers. Some people simply need a day off from the world — a taste of the Bahamas, or a little gambling — without changing their "home base." Cruises may be booked in advance directly through a cruise company or through a travel agent, risking no-refunds if the weather's amiss. It's also possible to wait until the chosen day, arriving early to stand in line for a vacant spot. Prices, as on longer cruises, include meals on board, activities, nightclub entertainment (tips and alcoholic drinks are extra), and access to casinos, which don't open until ships pass the 3-mile limit. High rollers are frequently seen queuing up outside closed casino doors. Kids under 11 usually sail free on all ships; inquire when making reservations.

DISCOVERY This is the largest day cruise liner hereabouts, debarking from Port Everglades, Ft. Lauderdale. It offers daytime and evening "cruises to nowhere" or to Freeport, Grand Bahama Island. Buffet dining is included; à la carte dining is an additional charge. Information: *Discovery Cruises,* 1850 Eller Dr., Ft. Lauderdale, FL 33316 (phone: 305-525-7800 or 800-937-4477).

SCANDINAVIAN DAWN The *SeaEscape* sails from Port Everglades, Ft. Lauderdale. It has daytime and evening "cruises to nowhere" or to Freeport, Grand Bahama Island. Buffet dining or à la carte at no additional charge. Information: *SeaEscape Cruises,* 8751 W. Broward Blvd., Suite 300, Plantation, FL 33324 (phone: 800-432-3939 in Florida or 800-826-6842 elsewhere in the US).

TROPIC STAR This recent entry in the day-cruising market sails to Freeport, Grand Bahama Island, from Miami; it also offers evening "cruises to nowhere." Buffet-style meals are included in the fare. Children 2 to 15 sail at a reduced rate. Information: *Starlite Cruises,* 1007 N. America Way, Miami, FL 33312 (phone: 305-539-3500 in Dade County; 800-354-5005 elsewhere).

A Shutterbug's View

With all its pastels, seascapes, and picturesque neighborhoods, Miami is a very photogenic city. There is architectural variety: Art Deco is juxtaposed with modern, ornate with ordinary, and a skyline bristling with the temples of modern commerce with the seashore reaching to meet it. There is also natural variety: Flowers embroider a park footpath, a palm tree waves in the breeze, and a sunrise sparks the horizon over the ocean. There's human variety as well: Immigrants exchange the latest news from the Old Country in Spanish, ruddy fishermen return with their catch, and beachcombers flaunt their tans on the boardwalk. The thriving city, the shimmering sea, the parks, the people, and traces of rich history make Miami a fertile stomping ground for shutterbugs. With backdrops like these, even a beginner can achieve remarkable results with a surprisingly basic set of lenses and filters. Equipment is, in fact, only as valuable as the imagination that puts it into use.

LANDSCAPES, SEASCAPES, AND CITYSCAPES Miami's populated beaches and historic buildings are most often visiting photographers' favorite subjects. But the city's green spaces and waterways provide numerous photo possibilities as well. In addition to the historic hotels, churches, and the Art Deco District, be sure to look for natural beauty: at the Fairchild Tropical Garden, the well-manicured plots of flowers in the public parks, and the rolling waves of the Atlantic.

Although a standard 50mm to 55mm lens may work well in some landscape situations, most will benefit from a 20mm to 28mm wide-angle. The Ft. Lauderdale skyline from the top of the *Pier 66* resort, for example, is the type of panorama that fits beautifully into a wide-angle format, allowing not only the overview, but the opportunity to include people or other points of interest in the foreground. A fruit stand, for instance, may be used to set off a view of a street in Little Havana; or people can provide a sense of perspective in a shot of a café in the Art Deco District.

To isolate specific elements of any scene, use your telephoto lens. Perhaps there's a particular carving in a historic building that would make a lovely shot, or it might be the interplay of light and shadow on the façade of an old Spanish church. The successful use of a telephoto means developing your eye for detail.

PEOPLE As with taking pictures of people anywhere, there are going to be times in Miami when a camera is an intrusion. Your approach is the key: Consider your own reaction under similar circumstances, and you have an idea as to what would make others comfortable enough to be willing subjects. People are often sensitive to having a camera suddenly pointed at them, and a polite request, while getting you a share of refusals, will also provide a chance to shoot some wonderful portraits that capture the spirit of the area as surely as the scenery does. For candid shots, an excellent lens is a zoom telephoto in the 70mm to 210mm range; it allows you to remain unobtrusive while the telephoto lens draws the subject closer. And for portraits, a telephoto can be used effectively as close as 2 or 3 feet.

For authenticity and variety, select a place likely to produce interesting subjects. The *Bayside Marketplace* is an obvious spot for visitors, but if it's local color you're after, visit the boardwalk in Ft. Lauderdale, Little Havana, or Coconut Grove. Aim for shots that tell what's different about Miami. In portraiture, there are several factors to keep in mind. Morning or afternoon light will add richness to skin tones, emphasizing tans. To avoid the harsh facial shadows cast by direct sunlight, shoot in the shade or in an area where the light is diffused.

SUNSETS While the sun doesn't set over the ocean in Miami, there are days when the last golden rays reflect off a lone sailboat, or when a fiery light hits the *Adrian* hotel's pink and turquoise façade, crowned with magical clouds of pink and lavender, purple and red.

When shooting sunsets, keep in mind that the brightness will distort meter readings. When composing a shot directly into the sun, frame the picture in the viewfinder so that only half of the sun is included. Read the meter, set, and shoot. Whenever there is this kind of unusual lighting, shoot a few frames in half-step increments, both over and under the meter reading. Bracketing, as this is called, can provide a range of images, the best of which may well be other than the one shot at the meter's recommended setting.

Use any lens for sunsets. A wide-angle is good when the sky is filled with color-streaked clouds, when the sun is partially hidden, or when you're close to an object that silhouettes dramatically against the sky.

Telephotos also produce wonderful silhouettes, either with the sun as a backdrop or against the palette of a brilliant sunset sky. Bracket again here. For the best silhouettes, wait 10 to 15 minutes after sunset. Unless using a very fast film, a tripod is recommended.

Orange, magenta, and split filters are often used to accentuate a sunset's picture potential. Orange will help turn even a gray sky into something approaching a photogenic finale to the day, and can provide particularly beautiful shots linking the sky with the sun reflected on the ocean. If the sunset is already bold in hue, however, the orange will overwhelm the natural colors — as will a red filter — but will produce dramatic, highly unrealistic results.

NIGHT If you think that picture possibilities end at sunset, you're presuming that night photography is the exclusive domain of the professional. If you've got a tripod, all you'll need is a cable release to attach to your camera to assure a steady exposure (which is often timed in minutes rather than fractions of a second).

For situations such as evening concerts or nighttime harbor cruises, a strobe does the trick, but beware: Flash units are often used improperly. You can't take a view of the skyline with a flash. It may reach out as far as 30 feet, but that's it. On the other hand, a flash used too close to a subject may result in overexposure, resulting in a "blown out" effect. With most cameras, strobes will work with a maximum shutter speed of 1/125 or 1/250 of a second. If you set the exposure properly and shoot within range, you should come up with pretty sharp results.

CLOSE-UPS Whether of people or of objects such as Art Deco spires, close-ups can add another dimension to your photography. There are a number of shooting options, one of which is to use a 70mm or a 210mm lens at its closest focusable distance. Unless you're working in bright sunlight, a tripod will be worthwhile. If you are very near your subject and there is a good deal of reflective light, it may pay to underexpose a bit in relation to the meter reading.

If you do not have a telephoto lens, you can still shoot close-ups using a set of magnification filters. Filter packs of one-, two-, and three-time magnification are available, converting your lens into a close-up lens. Even better is a special macro lens designed for close-up photography. It's tough to get broad perspectives in Miami, where the highest elevations are bridges — not a hill in sight. But that doesn't stop anybody, as you'll notice by all the professional photographers toting heavy equipment around. Below, a few of Miami's most photogenic places.

A SHORT PHOTOGRAPHIC TOUR

THE BEACHES Best views of the beach are anywhere on Miami Beach, but standing slightly elevated on the boardwalk that runs between 21st and 46th streets affords a better perspective.

SOUTH BEACH Stroll along the ocean side of Ocean Drive rather than trying to snap pictures from a moving car in the Art Deco District. Colorful spots are at 13th Street, where you'll see the *Carlyle* hotel on the south corner with its buff and mauve exterior and green-trimmed "eyebrows" and the *Cardozo* on the north corner, bedecked in white and peach with brownstone pillars and "eyebrows." Though not open to the public, the exteriors are accessible and photogenic. Or at 8th Street, you can shoot the pink and turquoise *Adrian* and include the *Tudor* (down the street at Collins Ave.), with its rounded entry and neon-lighted finial. Approaching from the west by car, you may be able to capture the three signature tall hotels, with their unique towers, in one shot around 17th Street: from north to south, the *Ritz Plaza,* the *Delano,* and the *National.*

CRUISE SHIPS For a fantastic view of a half-dozen cruise ships with Miami skyscrapers in the background, drive across MacArthur Causeway (A1A) between Miami and Miami Beach and pull in at the sign for *Chalk's Flights.* There are parking spots, and it's much safer than parking along the narrow roadside. The largest number of ships are docked on Saturdays and Sundays. Catch them pulling out in the late afternoon, decks lined with smiling and waving passengers. Just remember not to shoot directly into the sun.

DOWNTOWN For terrific views of downtown Miami, including *Bayside,* visit the *Inter-Continental* hotel's fifth-floor pool area or jogging track (100 Chopin Plaza; phone: 305-577-1000 or 800-327-3005).

FT. LAUDERDALE The best view of Ft. Lauderdale is atop the *Pier 66* resort (2301 SE 17th St., Ft. Lauderdale; phone: 305-525-6666) in the *Pier Top Lounge.* The tower's top revolves once every 66 minutes, providing wonderful vistas of the ocean, Intracoastal Waterway, and canals.

Directions

Introduction

To most tourists, Miami means miles and miles of beach, splendid swaths of white sand that seem to go on from here to tomorrow. But for those who can pry themselves away from the beach, there's a whole other Miami just waiting to be discovered. This other Miami — small neighborhoods, historic churches and landmarks, and picturesque cafés and shops — is best explored on foot; other vistas cover a broader area and require a car.

Whether you're walking or driving, pay careful attention to names of streets; it makes a big difference whether the "20th" you're seeking is a street or an avenue, or you'll find yourself in the completely wrong spot. The first tour begins in South Beach, the Art Deco District at the southern tip of Miami Beach. From there we proceed west, back to the mainland, then to South Miami and over to Key Biscayne before heading to the Cubanized area of Calle Ocho. To its west is the lovely suburb of Coral Gables, and farther south lies Coconut Grove, Florida's oldest and most bohemian neighborhood. Just for fun, we've thrown in a Cowboy and Indian tour in Ft. Lauderdale before moving north to luxurious Palm Beach for a glimpse at the lifestyles of its rich and often famous — though sometimes notorious residents.

And for those who'd like to journey farther, there are visits to the secluded, but oh-so-beautiful, Florida Keys and to the almost otherworldly, farthermost reaches of the Everglades. As we said, Miami is much more than just another pretty beach.

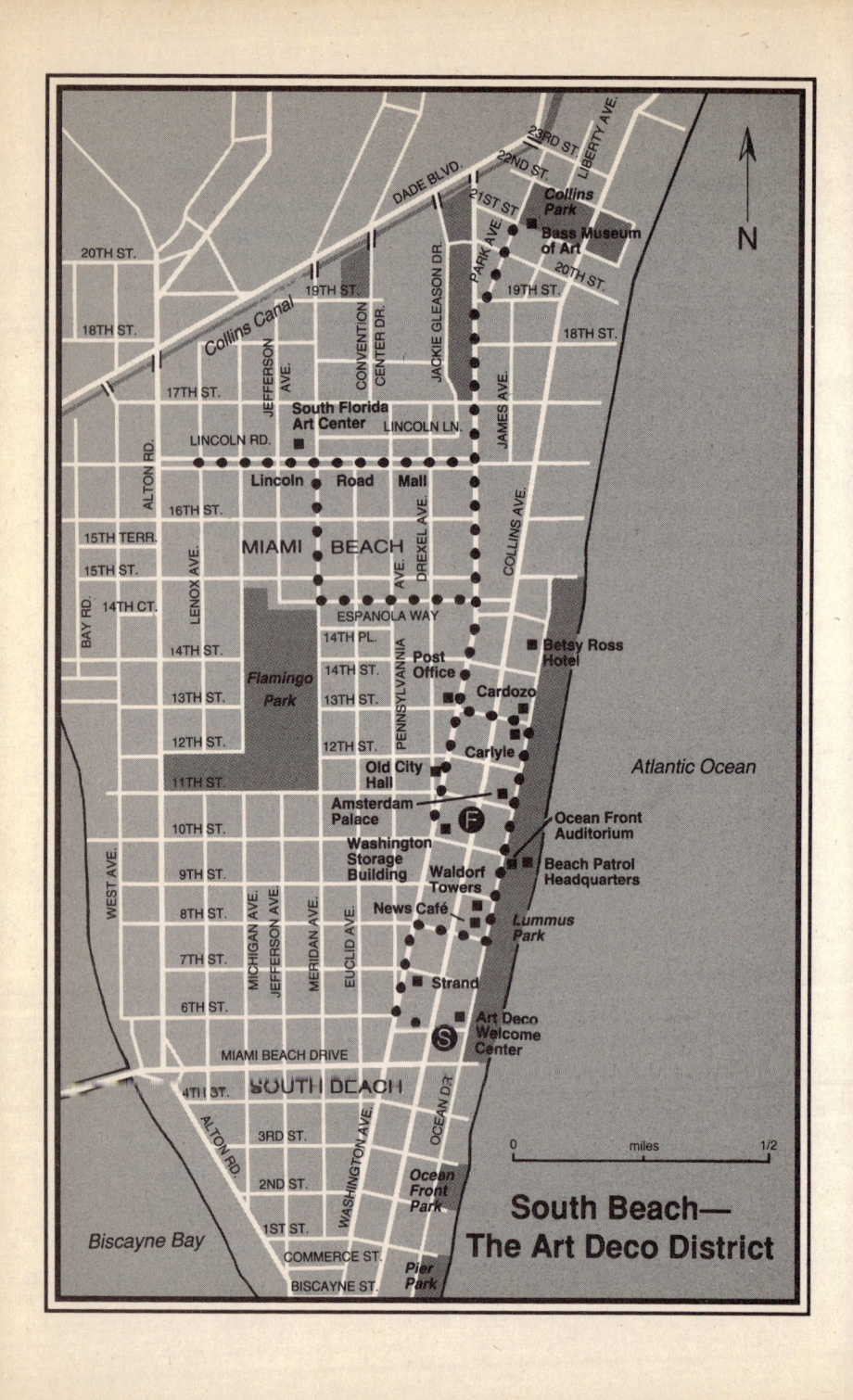

South Beach—The Art Deco District

Tour 1: South Beach – The Art Deco District

One of the oldest Miami Beach neighborhoods is again in the limelight. Miami Beach originally was developed as a coconut plantation, and although the enterprise failed, many beachfront coconut palms remain. In the 1920s, Carl Fisher began developing the beach as a vacation area for well-heeled sun worshipers. He dredged the mosquito-ridden mangrove swamps and built the first bridge to the mainland. (Above 15th Street, Fisher enforced the "Caucasian Clause," which prohibited blacks and Jews from buying property or staying in hotels. He made some notable exceptions, however, permitting Bernard Gimbel, the department store founder, to stay at his *Flamingo* hotel, and John Hertz, founder of the Yellow Cab Company, to buy land.)

Most of the construction in this area occurred just after World War I. But Miami's initial building boom went bust; the Hurricane of 1926 struck, destroying what had been built, and the Depression followed. Undaunted, Miami developers tried again in the late 1930s — and this time, for a while at least, succeeded. During this era, the first of two major periods of Art Deco construction and design was prevalent. Classical Art Deco, based on the French decorative movement, was characterized by elaborately designed fountains and rich surface ornamentation, but used tropical themes — palm trees, flowers, dolphins, flamingos — and soft pastels to adorn and reflect its resort setting. The second period, known as Art Moderne, followed, until World War II brought all frivolous construction to a halt. Influenced by industrial design, Art Moderne was characterized by minimal ornamentation, rounded corners, and cantilevered window shades called "eyebrows." Following the sleek designs of cars and planes from the Art Moderne period, the tropical element in Miami's version of the design movement evolved in the form of ocean liner motifs.

When Miami got back to building after the war, it was the softer, more decorative, classic themes that prevailed. Most buildings were originally painted white, with warm pink and yellow trim. Today, however, many have been daubed with ice-cream-soda colors of raspberry pink, banana yellow, and blueberry blue. Beth Dunlop, the architecture critic of the *Miami Herald*, claims the experiment began here in the 1980s, and the imaginative coloration then spread throughout South Florida.

The Art Deco District, referred to by locals as South Beach and increasingly as SoBe, is once again enjoying a rebirth. Thanks to the efforts of preservationists, spearheaded by the late Barbara Baer Capitman (who founded the Miami Design Preservation League), many buildings were saved from the wreckers' ball. The area was officially designated as the Art Deco District in 1979 and placed on the National Registry of Historic Places — it's the country's largest collection of Art Deco architecture in one area. About 650 important buildings are within a walkable square mile, bordered by the ocean on the east and Flamingo Park on the west, and running from 6th to 23rd Streets. The Art Deco District today, though, is more than a collection of historic buildings. The recently refurbished hotels have become fashionable; restaurants are receiving critical acclaim; and nightspots stay open until the wee hours. (On the down side for hotel guests who aren't night owls, the street noise often continues until about 4 AM.) Groups of high-fashion models and photographers fly in from New York, Paris, and Frankfurt to do shoots for magazines and clothing catalogues. There's an excitement here that sometimes leaves the resident senior citizens shaking their heads in wonder.

If you're driving in from the west, be sure to look up and see the three signature high-rise hotels around 17th Street and Collins Avenue: the *Ritz Plaza,* the *Delano,* and the *National.* Streetside parking may be a problem, with few metered spots; try the municipal parking garages on 13th Street between Ocean Drive and Collins Avenue or the one near *TOPA,* Lincoln Road Mall Parking. In addition, most major restaurants along Ocean Drive offer valet parking.

Start your tour at the *Art Deco Welcome Center* (1244 Ocean Dr.; phone: 305-672-2014); open daily from 11 AM to 6 PM. You can go at your leisure or join the 90-minute Saturday-morning walking tour (cost is $6 per person) or 2-hour Sunday morning bicycle tour ($5 per person; an additional $5 for bike rental) led by local historians (admission charge), with colorful anecdotes spicing up the history. You'll see the *Cardozo* hotel (where Frank Sinatra filmed the 1959 movie *Hole in the Head*) and Española Way (where — legend has it — Desi Arnaz made the rumba a dance craze). Pick up maps and books here, too, including the *Miami Beach Art Deco Guide* by Keith Root ($10), which has six self-guided tours and a glossary of architectural terms. Or proceed on your own, remembering to look up to spot the characteristic parapets and finials.

Remember that streets progress logically, with numbered streets running east-west; street addresses reflect the closest numbered cross street.

On Ocean Drive, the majority of hotels line the street facing palm-studded Lummus Park and the beach. Walk north on Ocean Drive's broad sidewalks, building after building, it's an Art Deco–phile's delight. Some structures have been turned into chic hotels and stylish eateries, others are home to senior citizens, and still others are undergoing renovation. There also are a few shops selling funky clothes and beach articles; please note that here and elsewhere in the Art Deco District, clothing shops may not open until late morning (11 AM), but remain open into the evening (until 9 or 10 PM). Plan to have breakfast or lunch at one of the popular outdoor places such as the *News Café* (800 Ocean Dr.) or *Larios on the Beach* (820 Ocean Dr.), the Cuban eatery owned by Gloria and Emilio Estefan.

At No. 860, the 1937 *Waldorf Towers* sports Art Deco "eyebrows" to shield it from the sun, and a unique rooftop tower. Notice the *Breakwater*'s vertical neon sign and racing stripes (No. 940). A pool links this hotel and the *Edison* (No. 960), which shows a Mediterranean Art Deco Revival influence.

If you've resisted strolling over to the beach until now, detour to the Beach Patrol Headquarters behind the auditorium at 10th Street. The building resembles a ship, typical of the Nautical Moderne style. Its seaside face, with porthole windows and metal ship railings, recalls the *Normandie*, the Art Deco *French Line* cruise ship. Inside, lectures and films are often presented; outside, roller bladers perfect their skills.

The *Amsterdam Palace* (1116 Ocean Dr.) has been generating much publicity since it was bought by Italian designer Gianni Versace, who is converting it into three single-family residences and perhaps a retail establishment for his haute and high-priced togs. It looks a bit out of place architecturally, with its arched entrance and windows, barrel-tile roof, and wrought-iron balconies. In fact, it was built in 1930 in a Mediterranean Revival style, modeled after the colonial Alcázar de Colón, home of Diego Columbus (Christopher's brother) in the Dominican Republic. Not open to the public, its exterior is still well worth noting.

At the corner of 13th Street stand two Art Deco landmarks: On the south side is the *Carlyle,* painted buff and mauve with green-trimmed eyebrows; on the north side is the white and peach *Cardozo,* with brownstone eyebrows and porch pillars, and a terrific-looking lobby.

Most of the 15 or so restaurants along this stretch are popular among locals who sit either at tables on the broad sidewalk or in the slightly more formal indoor dining rooms. Despite their pleasant ambience, the culinary creations are often pedestrian. For first-rate fare, try the highly acclaimed *A Mano* restaurant in the *Betsy Ross* hotel (1440 Ocean Dr.; phone: 305-531-6266), offering innovative dishes prepared with local and Caribbean ingredients — try the grouper brushed with rum and sweet red pepper purée and served with mango *mojo* (relish), or the outrageous venison with porcini. For more information see "Eating Out" in *Miami,* THE CITIES.

Turn west on 13th Street. At Collins Avenue, you'll see the Mediterranean Revival *Alamac,* with barrel-tile roof. At the northwest corner of 13th and Washington Avenue sits the still-functioning 1937 main post office, with a lantern finial crowning its dome. Climb the pink marble steps and enter through the brass doors for a peek into the impressive rotunda lobby. For an interesting detour, go 1 block south on Collins Avenue to 12th Street to see the *Marlin* hotel; its interior decor — considered by locals to be anything from weird to wonderful — is worth a look (see also

"Checking In" in *Miami,* THE CITIES). To return, go 1 block north to 13th Street and 1 block west to Washington.

Continue north on Washington, veering northeast on Park Avenue (it begins at 19th Street). At the corner of 21st and Park is the *Bass Museum of Art,* built in 1930 of Key stone (taken from the Florida Keys). Outside adornments include carved seagulls on the roof and bas-relief panels with nautical themes over doorways. Housed here are two enormous 17th century Flemish tapestries, along with works by Botticelli, Ghirlandajo, Rembrandt, and Rubens. The architectural and Oriental collections have recently been expanded. Open Tuesdays through Saturdays 10 AM to 5 PM and 1 to 5 PM Sundays; admission charge. Also at the corner of 21st and Park is the *Plymouth;* though it's now a run-down residential hotel, it's worth taking a look into the lobby to see the 1939 Rousseau-esque mural, depicting an idyllic tropical land with visions of skyscrapers rising in the background. Return to Washington Avenue.

Go south on Washington; between 17th and 16th Streets is *Lincoln Road Mall.* Built by Carl Fisher as an artery to the island's first commercial area, the road is still lined with many Art Deco buildings. In 1960, the city hired Morris Lapidus, the architect who designed the *Fontainebleau* hotel, to design new landscaping for the now pedestrians-only street. Today, many of the once fashionable stores along here are closed, but the west end is enjoying a retail revival. Walk west to the Miami Beach Community Church (500 Lincoln Rd.); built in 1921, it is the city's first church. Pass the headquarters for the *New World Symphony* (541 Lincoln Rd.) to Meridian Avenue (the 800 block). Between this block and Lenox Avenue, about 100 artists work in studios and galleries. The *South Florida Art Center* (810 Lincoln Rd.) owns three buildings housing a gallery and rotating exhibits, and leases space to artists. Also here are the home of the *Miami City Ballet* (909 Lincoln Rd.); a branch of *Books & Books* (933 Lincoln Rd.), selling (what else?) books and offering a film series; plus about ten restaurants, from fine Italian dining spots to casual cafés, including *Lazy Lizard* and *Key East.* Some cafés offer live music.

Turn south on Meridian Avenue; between 15th and 14th Streets is Española Way. Turn east and stroll to the block between Drexel and Washington Avenues, known as the Spanish Colony. This block has been refurbished, bringing to life the coral-painted Spanish Renaissance–style buildings with their iron balconies, red-tile roofs, and gaslight streetlamps. The alleged birthplace of the US rumba craze, today it's home to art galleries and vintage clothing and furniture stores. On the corner of Washington Avenue is the *Clay Hotel and International Youth Hostel* (1438 Washington Ave.; phone: 305-534-2988), where young travelers can often find lodging. At 1445 Washington Avenue, the 1938 *Cameo* theater hosts rap and reggae performers.

If you haven't sidetracked to the *Bass Museum* and Española Way — or even if you have — now continue south on Washington Avenue. On the west side (at No. 1130) sits the 9-story Old City Hall, dating from 1927. The Mediterranean-style building boasts barrel-tile roofs and Corinthian columns. Peek inside, where the Justice Center and University of Miami School of Continuing Education hold forth, to see the lobby's moldings and old brass fixtures.

On the east side, at the corner of 11th Street, is the *11th Street Diner* (1065 Washington Ave.; phone: 305-534-6373). Transplanted from Wilkes Barre, PA, the vintage steel diner (ca. 1948) serves such standard old-fashioned fare as meatloaf, along with more contemporary items, such as grilled dolphin and veggie melts.

At the corner of 10th Street stands the Washington Storage Building. Built in 1927 for summer storage serving winter visitors, it features ornate carved relief bands in the Spanish baroque style; it's now being restored by the Wolfson Foundation. Next year, the building will open as a museum and study center of the decorative and propaganda arts — intended to illustrate the destructive side of human nature — housing part of the Mitchell Wolfson, Jr., Collection of 50,000 objets d'art and rare books.

On the corner of 7th Street is a rounded building that originally was built for — and until recently housed — *Friedman's Bakery*. The 1934 building — which has appeared on the cover of *Progressive Architecture* — looks like a wedding cake, with stepped back "layers" and a parapet for the bride and groom. Painted white, with blue and green trim, it's now home to the *WPA* restaurant, a good stop for pizza, pasta, or burgers (phone: 305-534-1684).

Walk south on Washington past the *Strand* (No. 671), former home of the *Famous* restaurant, and featuring a ziggurat (jagged) parapet and pelican capitals.

Return to Ocean Drive and the Welcome Center, or hop in your car for yet another tour nearby.

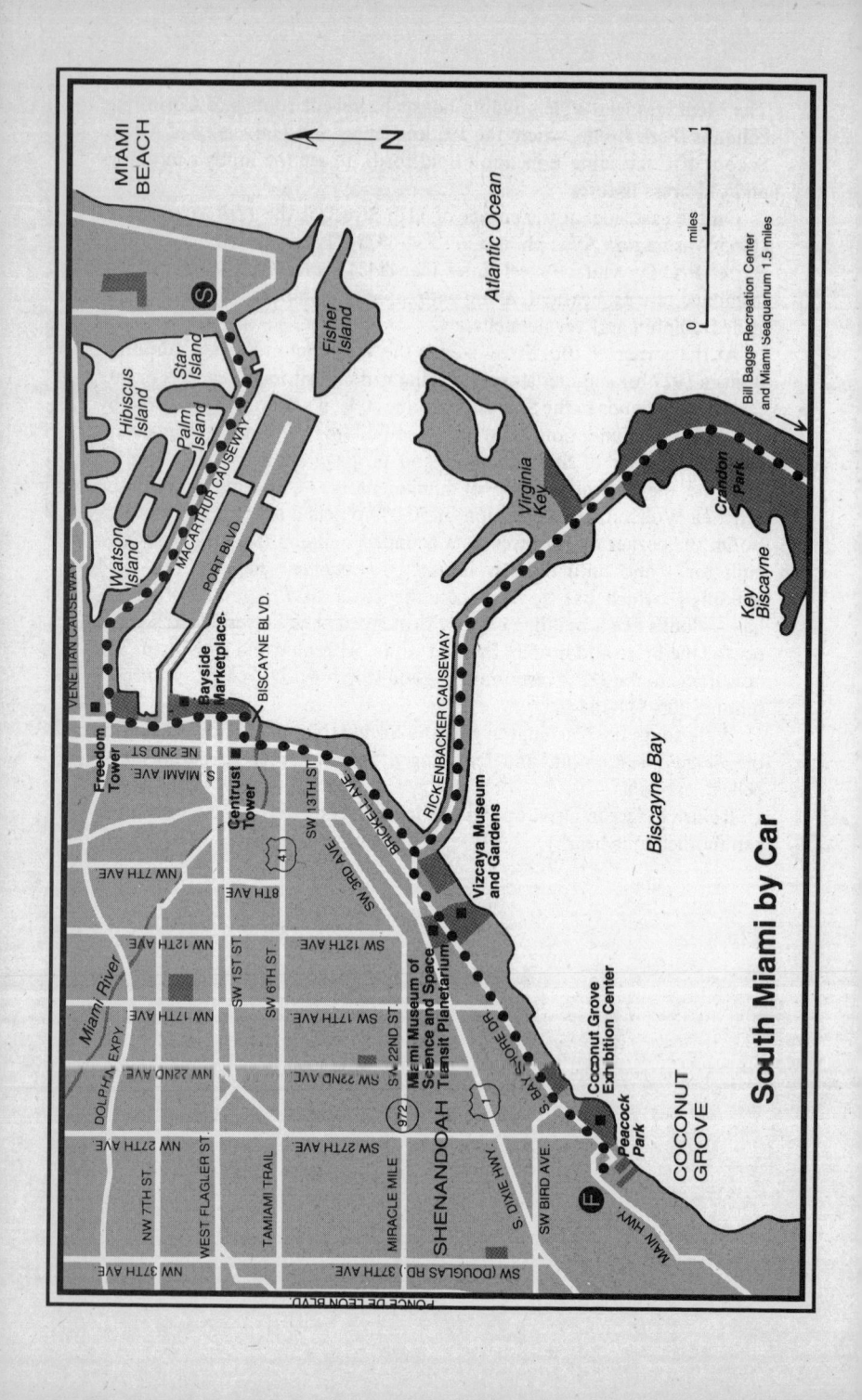

South Miami by Car

Tour 2: South Miami by Car

From Miami's South Beach, drive across MacArthur Causeway (Rte. 395). To the right, on the turquoise waters of Biscayne Bay, sit the private islands of Star, Hibiscus, and Palm, with their spectacular private homes and equally spectacular yachts. Most of us can't get past the guardhouses, but from Watson Island you can get a pretty good view. On the left, pass the ferry to the plush Fisher Island resort. Still on the left, note the string of cruise ships lined up at the Port of Miami, the world's busiest cruise port. Pull over at the sign to *Chalk's International Airlines* (a seaplane company), park the car, relax beneath the trees, and watch the huge cruise ships maneuver in and out of port. (For more information see "Special Places" in *Miami*, THE CITIES.)

Continue west to Route 1 (Biscayne Blvd.) and go south through downtown Miami. Notice the pink Freedom Tower (No. 600) on the right, a Spanish Renaissance–style building dating from 1925 and replicating Spain's Giralda Tower. Built for the *Miami News,* it received its nickname when it was used as the Cuban Refugee Emergency Center in 1962. Rescued from the wrecker's ball, it now houses offices.

On the left is the *Bayside Marketplace* (8396 NW S. River Dr.), where shoppers and diners can spend several hours. The Rouse-developed complex of 180 shops and eateries harbors many of the same shops as New York City's *South Street Seaport* or *Riverwalk* in New Orleans. But being able to sit and sup while watching a 1,035-foot ship trying to fit into a tight parking space is a distinctly Florida experience. And the food is definitely more Latin in flavor than in any other US place.

Continue south on Biscayne, and follow the signs to US 1 South. Note the downtown commercial area to the right, with additional skyscrapers constantly changing the skyline. Notice in particular I.M. Pei's International Tower, formerly Centrust Tower (100 SE 2nd Ave.), three graduated ellipses of glass that, when lit at night, look like a glowing waterfall. Pass the *Hyatt Regency* hotel (400 SE 2nd Ave.) on the right and immediately cross the Miami River — that is, unless the bridge is open, which can hopelessly back up traffic in this bustling business zone. Passing over the bridge, look to the right. Alongside the elevated track carrying *Metrorail* trains is *Miami Line,* a multicolored, neon, 300-foot, public sculpture by Rockne Krebs; it's particular striking at night.

On the other side, US 1 becomes Brickell Avenue. The area from SE 15th Street to SE 5th Street looks more like Wall Street with palm trees;

more than 2 dozen imaginatively designed buildings house several US and Latin American international bank headquarters. Unlike Wall Street, however, these sparkle with marble and mirror; some even have palm trees poking their tufted tops through the atria.

Continue south on Brickell past the pricey condominiums on the left, many boasting striking architecture. Villa Regina (1581 Brickell Ave.), an Isamu Noguchi–designed condominium building, has a rainbow-hued exterior decorated by Israeli artist Yaacov Agam. Another is the Atlantis (2025 S. Brickell Ave.), seen in opening shots of "Miami Vice," with its 5-story-high central courtyard housing a curved red staircase, full-size palm tree, and a hot tub. The Atlantis was designed by the progressive architecture firm, Arquitectonica.

If you're visiting sometime during mid-May through June, detour 1 block west of Brickell to South Miami Avenue, between SW 15th Road and SW 25th Road; the 4-lane, malled street is lined with huge royal poinciana trees, which, during that time, form a canopy of huge orange blossoms — an incredible sight. Not as splendid as before Hurricane Andrew (many trees have been uprooted or lopped off), but it's worth a visit. To check best and most specific blooming periods, call the Fairchild Tropical Garden (phone: 305-667-1651).

At the end of Brickell, there are two options: You can go left across the Rickenbacker Causeway to Key Biscayne (see below) to visit the *Miami Seaquarium,* or follow the signs to Bayshore Drive, past *Vizcaya Museum* (3251 S. Miami Ave.; phone: 305-579-2813) on the left. The opulent 1916 Italian Renaissance–style villa was the winter home of International Harvester Company's James Deering. Fronting on the bay, it rivals any mansion in Newport, Rhode Island (see "Special Places" in *Miami,* THE CITIES).

On the right is the *Museum of Science and Space Transit Planetarium* (3280 S. Miami Ave., Coconut Grove; phone: 305-854-4247). The science museum offers live demonstrations of scientific phenomena, 150 hands-on exhibits, and multimedia laser shows. For details, see "Special Places" in *Miami,* THE CITIES.

Continue south on Bayshore Drive past a high-rent condominium area. On the right, note *The Windward,* the large red sculpture by Alexander Leiberman, resting in front of the *Grand Bay* (at 27th Ave.), Florida's only Mobil 5-star hotel. On the left, with colorful nautical flags painted on its exterior, is the Coconut Grove Exhibition Center. Here sailboat masts seem to sprout like trees in a forest; the bay plays a major role in life hereabouts. Stop in at *Monty's* for a casual lunch on the deck, and stroll the dock at the marina to see the boats. Soon the road curves in front of Peacock Park (named for early settlers Charles and Isabella Peacock, who built the first hotel on South Florida's mainland), a small park with assorted ball courts. Continue to the next traffic light and make a hard left onto Main Highway, the heart of Coconut Grove.

FARTHER SOUTH: KEY BISCAYNE

From the southern end of Brickell Avenue, or from US Route 1 exiting at SE 26th Road, follow the signs eastbound to Rickenbacker Causeway to Key Biscayne (a key is a low island, or reef). Key Biscayne is a large island — once a coconut plantation — that's winter home to the rich and famous, and sometimes infamous (including actor Andy Garcia, businessman Charles "Bebe" Rebozo, and, once-President Richard Nixon); it's the site of the annual *Lipton Tennis Tournament* and two large public parks.

Cross the first bridge to a small island known as Windsurfer Beach. A good spot for windsurfing (what else?), aficionados bring their own gear or rent on the spot from *Sailboards Miami* (on Rickenbacker Cswy., just beyond the toll booths; phone: 305-361-SAIL or 305-361-3870). There are picnic facilities, public bathrooms, and parking; the beach isn't much by Miami standards, but, in addition to windsurfers, it also attracts fisherfolk, who cast their lines from the bridge.

Continue across William Powell Bridge to Virginia Key. On the right is the *Miami Seaquarium* (4400 Rickenbacker Cswy.; phone: 305-361-5705). Six daily shows feature Flipper (not the original trained dolphin of TV fame; he's long since gone to the aquarium in the sky) in the original lagoon set. For more information see "Special Places" in *Miami,* THE CITIES.

From here, drive over the next bridge onto Key Biscayne; you'll be on Crandon Boulevard. Pass the *Crandon Marina* (with charter boats available for half- or full-days). Plan on lunch or cocktails at *Sundays on the Bay,* a delightful spot with a dockside deck where diners can watch the boating scene while enjoying anything from a snack to first-rate continental fare (phone: 305-361-6777).

The road continues through a natural area of palmettos and sea grapes; this is Crandon Park (more about the park below). If you don't detour to the park, drive 1.5 miles from the *Seaquarium* to the *International Tennis Center* (phone: 305-361-8633) on the right. The Dade County facility offers 17 courts (6 night-lit) with an additional 7 clay courts expected to be completed this year. There's a pro shop with racquet rentals, and lessons with the pro ($40 per hour) or assistant ($30 per hour). Open daily 8 AM to 10 PM; court fees are $2 per person per hour, $3 at night.

This is the site of the annual *Lipton Tennis Tournament* (phone: 305-446-2200) in March, which draws almost 200,000 fans and top-ranked players from around the world.

Controversies have arisen over the 67,500-seat stadium at the *International Tennis Center*; much of the flack has come from the Matheson family heirs, whose antecedents donated the land to Crandon Park in 1940. They claim the intention was to leave the area in its natural state and have fought to reclaim it.

Pass through the center of Key Biscayne and turn right at the next traffic light onto Harbor Drive. Go 1.4 miles onto Mashta Island. (Developed by Dr. William J. Matheson in 1902, his daughter named the island "mashta," an Egyptian word meaning "home on the resting spot by the sea.") Circle around to the right to see the stunning residences, especially those on the northwest side; located right on Biscayne Bay, they enjoy a magnificent view of downtown Miami.

Go north on Crandon Boulevard. Before crossing the causeway from Key Biscayne to the mainland, on the right is the *Miami Marine Stadium* (3601 Rickenbacker Cswy.; phone: 305-361-6730 or 305-361-6732), a 6,500-seat roofed stadium hosting outdoor pop concerts, fireworks displays, and the annual 3-day *Budweiser Unlimited Hydroplane Regatta* in early June, purportedly the world's largest.

Also on the right are beaches; most have jet ski rentals, and all afford a fabulous view of downtown Miami's business skyline, South Miami's colorful condos, Dodge Island with its large ships and, if the night cooperates, a different view of that moon over Miami.

> **NOTE** The 900-acre Bill Baggs State Park (1200 Crandon Blvd.; phone: 305-361-5811) was one of the worst victims of Hurricane Andrew. Though it was closed as we went to press, it's worth checking for a progress report (see also "Special Places" in Miami, THE CITIES).

Tour 3: Coconut Grove

Park your car and continue on foot. Coconut Grove is Florida's answer to New York City's Greenwich Village, complete with shops selling high fashion and funky duds, elegant restaurants, and droves of casual eateries with tables spilling out onto the sidewalks. It's fun to stop at an outdoor café, nurse an ice cream cone or a beer, and watch the passing parade. Kids with punk hairdos flit by on skateboards, and seniors shop for antiques and paintings. Plenty of arty and intellectual types live in this area, along with descendants of early Bahamian settlers; at almost any time of the day or night, it's a great place to people watch, participate in an impromptu sing-along, or listen to the musicians who serenade on the street.

The *King Mango Strut Parade,* Coconut Grove's funky, not to mention funny, answer to the *Orange Bowl Parade*, takes place each December. A major tongue-in-cheek event, its marching groups may include strutters decked out as characters off the label of Fruit of the Loom underwear, transformed into bunches of grapes by purple and green balloons; there's always someone offering a spoof of the current president or mayor.

Art lovers come together in February, when the *Coconut Grove Arts Festival* draws hundreds of thousands to its juried outdoor exhibits. For more information, call the Chamber of Commerce (phone: 305-444-7270).

Stroll along Main and up and down the short side streets, peeking into boutiques and galleries. Sidewalk cafés offering light meals and snacks line every sidewalk. For more serious food, *Kaleidoscope* offers fine dining in a romantic enclosed garden, a balcony, or in air conditioned indoor dining rooms (see "Eating Out" in *Miami,* THE CITIES). Favorite dishes include grilled swordfish and roasted red snapper with honey-mustard glazed bananas.

On nearby Grand Avenue, *CocoWalk* is an upscale shopping center vying for visitors' bucks, with lots of trendy boutiques and eateries such as *Café Tu Tu Tango* and *Big City Fish* (see "Eating Out" in *Miami,* THE CITIES); unfortunately, the formerly upscale *Mayfair Mall* has lost numerous tenants, including its *Burdine*'s anchor store. Residents are hopeful of a turnaround.

On the west side of Main is the 1927 *Coconut Grove Playhouse* (3500 Main Hwy.; phone: 305-442-4000), which presented the American premiere of *Waiting for Godot,* only one of its triumphs. The theater often plays host to pre-Broadway try-outs and performs two cabaret shows each season. Recent offerings include *Fame: The Musical, Run for Your Wife,* and *Don't Dress for Dinner.* The playhouse also has a children's theater and an acting school.

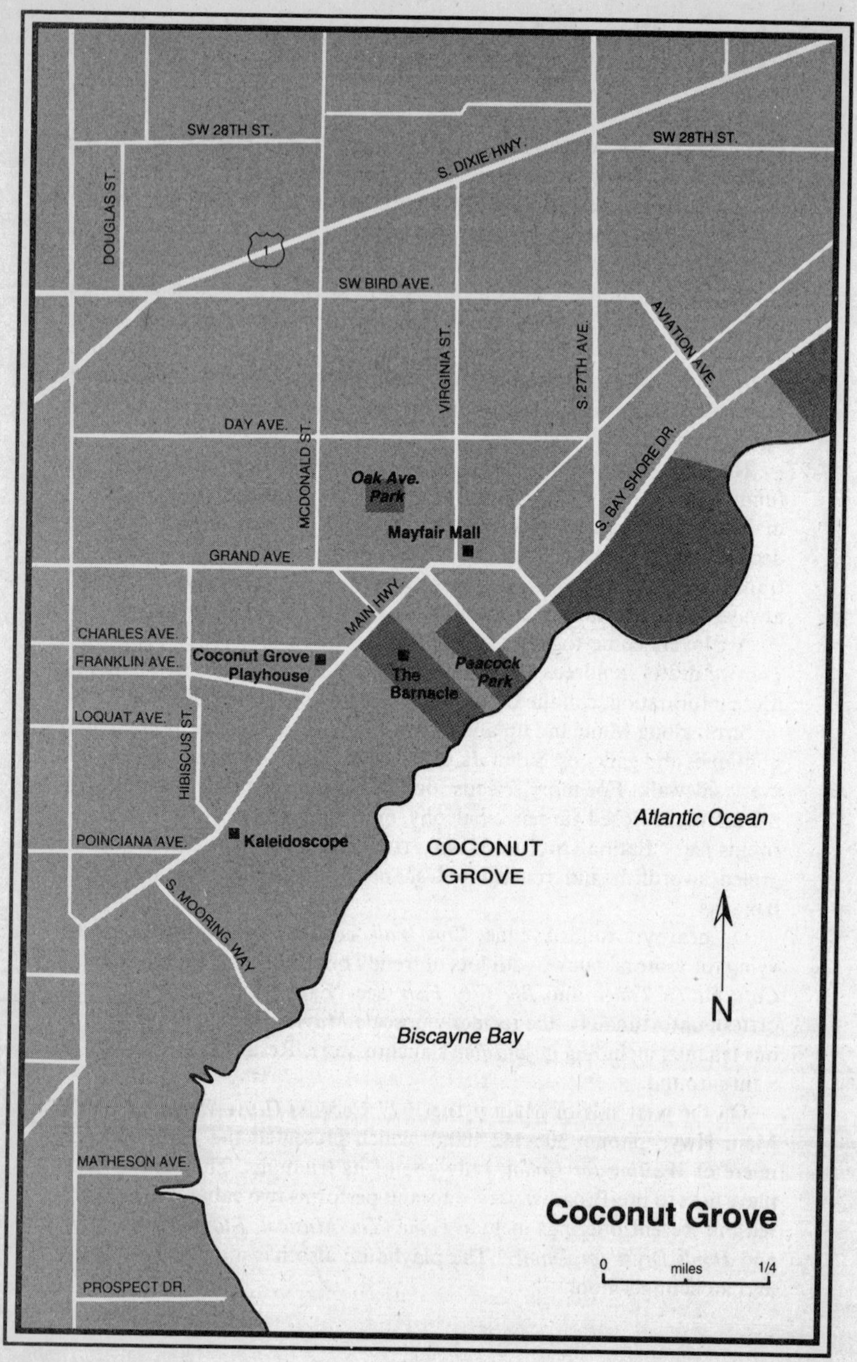
SW 28TH ST.
SW 28TH ST.
S. DIXIE HWY.
1
DOUGLAS ST.
SW BIRD AVE.
AVIATION AVE.
VIRGINIA ST.
S. 27TH AVE.
DAY AVE.
MCDONALD ST.
S. BAY SHORE DR.
Oak Ave. Park
Mayfair Mall
GRAND AVE.
MAIN HWY.
CHARLES AVE.
FRANKLIN AVE.
Coconut Grove Playhouse
The Barnacle
Peacock Park
LOQUAT AVE.
HIBISCUS ST.
Atlantic Ocean
POINCIANA AVE.
Kaleidoscope
COCONUT GROVE
S. MOORING WAY
N
Biscayne Bay
MATHESON AVE.
Coconut Grove
0 miles 1/4
PROSPECT DR.

On Charles Avenue are the original wood-frame houses built by the black Bahamians who emigrated here to work in the nearby coconut groves late in the last century; homes in the area, comprising Miami's first black settlement, date from 1889.

From Coconut Grove follow the next route in nearby Coral Gables, or head back to the beach and save it for another day.

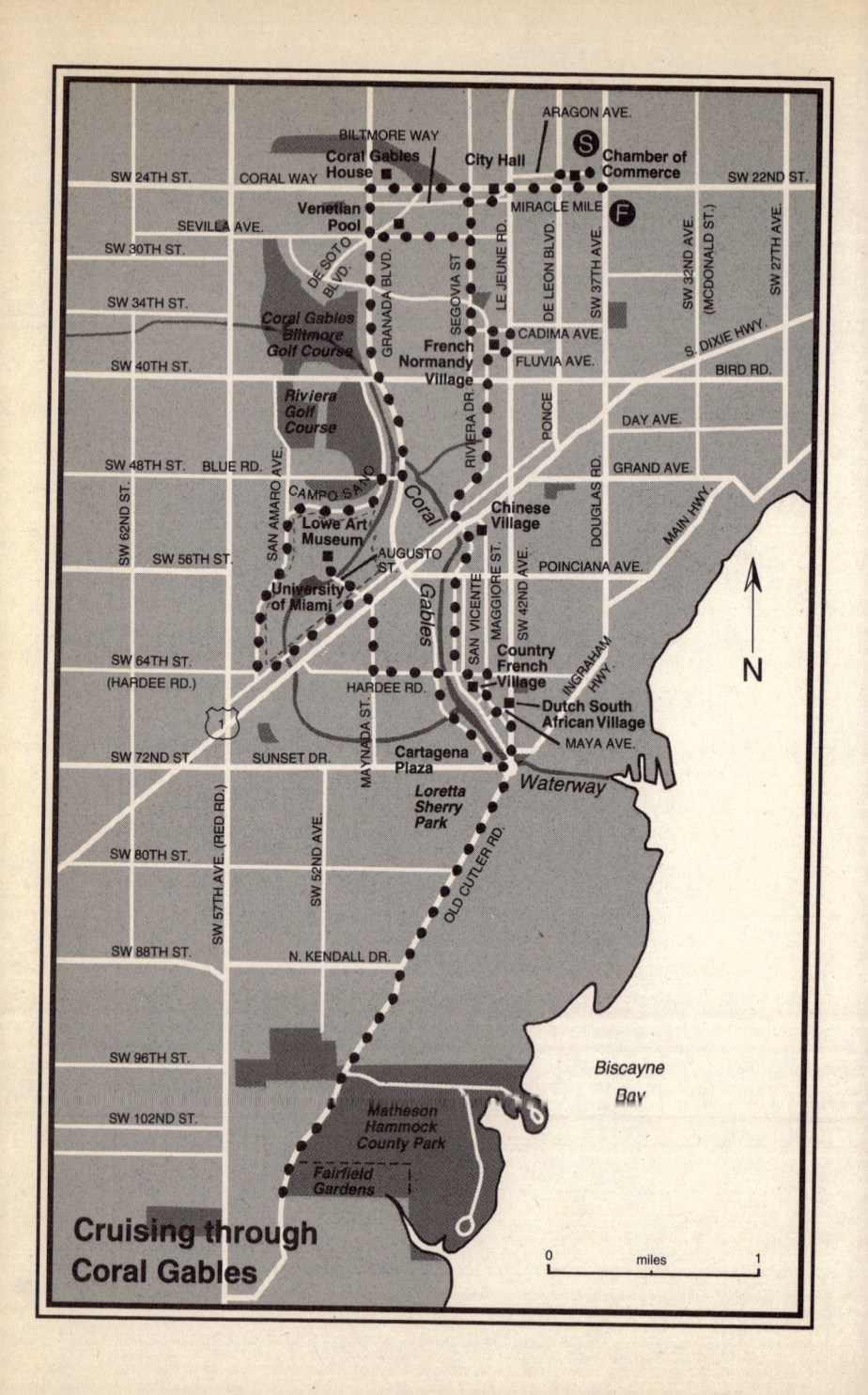

Cruising through Coral Gables

Tour 4: Cruising through Coral Gables

George Merrick developed this prime residential area in the 1920s, as part of his innovative concept of a perfectly designed city, patterning it on ancient communities with curving boulevards (which also make it very easy to get lost), and four grand entrances to the city built with Spanish-style spiral pillars. Merrick built more than 600 homes, and donated land for the city's first church, library, and what would become the University of Miami. Unfortunately, inflated land values wreaked havoc financially; the Hurricane of 1926 did the rest.

Today, however, the 12-square-mile city remains an area of great beauty, with lovely homes set among spacious gardens. Canals leading to Biscayne Bay run alongside it, and docked boats bob in the water. Many of the original buildings remain, and ongoing restoration projects are returning many buildings to their former grandeur. Coral Gables also is home to a number of multinational business offices, as well as numerous sophisticated restaurants.

Start the drive at the Chamber of Commerce building (50 Aragon Ave.; phone: 305-446-1657), where you can pick up maps and brochures. Go west on Aragon for 3 blocks to Le Jeune Road, then south on Le Jeune 1 block to the Miracle Mile (Coral Way). Make a half-right turn onto Biltmore Way. (Don't look for street signs at eye level or above in most of the Gables; look down — they're discreetly placed in whitewashed cornerstones on the ground.) Stop at the 1928 City Hall (405 Biltmore Way; phone: 305-446-6800), built of Key stone (oolitic limestone from the Florida Keys), with its curved, colonnaded façade. Peek inside to see some of the original fixtures, furnishings, and paintings.

Go west 2 blocks on Biltmore Way to Segovia Street and turn left. Then drive 3 blocks to Sevilla Avenue and turn right; proceed 4 blocks to De Soto Boulevard. At No. 2701, stop at the Venetian Pool, the only swimming pool listed in the National Registry of Historic Places. Restored to its former splendor, it was originally a limestone quarry; the 800,000-gallon pool is fed by underground artesian wells. The setting also boasts coral caves, a palm-fringed island, bridges, fountains, and painted gondola poles. Movie stars such as Esther Williams, queen of water ballet, and Johnny "Tarzan" Weismuller once backstroked here, and Paul Whiteman's orchestra provided background for dancers. A photo exhibit chronicles beauty pageants and celebrities' visits. Visitors may swim here (amenities include swimming, scuba, and snorkeling lessons, lockers, and a café), but the pool is extremely crowded during the summer, when kids from local camps come here to splash around. Open Tuesdays through Sundays year-round. Admission charge.

Circle back via Sevilla to Segovia Street; turn right and continue south 8 blocks to University Drive and turn left; immediately bear right into Cadima Avenue; notice the deep setbacks and unobtrusive low metal street lamps throughout the area. Unfortunately, some of the lovely large banyan and Indian fig trees suffered hurricane damage. Proceed 3 blocks and turn right onto Le Jeune. In this area, developer George Merrick created a residential district featuring "villages," each with a distinct architectural style. On the right, on Viscaya Court, are some of the occupied remains of his experiment. Here is the French Normandy Village, in a French architectural style, with white stucco houses, wooden beams, and shuttered windows. Circle back to Le Jeune, go 1 block south to Fluvia Avenue and turn right; proceed 1 block to Riviera Drive and turn left. Follow Riviera for 15 blocks, and cross US 1 (South Dixie Hwy.) to Menendez Avenue, the next street on the left. Here is the Chinese Village, the most bizarre of Merrick's communities, with blue-and-yellow-tile upturned roofs and doorways painted red and yellow. Circle around the village and return to Riviera Drive. Go south .65 miles to Hardee Road, then turn left. Go 1 block to San Vicente Street, where there are examples of the Country French Village on the left, sporting red tile roofs and stucco façades with wooden beams. Continue 1 block to Maggiore Street and turn right, then go 2 blocks to San Vicente and turn left. At the third corner on the left, at Maya Avenue, stands the Dutch South African Village, with homes of white stucco and curlicued gables.

Circle around, returning to Le Jeune, and turn right. Go 2 blocks, passing over the canal. Stop at the tiny Loretta Sherry Park on the right. Here are some lovely, large homes (and equally lavish yachts), typical of the upscale residential area. Continue around the circle (Cartagena Plaza) to Old Cutler Road. Go south 2 miles. On the left is the entrance to the Matheson Hammock County Park. Walk along its winding trails through native forest to a manmade lagoon overlooking Biscayne Bay, where you can take a dip. Although the buildings were destroyed by Hurricane Andrew, the park has reopened. Facilities include a beach, picnic area, snack bar, and showers. Open sunup to sundown; parking charge (phone: 305-666-6979).

About a half-mile farther south on Old Cutler Road, on the left side, is Fairchild Tropical Garden, where something's always in bloom, such as red-edged impala lilies or red silk cotton trees. The 83-acre grounds, supposedly the largest tropical botanical garden in the continental US, afford visitors hours of beauty and tranquillity. Along with one of the world's largest collections of palms, there's also a rain forest and a rare plant house. Stroll leisurely around the 11 lakes, with benches for contemplation thoughtfully provided. Guided walking and tram tours are available at no charge. Other features include a snack bar open on weekends, and a bookstore focusing on horticulture. Open daily; closed *Christmas*. Shirts and shoes must be worn; admission charge (phone: 305-667-1651).

Return 2.2 miles on Old Cutler Road to Cartagena Plaza. Circle it to the first right, which is Sunset Drive, and take the first right after that, on to Granada Boulevard. Follow it for .7 miles to Hardee. Go .3 miles west on Hardee, passing a section between Cellini and Leonardo Streets where a new French-looking community mimics Merrick's older experiment. Proceed to Maynada Street and turn right. Continue for .35 miles to Augusto Street. Follow Augusto across US 1 and Ponce de León Boulevard, known locally as just Ponce. On the right is the *Lowe Art Museum*, on the University of Miami campus (1301 Stanford Dr.; phone: 305-284-3535), displaying a permanent Renaissance art collection and changing displays. (Open Tuesdays through Saturdays, and Sunday afternoons; closed major holidays; no admission charge.)

Leaving the museum, you'll still be on the campus of the University of Miami, a major university with a large undergraduate enrollment and graduate schools in law, the Rosenstiel School of Marine and Atmospheric Science, and the highly regarded University of Miami/Jackson Memorial Medical Center — not to mention the famed *Hurricanes* football team. Return to Ponce, turn right, and proceed to the third traffic light, San Amaro Avenue. Turn right, keeping your eyes peeled for one of those famous *Hurricanes,* and go .9 miles to Campo Sano. Turn right and proceed east for .5 miles to University Drive. Go north (left) and, at the next corner, turn right on Blue Road. Cross the canal; the first light is Granada Boulevard. Turn left and continue north for 1.5 miles to Coral Way.

Turn right on Coral Way. In the first block, on your left, is the Coral Gables House (No. 907), built in 1907 as the Merrick family home. Built of oolitic limestone, the interior still boasts many of its original furnishings from the 1920s. Other pieces reflect the varied history of the city. Open Sundays and Wednesdays, or by appointment. Admission charge (phone: 305-460-5360).

Continue east on Coral Way; turn right at Segovia (the next traffic light). The next corner on the left is Biltmore Way. Take it back into Coral Way. The area between Le Jeune Road and Douglas Road is known as the Miracle Mile, although parts of it are somewhat less than a miracle today; nevertheless, it's an attractive pedestrian thoroughfare with 160 shops and eateries. Some upscale specialty shops are already in place and plans are afoot to lure additional European retailers.

While in the shopping mode, pop into *Books & Books* around the corner at 296 Aragon Avenue (phone: 305-442-4408). Owner Mitch Kaplan regularly schedules readings and lectures by such well-known writers as Susan Sontag (the late Isaac Bashevis Singer was also a speaker here), plus photographic art exhibits. Open daily.

Coral Gables boasts several fine restaurants. The two listed below serve both lunch and dinner. *St. Michel* (162 Alcazar Ave.; phone: 305-446-6572) is a bistro in a charming 1926 bed and breakfast establishment. *Yuca* (177 Giralda Ave., Coral Gables; phone: 305-444-4448), is another fine neighborhood eatery. For more about both restaurants see "Eating Out" in *Miami*, THE CITIES.

Tour 5: Little Havana

From downtown Miami, drive south on Biscayne Boulevard, following signs around to Brickell Avenue (Rte. 1). Cross the Miami River and continue to SE 7th Street. Turn right and proceed to SW 13th Avenue and park. Walk 1 block south to the corner of SW 8th Street (Calle Ocho, the heart of Little Havana) and SW 13th Avenue, where you'll find the Brigade 2506 Memorial. This monument to those who died in the unsuccessful 1961 Bay of Pigs invasion of Cuba symbolizes the political outlook of many who settled here in the 1950s. (For a thorough background, read Joan Didion's *Miami*.)

Earlier called Shenandoah, this neighborhood was mainly a middle class Jewish community until the 1950s, although a large Hispanic group had settled here before the refugees from Castro's reign arrived. Many of the Jewish shops gradually became Hispanic, although some of the older signs still are visible; a grocery selling pork is the former site of a kosher butcher. Today, many of the original middle class Cuban residents have moved on to more affluent neighborhoods, and other Hispanic groups have settled here. Now more Nicaraguans live here than Cubans, and the area long known as Little Havana increasingly is called the Latin Quarter.

From the monument, walk west along Calle Ocho. Here is *Los Pinareños,* an open-air market (1334 SW 8th St.) selling sugarcane stalks, *plátanos* (bananas, in this case the kind cooked as a vegetable), and green coconuts. As you stroll, look down and notice the red-brick sidewalk, dubbed the Hispanic Walkway of Stars. Squares are dedicated to various Hispanic stars, such as Gloria Estefan, María Conchita Alonso, and Julio Iglesias.

At the corner of SW 14th Avenue, note the *McDonald's* restaurant. Because new buildings must adhere to the Spanish architectural style, this one has a red-tile roof and blue tiles on its stuccoed exterior. It may be the only *McDonald's* that serves *café con leche.*

At the corner of SW 15th Avenue, in Máximo Gomez Park, elderly men in *guayaberas* sit at outdoor tables under roofed areas playing dominoes and chess. Hispanic music fills the air. Although this is a city park, visitors can enter only with a membership card and they must be males above age 55.

For an inexpensive lunch, pop into *El Pub* (SW 16th Ave.). Pick up a shot glass of coffee at the window or be seated at an inside table. Try a Cuban sandwich consisting of ham, cheese, pickles, and mustard on Cuban bread. Or a cup of *café con leche,* so strong that the spoon you mix it with may come out bent. (Stand in the same line for coffee and lottery tickets.)

SW 17th Avenue is the boundary of Little Havana (after this, it be-

Little Havana

- El Credito
- Botanica la Abuela
- Brigade 2506 Memorial
- Los Pinareños
- McDonald's
- El Pub
- Maximo Gomez Park
- Cuban Museum of Art and Culture

SW 11TH AVE
SW 12TH AVE
SW 12TH CT
SW 13TH CT
CUBAN MEMORIAL BLVD
SW 12TH ST
SW 14TH AVE
SW 15TH AVE
SW 16TH AVE
SW 17TH AVE
SW 8TH ST / CALLE OCHO
SW 9TH ST
SW 10TH ST
SW 11TH ST
SW 11TH TERR

LITTLE HAVANA

N ←

0 1/8 miles

comes Little Managua); cross the street and retrace the route on the opposite side. The *Dunkin Donuts* at 16th was the first in the country to serve *café con leche;* it also bakes guava doughnuts. *La Casa de Los Trucos* (House of Tricks), between 13th and 14th, does big business in satin and sequined costumes — especially at *Halloween.*

Stop in at *Botánica la Abuela* (roughly translated, it means Grandma's Botany; it's at No. 1122). There are a few *piñatas* and dolls here, but the stock of candles, roots, and oils used for *santería* (religious) purposes is even more fascinating — it's a creed combining voodoo and Catholicism. An Amazonian Indian is on hand, with feathers and other paraphernalia piercing his ears and nose.

At 11th Avenue, stop at *El Crédito* and watch cigars being made at Miami's largest hand-rolled cigar factory (1106 SW 8th St.; phone: 305-858-4162). The business began in Havana in 1907, and opened here in 1969. Today, the tobacco is imported mainly from the Dominican Republic and Mexico. Closed Sundays.

Return to your car and drive to SW 13th Street (Ronald Reagan Ave.) on 12th Avenue to visit the *Cuban Museum of Arts and Culture.* Originally designed to showcase Cuban heritage, it now focuses on the entire Hispanic community, with 200 paintings and drawings in its permanent collection. Open Wednesday through Sunday afternoons. No admission charge (1300 SW 12th Ave.; phone: 305-858-8006).

Take SW 12th Avenue north to SW 7th Street. Turn left and proceed to SW 19th Avenue, then left to SW 8th Street and turn left. On your right is a wonderland of *piñatas* at *La Casa de Las Piñatas* (1756 SW 8th St., 2nd floor; phone: 305-649-4711). The standard Mexican paper donkeys are available, but hanging throughout are fantastic creations such as a Ninja Turtle *piñata* holding five of the creatures, or a tableau of a beauty pageant, complete with beauty queen, emcee, and television cameraman. These decorations are swung in the air and then hit with long sticks so the candy inside spills out — a tradition at children's parties, especially at *Quinces,* the often lavish parties thrown for 15-year-old girls (akin to a "Sweet 16" party). *Piñata* prices range from $25 to $500. The store is busiest in summer and is closed for *Christmas.*

Try a typical Cuban meal — spiced pork, paella, or *arroz con pollo,* and flan for dessert — plus nightly flamenco shows at *Málaga* (740 SW 8th St.; phone: 305-858-4224) or *Versailles,* open daily till the wee hours (3555 SW 8th St.; phone: 305-445-7614). Flamenco shows also take place at *Centro Vasco,* which serves Spanish-Basque dishes (2235 SW 8th St.; phone: 305-643-9606). Hispanic families like the more sophisticated cuisine at *Casa Juancho* (see "Eating Out" in *Miami,* THE CITIES).

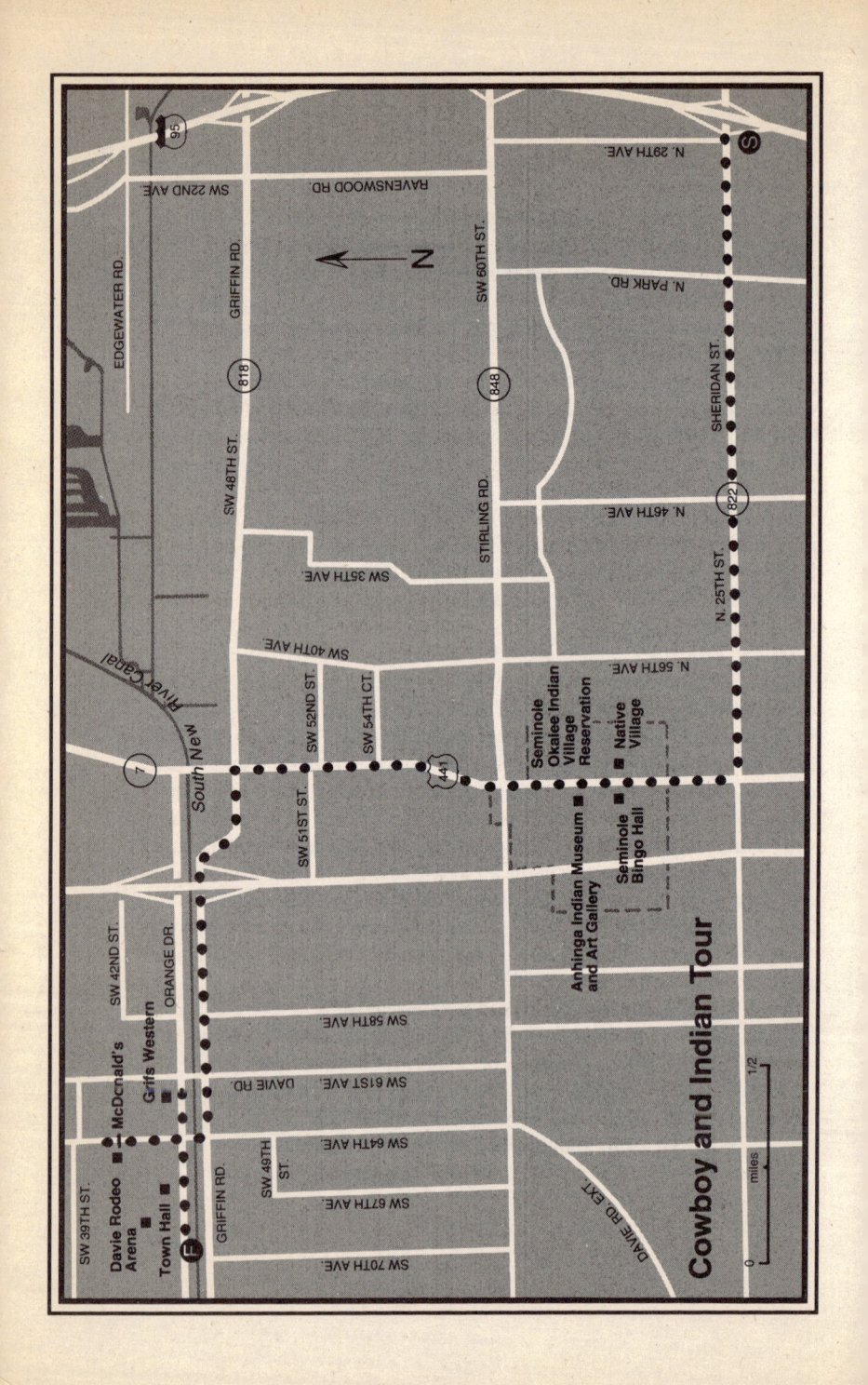

Cowboy and Indian Tour

Tour 6: Cowboy and Indian Tour

For a change from the sun and surf of South Florida, head west to the land of cowboys and Indians — just south of Ft. Lauderdale. Here the Seminole Tribe of Hollywood (Florida) have a reservation. The tribe is a fairly recent arrival historically, having relocated here in the early part of the 18th century. An amalgamation of the Creek, Oconee, and other tribes, the confederation took the word "is-te-seminole," meaning separatists, to differentiate themselves from other Florida Indians who had become tolerant of white settlers. Today, they too have intermarried with other area residents.

Many residents have developed industries appealing to tourists. Some seem tacky, but despite the kitsch, they offer insights into earlier lifestyles. The year's major event is the *Seminole Indian Tribal Fair* (held in mid-February), featuring Native American food, art, and tribal dancing from all over North America; there's also a rodeo. For information, call 305-584-0400.

From US 1 or I-95, drive west on Sheridan Street (State Rd. 822) in Hollywood to US 441 (also called State Rd. 7) and turn north. After about 10 blocks, be on the lookout for the *Native Village* (3551 N. State Rd. 7; phone: 305-961-4519), a commercial enterprise on the right; it's run by Bobbie Billie, the chief's wife. After passing through the gift shop, wander through a jungle-like setting of small lakes, waterfalls, and dripping foliage. Tropical birds call out, a roar blasts from three caged Florida panthers — a protected, endangered species — and in the snake pit, a trainer approaches a rattlesnake — very carefully. The man describes the various venomous snakes slithering about, and then provokes a non-venomous type into biting him. But the most excitement is generated at the alligator wrestling exhibit. The trainer enters the pit, describing the native animal's characteristics, and then pries his mouth open to reveal 80 large teeth. The trainer's hand darts in and out of the huge mouth and the animal snaps his jaws shut — usually *after* the trainer's hand has been withdrawn. Open daily; admission charge.

On the west side of the street is the *Seminole Bingo Hall*. Although high-stakes bingo is illegal elsewhere in Florida, it's permitted here because the land is a federally protected Indian reservation. The enclosed hall, seating 1,400, attracts players hopeful of winning $100,000 jackpots. Open daily; admission charge. (4150 N. State Rd. 7; phone: 305-961-3220).

A few blocks north is a complex of *chickee* huts, including an open-air haircutting salon. Stop in at the *Anhinga Indian Museum and Art Gallery*

(5791 S. State Rd. 7; phone: 305-581-0416) for nicely crafted pottery, colorful appliquéd Indian skirts and jackets, and beaded jewelry. Open daily.

Continue north to Griffin Road and turn west. Drive along the South New River Canal to Davie Road (SW 64th Ave.) and you're in cowboy territory. When the area was developed in the early part of the 20th century, it was dotted with orange plantations, sugarcane fields, and dairies where cattle were raised. The cattle herders evolved into cowboys, and others who love horsing around followed suit.

Today, visitors can still spot many equestrians, usually clad in cowboy-cut jeans and Stetson hats, riding their steeds through the streets. Shops advertise boot and saddle repairs, and shopping centers are designed to look like porches at a ranch. *Boot Barn* (7138 Stirling Rd.; phone: 305-435-BOOT) carries such brands as Tony Lama, with handmade boots made of snake, alligator, lizard, buffalo, elk, and elephant (closed Sundays). Ranches abound where horses are boarded, and riders can rent mounts by the hour or by the day. The region's heritage leaps to life during the annual *Orange Blossom Festival* held in late March, a week-long celebration featuring rodeos, food, and music.

Turn right on Davie, cross over the canal, and immediately turn right on Orange Drive. Stop at *Grifs Western* (6211 SW 45th St.; phone: 305-587-9000), a 20,000-square-foot emporium featuring saddles, hats, western shirts, and seemingly miles of boots, priced from $80 to $600. There are hitching posts out front for those arriving on horseback. Open daily.

Return to Davie and turn right. On the left, at SW 41st Street, stands a ranch-style *McDonald's*. Out back, riders park their horses at hitching posts in the Golden Arches' corral, where the nags slurp from water troughs while their riders put on the feed bag inside.

Retrace the path on Davie to Orange Drive and turn right. On the right is the Town Hall, a western-style complex of rough-hewn cedar. (The fire and police stations down the road bear similar façades.) In back of Town Hall is the covered *Davie Rodeo Arena,* where 5,000 folks can watch cowboys compete in bareback riding, calf roping, steer wrestling, tie-down roping, bull riding, and girls' barrel racing every Wednesday night at 8 PM and occasionally at other times. For information, contact *Davie for Horses* (phone: 305-797-1145). The *Five Star Pro Rodeo* monthly series features professional rodeo cowboys from around the country, and points for the events go toward the *National Finals Rodeo* in Las Vegas. The *Florida State Championship Rodeo* takes place here each December. (4201 SW 65th Way; phone: 305-437-8800).

If you can't wait to get in the saddle yourself, mosey up to one of the area stables. You can rent horses at the *Bar-B Ranch* (4601 SW 128th Ave., Davie; phone: 305-434-6175; open daily) or join a supervised ride at the *Stride-Rite Training Center* (5550 SW 73rd Ave., Davie; phone: 305-587-

2285); open daily. For more information, see "Horseback Riding" in *Ft. Lauderdale*, THE CITIES.

Those in the area at dinnertime who wish to sample authentic Southwestern food (not the standard Tex-Mex, fast-food variety) should stop in at the *Armadillo Café* (4630 SW 64th Ave., Davie; phone: 305-791-4866). The chefs have created culinary drama using Southwestern influences. Try the smoked duck with orange juice and wildflower honey sauce. Open for dinner Tuesdays through Sundays. For more details, see "Eating Out" in *Ft. Lauderdale,* THE CITIES.

For an experience unique to South Florida, a quick and easy visit to the Everglades awaits. Continue west on Griffin Road about 25 miles to US 27 (it's 18 miles west of I-95, a half-hour drive from 441) and the Everglades Holiday Park. A narrated airboat ride skims guests over the sawgrass through the park that conservationist Marjorie Stoneman Douglas termed a "River of Grass." Visitors will probably spot snoozing live alligators (sometimes a nest of babies), and flocks of 2-legged tropical denizens such as red-legged gallinules. There's an alligator wrestling show and wildlife exhibit, plus Seminole crafts sold in a straw hut. Learn about Native American food and clothing, as well as the Indian uprisings. The park is open for wandering, fishing, and 1-hour airboat tours. Admission charge for tours (21940 Griffin Rd.; phone: 305-434-8111). Another option is the Sawgrass Recreation Area, where fishing boats can be rented for $35 for 4 hours; 1½-hour guided airboat tours cost $13.50 for adults, $7.75 for children under 12, including a stop at an Indian village. Nature walks are available and there's a store. Open daily (5400 US Rte. 27; phone: 305-389-0202). For more information see *Tour 9: Everglades National Park,* below.

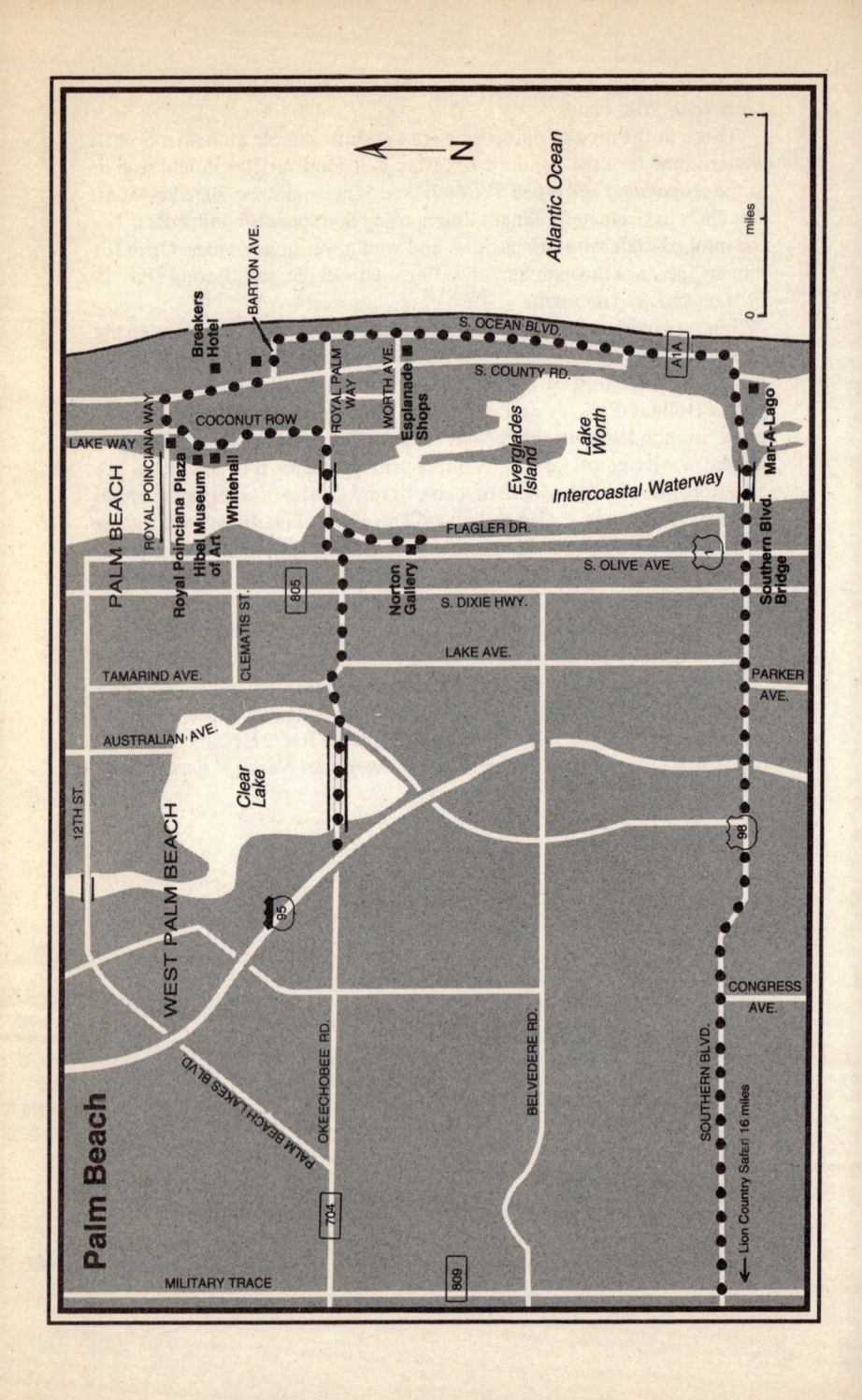

Palm Beach

N ←

0 1 miles

- Atlantic Ocean
- Breakers Hotel
- Barton Ave.
- S. Ocean Blvd.
- S. County Rd.
- A1A
- Royal Palm Way
- Worth Ave.
- Esplanade Shops
- Coconut Row
- Lake Way
- Royal Poinciana Way
- Royal Poinciana Plaza
- Hibel Museum of Art
- Whitehall
- Palm Beach
- Everglades Island
- Lake Worth
- Intercoastal Waterway
- Mar-A-Lago
- Flagler Dr.
- S. Olive Ave.
- Southern Blvd. Bridge
- Clematis St.
- 805
- Norton Gallery
- S. Dixie Hwy.
- Tamarind Ave.
- Lake Ave.
- Parker Ave.
- Australian Ave.
- Clear Lake
- 12th St.
- West Palm Beach
- 95
- 98
- Congress Ave.
- Okeechobee Rd.
- Palm Beach Lakes Blvd.
- 704
- Belvedere Rd.
- 809
- Military Trace
- Southern Blvd.
- ← Lion Country Safari 16 miles

Tour 7: Palm Beach

Another day might be spent viewing the area where the rich, famous, and infamous winter in Palm Beach. There also are several interesting sights along the way. (It's an easy drive north to Palm Beach; just be sure to avoid I-95 during rush hours.)

Take I-95 North (for those in the western region of South Florida, Florida's turnpike is less heavily trafficked). For a short diversion, exit at Palmetto Park Road (Exit 38) and go east for 2 miles to Federal Highway (Route 1). Turn left and pass one traffic light. On the right, turn into Mizner Park, a stunning complex of pink buildings with orange barrel-tile roofs, green balconies, brick roads, and splashing fountains. Visitors might want to browse among boutiques and outdoor cafés in this multi-use center. Also worth a stop is *Liberties* (309 Plaza Real; phone: 407-368-1300), a giant book and music store that features frequent readings by celebrity authors. Open to midnight or beyond.

Return to I-95 North and continue to Southern Boulevard, Route 98 (Exit 50). Those traveling with children, or who simply love animals, should go west 18 miles to *Lion Country Safari* (Southern Blvd. W., West Palm Beach; phone: 407-793-1084). Occupants remain in their cars and drive through more than 500 acres, where they pass prides of lions and herds of antelope in re-creations of African areas such as the Serengeti Plains and Skukuza Veldt.

If you stop, a rhinoceros may lumber alongside the car. As a pickup truck deposits a load of sapling trees for the African elephants' lunch, adult elephants protectively circle their babies. Paddleboat and kiddie rides, plus a snack bar, are available on the premises. Plan to spend several hours. Open daily, with the last cars admitted at 4:30 PM; admission charge.

After the safari, return to Southern Boulevard and go east for 19.2 miles. Follow the Southern Boulevard Bridge across the Intracoastal Waterway; note the winter waterfront mansions on the left. The closest one, with a pink 75-foot Moorish tower, is Mar-A-Lago, the estate currently owned by Donald Trump, but originally built for the late Majorie Merriweather Post, heiress to the Post cereal fortune. The 118-room mansion is listed on the National Register of Historic Places. You're now on the island of Palm Beach, one of the barrier beaches along South Florida's east coast. Proceed around the traffic circle, following signs for Route A1A North (South Ocean Blvd).

Continue north on South Ocean Boulevard past Mar-A-Lago. The ocean is on the right. On the left, the strip is dotted with elegant mansions owned by members of European royalty or giants of American industry.

The mansions' architecture — in Spanish, French, and Italian styles — recalls the landscape along the Riviera.

At 1.65 miles from the traffic circle, look to the left for the street sign marked Worth Avenue. This famed street is well worth a visit. If there are no vacant parking meters, there's a parking lot (with valet parking) in the *Esplanade Shops* about half a block down on the left, just east of *Saks Fifth Avenue*. (Or try the outdoor lot a few blocks away on Peruvian Avenue.)

Whether you're a world class shopper or just the window-shopping type, these few blocks along Worth Avenue should not be missed. The 200 glamorous stores — and the elegantly dressed shoppers who frequent them — are reminiscent of Beverly Hills' Rodeo Drive (in fact, the Palm Beach version has been around a lot longer), although one recent visitor from Beverly Hills noticed more Rolls-Royces here in a day than he ever spotted back home. In addition to its pricey shops, Worth Avenue's architectural beauty is worthy of note.

Basically, the 4-block-long street is lined with 1- and 2-story shops built by 1920s architect Addison Mizner, in the Spanish Revival style he thought the region's history and climate demanded. Mizner was responsible for many grand homes throughout the area as well, for families such as the Vanderbilts and the Phippses. Buildings are white stucco with orange barrel-tile roofs, dripping with cerise bougainvillea. Arched galleries face miniature royal palm trees; and everything is spotless and subdued. At the eastern end, the 2-story *Esplanade Shops*, with their Spanish tiles and water fountains, add further charm to the scene.

One of the top restaurants for a fashionable lunch or dinner is award-winning *Café L'Europe* (150 Worth Ave.; phone: 407-655-4020) on the second floor of the *Esplanade*, serving French and continental fare (such as sautéed Florida snapper or grilled medallions of veal with tarragon sauce) in an elegant setting of rich woods, leaded glass, heavy lace curtains, and crystal. There is a caviar bar (with five varieties of caviar) and champagne bottles in silver top-hat wine buckets. Open for lunch Mondays through Saturdays and dinner daily.

Don't miss the "vias," charming side courtyards off the street hosting additional shops and eateries, with gurgling fountains and lush flower beds.

High-fashion shops include *Martha's, Valentino Boutique, Polo by Ralph Lauren, Brooks Brothers, Salvatore Ferragamo, Sonia Rykiel,* and *Saks Fifth Avenue*. Leather goods are at *Gucci* and *Mark Cross*. Jewelry can be purchased at *Cartier* and *Van Cleef & Arpels*. Artworks can be found at *Wally Findlay Galleries* and *Holsten Gallery*. High-priced toys are at *F.A.O Schwarz*. There's also a thrift shop where you just might find a cast-off sequin gown formerly owned by a society czarina.

When you've had your fill of shopping and staring, you can either rent a bike at *Palm Beach Bicycle Trail Shop* (223 Sunrise Ave.; phone: 407-659-4583) where you'll get a map showing how you can see many of the mansions up close, or drive east along any of the streets, returning to Ocean Boulevard. Take the boulevard north as far as it goes (Barton Avenue). Ahead is a white-pillared house that belongs to cosmetics magnate Estée Lauder. Local lore has it that if the guards stand at the doorway, she's in residence. Beyond that lies the Kennedy compound, which isn't visible from the street. (Don't expect to approach any of these well-guarded private homes.)

Follow Barton left to South County Road (the first traffic light) and turn right. At the second light (Breakers Row), turn right into the *Breakers* hotel and park near the fountain. This 528-room stucco hotel, built in 1926 (after two former wooden incarnations burned down), is reminiscent of a European palace with its Italian Renaissance–style antique furniture and hand-painted ceilings. Notice the 15th-century tapestries in the lobby. If your visit coincides with the "season," you may spot one or several of the many movie stars and heads of government who stay here. Have lunch in the *Beach Club,* overlooking the ocean, or in the *Fairways Club,* overlooking the golf course (1 S. County Rd., Palm Beach; phone: 407-655-6611).

Once refreshed, return to your car. Go back on South County Road to the next light, Royal Poinciana Way, and turn right. At the next light (Coconut Row), turn left. On the right pass *Royal Poinciana Plaza,* a low-key complex housing the *Royal Poinciana Playhouse,* stores, and restaurants. In the "famous-for-all-the-wrong-reasons" category is *Au Bar* (336 Royal Poinciana Way; phone: 407-832-4800; closed Mondays), the rendezvous spot that figured in the 1992 William Kennedy Smith rape trial (Smith was acquitted), it remains a good watering hole. For a quick snack, stop at *Too-Jay's* for New York–style delicatessen sandwiches, unusual salads, and fantastic pastries such as their killer chocolate cake (phone: 407-659-7232; open daily for breakfast, lunch, and dinner). The *Hibel Museum of Art* (150 Royal Poinciana Plaza; phone: 407-833-6870) mounts the works of 76-year-old artist Edna Hibel — original oils, lithographs, bronze sculptures, and collectible plates. The first female artist to be awarded the medal of honor by Pope John Paul II, Edna Hibel also has been honored with a fellowship to the World Academy of Art and Science. Open Tuesdays through Sundays; closed Mondays; no admission charge.

Exit the *Royal Poinciana Plaza;* shortly ahead on the right is the 73-room *Henry Morrison Flagler Museum.* Called "Whitehall," the mansion was the home of Henry Morrison Flagler, a co-founder of the Standard Oil Company who brought what is now the *Florida East Coast Railroad* south through the state to Key West. (He subsequently opened resorts throughout Florida, and is credited with establishing Palm Beach and aiding development of Miami Beach and Key West.) He built this home in 1901 for his third wife, who was 38 years his junior. (One of his tokens of affection was a pearl necklace with a clasp enhanced by a 12-carat diamond.)

A vacation home like those in Newport, Rhode Island, Whitehall cost

$2.5 million to build and $1.5 million to furnish. (In 1994 dollars, that would run over $70 million to build and over $42 million to furnish.) Its 110-foot-long foyer is decorated in seven kinds of marble. Features include gilded moldings, ceiling murals, museum-quality furnishings, enormous Baccarat crystal chandeliers, columns, fireplaces, and artworks. Children will enjoy the doll room with its antique doll collection. There are costume collections dating from 1895 to 1915, and other collections, including lace and silver. Allow about 1½ hours for a tour. Open Tuesdays through Sundays; closed Mondays, *Christmas* and *New Year's*. Admission charge. Coconut Row, Palm Beach (phone: 407-655-2833).

Continue south on Coconut Row and turn right on Royal Palm Way (towering royal palms line both sides of this especially striking street); continue over Royal Palm Bridge. Exit the bridge and turn left onto Flagler Drive. Proceed .3 miles to Diana Place on the right, site of the 1-story, buff-colored *Norton Gallery,* with its permanent collection of French Impressionist, Chinese, and American art, plus traveling exhibitions. Closed Mondays. Donation requested. (1451 S. Olive Ave., West Palm Beach; phone: 407-832-5194).

Return north on Flagler to the bridge (Lake View Ave.) and turn left. Staying on the right side of the road as it crosses Dixie Highway (US 1), the road curves right and then continues straight as Jessamine Street. Continue west across the railroad tracks, and straight ahead (after the third light from the bridge) note the $52-million *Kravis Center for the Performing Arts* (701 Okeechobee Blvd., West Palm Beach; phone: 407-832-SHOW or 800-572-8471). Offerings include opera and ballet performances, such as the *Bolshoi Ballet,* plus national companies of Broadway shows.

At this point, Lake View Avenue has turned into Okeechobee Boulevard. From the corner of Okeechobee and Tamarind Avenue, continue west on Okeechobee for 1 mile, until you see the signs for I-95 southbound. Now, retrace the route back to your hotel, or perhaps stay and sample the elegance of the *Breakers* at dinner. Its *Florentine* dining room, where diners sit beneath 25-foot-high, frescoed, beamed ceilings patterned after the Palazzo Davante in Florence, also is open to non-guests. Sample the famed wine list and dance to live orchestra music. Men are required to wear jackets. Open daily 6 to 10 PM. 1 S. County Rd. (phone: 407-659-8480).

Tour 8: Florida Keys and John Pennekamp Coral Reef State Park

Curving 150 miles out into the Gulf of Mexico from the southern tip of mainland Florida, the Florida Keys dot the waters like an ellipsis following a phrase. And in many ways this archipelago is an afterthought to that great landmass above, centered around Miami, with its glittering nightlife and crowded swimming beaches. The 45 principal islands that make up the Keys are generally tucked soundly away by 11 PM, have very few swimming beaches despite the availability of water (the shallow waters, coupled with fierce coral, discourage swimming), and few glamorous resorts. A 7-story hotel — a midget by Miami standards — is a skyscraper hereabouts. The Keys are an easy day's drive from Miami; a fun way to view the multicolored water from the air and save driving time is provided by *Chalk's International Airlines,* whose seaplanes depart from Miami and Ft. Lauderdale and splash down right off of Duval Street in Key West (phone: 305-371-8628 or 305-359-7980). For those who would like to stay overnight, our choice of hotels is listed below.

What the Keys do have, however, are some of the finest seascapes around — the blue waters of the Atlantic to the east and south and the green seas of the Gulf of Mexico on the northwestern side. As you drive along the Overseas Highway (US 1), a toll-free highway that spans the islands with 43 bridges (some only 100 feet long, one stretching more than 7 miles), you are surrounded by sea and sky on all sides. Even on the Keys themselves, many of which are only a few hundred yards wide, you can see through the mangroves, Caribbean pine, and silver palmetto to the sea, which is the overwhelming presence here. And though you can't see it from a car, the view is even more dramatic below the water's surface.

The Keys are surrounded by an offshore coral reef. The *Florida Keys National Marine Sanctuary,* measuring 2,800 square nautical miles, extends from Dade County west to the Dry Tortugas (it's actually the same reef that continues northward past Ft. Lauderdale, with some gaps along the way). Located an average of 5 to 8 miles offshore, the reef escaped major damage from Hurricane Andrew; in the northern section, however, some branching coral was damaged and some soft coral was dislodged. There are dive shops all along the route (some indicated by the red-and-white-striped "divers down" flags) which arrange private or group snorkeling expeditions to nearby reefs where you stalk (swim after) your prey.

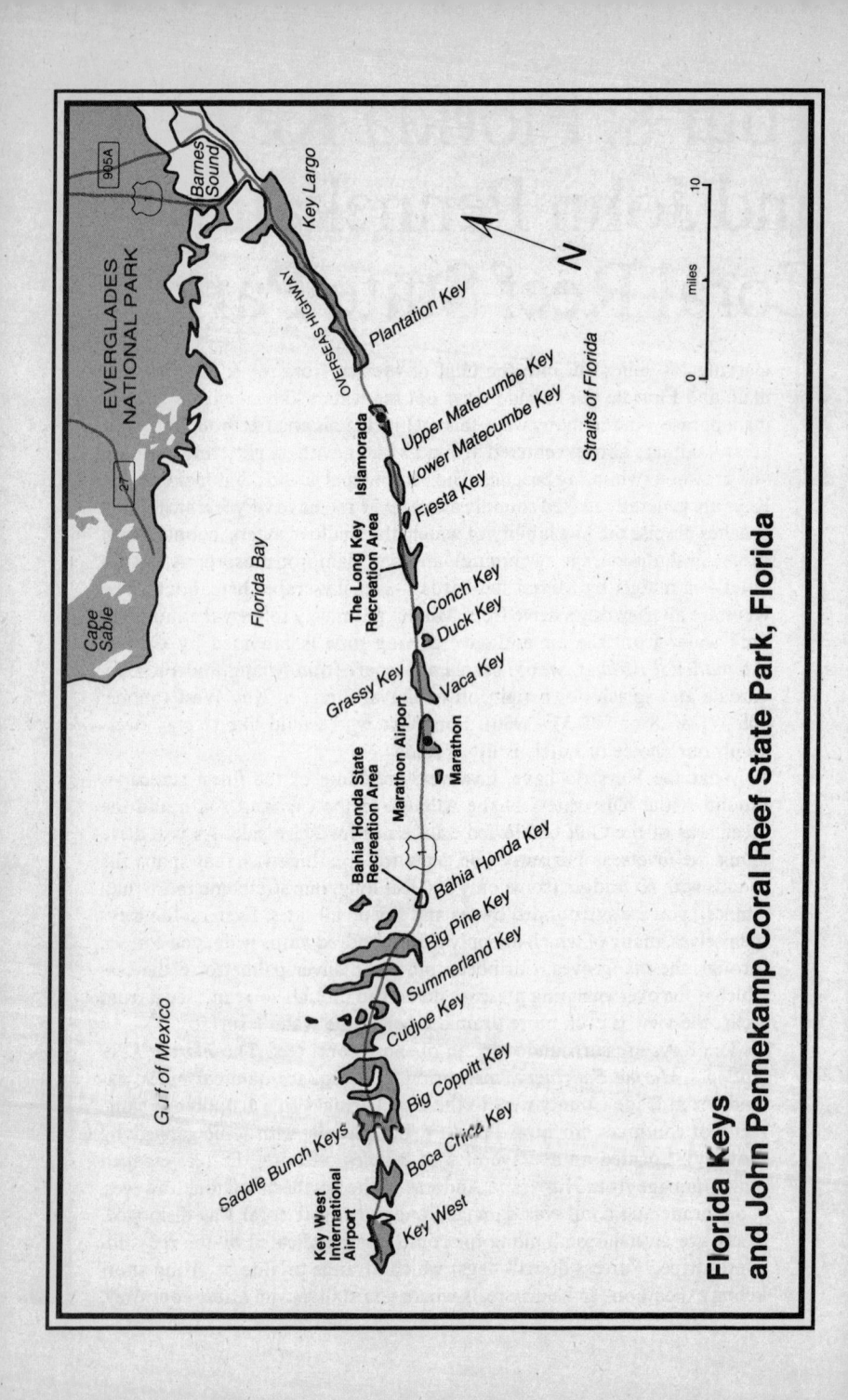

**Florida Keys
and John Pennekamp Coral Reef State Park, Florida**

The best section of the reef can be seen close up at the *John Pennekamp Coral Reef State Park* in Key Largo. It is a slightly hallucinogenic underwater scene, as bright blue and green tropical fish move in and out of the sculptured reefs of white, pink, and orange coral.

The story of the Overseas Highway is interesting. During the late 1880s, Henry Flagler, an associate of John D. Rockefeller, aimed to establish a "land" route to Cuba by extending the *Florida East Coast Railroad* line to Key West. From there he planned a ferry shuttle for the final 90 miles to Havana. He invested some $20 million in the construction of tracks, but the 1929 crash destroyed his project and the *Labor Day* hurricane of 1935 wiped out most of what remained of the tracks and roadbed. At that point, the government stepped in and began building the Overseas Highway along the same route. In 1982, 37 bridges were replaced with wider, heavier spans, including the well-known Seven-Mile Bridge at Marathon.

Of the 45 keys linked by the highway, several are major islands with accommodations, restaurants, shops, and their own unique characteristics. Much of this local flavor has to do with the natives of the area. They're Floridians, but they call themselves "Conchs." Descended from London Cockneys who settled in the Bahamas, the Conchs also incorporate Cuban, Yankee sailor, and Virginia merchant blood. Conchs always have been people of the sea — fishermen, boatmen, spongers (they dive for sponges), and underwater salvagers. (They hardly could be otherwise, living as they do, surrounded by water.) And when you are in their territory, you can easily share their pleasures.

Fishing is king in these parts, with over 300 varieties of fish in the surrounding waters. Besides the challenges to anglers, the availability of fresh fish has stimulated Keys chefs to dream up such creations as conch chowder and, in their land-bound flights of fancy, Key lime pie — which must be yellow, not green, to be genuine.

Key Largo is the first of the keys and the longest, but what is most interesting here is underwater. Running parallel to the Key for 21 miles is the country's only underwater state park, and the largest living coral reef in the continental US. The park is a snorkeler's and scuba diver's heaven, encompassing 165 square miles of the Atlantic Ocean, hundreds of species of tropical fish, and 55 different varieties of coral. Laws forbid taking anything from the water so that the area will be preserved for others to see.

To get an overview of the reef and surrounding sea, take a glass-bottom boat tour operated by the John Pennekamp Coral Reef State Park (phone: 305-451-1621), which sails three times daily (cost is $14 for adults, $7.50 for children under 12). It provides valuable insights on the ecological balance of the reef and journeys several miles out onto the high seas to the reef's most spectacular section, where you'll see beautifully colored coral formations and other marine life, including barracuda, giant sea turtles, and sharks.

You also can venture into the water for snorkeling and scuba diving tours of the reef. Gear can be rented at one of Key Largo's many dive shops or at park headquarters.

Closer to shore, water trails for canoeing in the mangrove swamp offer alternatives for those who want to stay above water. For those who want to go in, the swimming beach has a roped-off area that is good for a dip or some casual skin diving.

There are 47 campsites, all with tables, charcoal grills, electrical hookups, and water. Reservations for the sites should be made up to 60 days in advance — the park is a very popular destination. Admission is $3.25 for the vehicle and driver; additional charge for other passengers. Stop by the visitors' center. Reservations and information: John Pennekamp Coral Reef State Park, PO Box 487, Key Largo, FL 33037 (phone: 305-451-1202; for concession and equipment rental information, 305-451-1621).

Islamorada, in Upper Matecumbe Key, is a sport fishing center in an area that's famous for fishing; its many coral reefs in the surrounding shallow waters attract scuba and skin divers as well. The Underwater Coral Gardens, two colorful coral deposits and the wreck of a Spanish galleon, offer underwater exploration and photography and can be reached by charter boat.

Also stop at Long Key for some underwater hunting (in season) of crawfish — lobster-like crustaceans without the pincers. The Long Key State Recreation Area (Long Key Park, mile marker 67.5, Long Key; phone: 305-664-4815) features 60 campsites, picnic areas with tables, barbecue grills, fresh water, and nature trails through the mangrove swamps.

Marathon, the large key midway down the archipelago, has been developed as a tourist center and has an airport and an 18-hole golf course. Nevertheless, Marathon retains much of the original character of a fishing town. There are over 80 species in the gulf and ocean waters which can be taken with rod and reel or nets from charter boats or the key's bridges. For information on the many fishing contests held throughout the year, write to the Chamber of Commerce (3330 Overseas Hwy., Marathon, FL 33050; phone: 305-743-5417 or 800-842-9580). The competition is tough and the fish are smart. *Hall's Diving Center* (1994 Overseas Hwy.; phone: 305-743-5929) is a good place to rent gear.

Big Pine Key, the largest of the Lower Keys, contains 7,700 acres thick with silver palmetto, Caribbean pine, and cacti. Tiny Key deer were thought to be extinct until they reappeared here, and it also is possible to spot the endangered great white heron.

At Bahia Honda Key, the 740-acre Bahia Honda State Recreation Area (5 miles east on US 1) has 80 campsites, 6 cabins, boating, picnicking, and coral-free swimming (phone: 305-872-2353).

And last, but not least, Key West, the southernmost community in the US and the point closest to Cuba, combines Southern, Bahamian, Cuban, and Yankee influences in a unique culture that can be seen in its architecture, tasted in its often quirky food, and felt in its relaxed, individualistic atmosphere. Traditionally, fishermen, artists, and writers have been drawn to this tranquil slip of sand and sea. Ernest Hemingway, among its early devotees, lived here during his most productive years, when he wrote *To Have and Have Not, For Whom the Bell Tolls, Green Hills of Africa,* and one of his greatest short stories, "The Snows of Kilimanjaro." His Spanish colonial-style house of native stone, surrounded by a lush garden of plantings from the Caribbean, is now a museum with many original furnishings and Hemingway memorabilia, along with descendants of Hemingway's pet cats (907 Whitehead St.; phone: 305-294-1575). Among others who have been attracted to Key West are John James Audubon, Tennessee Williams, John Dos Passos, Robert Frost, and President Harry S. Truman, who established a "Little White House" here. It is now a museum filled with Truman's original furniture and artifacts (open daily; admission charge; 111 Front St.; phone: 305-294-9911).

To get your bearings, take the *Conch Tour Train,* a 90-minute narrated tram ride that covers 14 miles, passing all the local highlights. The train leaves from Mallory Square and North Roosevelt Boulevard, next to the Welcome Center where there's free parking (phone: 305-294-5161). Purchase tickets at the bright yellow kiosk on the corner of Duval and Front Streets. Since Key West is best for strolling, you can later visit the places that sounded most interesting — for example, the wooden gingerbread architecture influenced by Bahamian settlers and New England sea captains — or walk to the galleries, craft, and shell shops.

The area also has the dubious distinction of having more T-shirt shops per square foot than anywhere else in the Miami/Ft. Lauderdale area. There's also *The Cat House,* a shop filled with toys, snacks, and other items for cats — plus feline-oriented T-shirts, calendars, and knickknacks for cat lovers (411 Greene St.; phone: 305-294-4779).

Another great orientation is provided by *Old Town Trolley Tours.* The narrated daily tours pick up passengers at 12 stops; the $13 price permits full-day on-again, off-again privileges until the loop is completed (phone: 305-296-4444, 305-296-6688, or 800-284-4482). The best tours are daily walks operated by *Lowder City Tours* (phone: 800-354-1961). Knowledgeable guides lead participants through streets and into hidden gardens, while dispensing colorful anecdotes. *Discovery Tours'* boat leaves from *Lands End Marina* (phone: 305-293-0099). Unlike glass-bottom boats, *Discovery* craft have a below-deck viewing room where passengers look through eye-level windows lining the hull. Thrice-daily trips visit the coral reef, while a sunset cruise stops at the reef, then sails to Mallory Dock in time to watch the sun go down. In fact, the main tourist attraction in these parts is the *Sunset Celebration* at Mallory Square. Locals and visitors watch as the sun sinks, hoping to spot the green flash. Artisans, jugglers, and flame swallowers add to the color as shrimp boats head home. Numerous glass-bottom boats ply the water as well. A favorite is the long-established *Fireball,* with two boats that sail daily from the foot of Duval

Street (phone: 305-296-6293 or 305-294-8704). The catamaran *Stars & Stripes*, a replica of the *America's Cup* winner, offers twice-daily sails to a deserted island and off-boat snorkeling, plus a sunset sail; the boat departs from *Lands End Marina* (phone: 305-294-PURR or 800-634-MEOW).

At the *Lighthouse Museum* (open daily; admission charge; 938 Whitehead St.; phone: 305-294-0012), you can climb the 90-foot-tall 1847 lighthouse for panoramic island views and visit the furnished Lighthouse Keeper's Quarters. The *Audubon House & Gardens* (open daily; admission charge; 205 Whitehead St.; phone: 305-294-2116), where the artist John James Audubon worked on paintings of Florida Keys wildlife in 1831 and 1832, has a complete set of his *Birds of America* engravings. The lovely gardens showcase numerous tropical plants. Restored by the philanthropic Wolfson family who hail from these parts, *Audubon House* also encompasses the home and belongings of a wealthy 19th-century sea captain and wrecker. Wrecking was an important industry among early Conchs; the industry is explained through talks and pictures at the *Wrecker's Museum* (closed *Christmas;* admission charge; 322 Duval St.; phone: 305-294-2116). The oldest house in Key West (dating from 1829 and also owned by a sea captain), it harbors furniture, documents, a charming furnished dollhouse, ship models, and a "blacklist" of 19th-century wreckers whose licenses were revoked.

The *Historic Key West Shipwreck Museum* in the brick building that was the original City Hall (open daily; admission charge; 510 Greene St.; phone: 305-292-9740) contains mementos from the merchant ship *Isaac Allerton*, sunk in 1856. Displayed here are glass bottles, ivory toothbrushes, and parts of the ship, whose demise was known as "the richest single salvage of the era." The island's oldest house of worship, the *Cornish Memorial AME Zion Church* (702 Whitehead St., Bahama Village; phone: 305-294-2350), dates from 1864. The *East Martello Museum* (open daily; admission charge; 3501 S. Roosevelt Blvd; phone: 305-296-3913), housed in a Civil War fort, details colorful island history, including tales of weird inhabitants such as "the mad scientist of Key West," who "reconstructed" his dead wife using wax and wire, hoping to bring her back to life. More treasures await at the *Mel Fisher Maritime Heritage Society Museum,* housed in the former navy warehouse. It displays loot salvaged from the Spanish ships *Atocha* and *Santa Margarita,* sunk in a 1622 hurricane. On view are hoards of silver bars, gold chains, emerald and diamond jewelry, and trade beads and shackles from the *Henrietta Marie,* an English merchant slaver, which sank in 1701. The museum is open daily; admission charge (200 Green St.; phone: 305-294-2633).

Fishing dominates sports here as elsewhere in the Keys. In addition to fishing, there is a collection of local marine life at the *Key West Aquarium* (open daily; admission charge; 1 Whitehead St. on Mallory Sq.; phone: 305-296-2051). For snorkeling and scuba diving around the coral reefs, the *Key West Pro Dive Shop* sponsors trips and rents gear (1605 N. Roosevelt

Blvd., PO Box 580, Key West, FL 33040; phone: 305-296-3823). Golfers can tee off at the 18-hole *Key West Resort Golf Course* (phone: 305-294-5232). Greens fees, including cart, average $40; there's a resident pro. The area also boasts 9 public tennis courts: 6 that are lighted (Truman Ave. and Jose Marti Dr.; open from daylight to 11 PM) and 3 that are unlit (Atlantic Ave. and Reynolds St.).

Information: *Key West Chamber of Commerce,* 402 Wall St., Key West, FL 33040 (phone: 305-294-2587 or 800-648-6269). Area information: *Florida Keys Visitors Bureau,* PO Box 1147-PR, Key West, FL 33041 (phone: 800-FLA-KEYS).

Antonia's (615 Duval St.; phone: 305-294-6565) is one of Key West's most popular restaurants. Outstanding meals also are served at *Louie's Backyard,* either inside or on the large deck under a huge banyan tree, overlooking the ocean (700 Waddell Ave.; phone: 305-294-1061), and at the *Pier House* restaurant (see below), where the Key lime pie may be the best anywhere. Fans of singer Jimmy Buffett can stop at his *Margaritaville Café* (500 Duval St.; phone: 292-1435) for the eponymous thirst-quencher, a light meal, and the possibility of bumping into Buffett, who appears here from time to time. And Hemingway fans never miss a pilgrimage to *Sloppy Joe's* (phone: 305-294-5717), the Duval Street bar once frequented by the writer himself; current regulars are not of the literary persuasion.

Below are some suggested overnight stays in the Keys.

Cheeca Lodge, Islamorada Low-key elegance makes this 27-acre seaside hideaway a romantic pleasure. There are 203 rooms and suites. Other amenities include a dining room and open-air grill, 2 pools, a manmade lagoon with a sand beach and waterfalls, 6 lighted tennis courts, and a 9-hole, par 3 golf course designed by Jack Nicklaus. "Camp Cheeca" has won awards for its environmentally conscious program for kids. Water activities — such as fishing, snorkeling, and parasailing — also are available. Marker 82, PO Box 527, Islamorada, FL 33036 (phone: 305-664-4651 or 800-327-2888; fax: 305-664-2893).

La Concha Holiday Inn, Key West In the heart of Old Town, this restored 160-room, 7-story Art Deco hotel first opened in 1926. Chenille bedspreads, four-poster beds, lace curtains, and antique furnishings abound, although plumbing and electronic equipment are modern. There's a restaurant, as well as 3 bars, boutiques, and a pool. A daily sunset celebration (weather permitting) takes place at the rooftop bar. 430 Duval St., Key West, FL 33040 (phone: 305-296-2991, 800-745-2191, or 800-HOLIDAY; fax: 305-294-3283).

Curry Mansion Inn, Key West This impeccably and authentically restored Victorian mansion features 21 rooms in an antiques-filled main house, as well as an L-shape guesthouse enclosing the pool and patio, where breakfast is served and evening cocktail parties are held (both complimentary). Guests have beach privileges at the *Pier House* and *Marriott's Casa Marina* (see below). 511 Caroline St., Key West, FL 33040 (phone: 305-294-5349 or 800-253-3466; fax: 305-294-4093).

Hyatt Key West, Key West With its own private beach and marina, this 4-story, 120-room hostelry in town offers a pool, a Jacuzzi, a small exercise facility, and 2 restaurants. 601 Front St., Key West, FL 33040 (phone: 305-296-9900 or 800-233-1234; fax: 305-292-1038).

Little Palm Island, Little Torch Key On a secluded island just off Key West is this charming hideaway, a member of the prestigious Relais & Châteaux group. There are 30 private one-bedroom cottages with thatch roofs and rustic but elegant furnishings, a swimming pool, and a fine restaurant. Tennis and golf facilities are nearby. Rte. 4, Box 1036, Little Torch Key, FL 33042 (phone: 305-872-2524 or 800-343-8567; fax: 305-872-4843).

Marriott's Casa Marina, Key West Built in 1921 by Henry Flagler, a charming full-service resort whose past guests have included Rita Hayworth, Ethel Merman, Al Jolson, and Gregory Peck. Along with its own beach, it now has 312 rooms, 2 restaurants, a pool, a whirlpool bath, 3 lighted tennis courts, a health club, and water sports. 1500 Reynolds St., Key West, FL 33040 (phone: 305-296-3535 or 800-228-9290; fax: 305-296-9960).

Ocean Reef Club, Key Largo Hurricane Andrew caused some water and landscaping damage, but the resort reopened last year almost completely restored to its original state. Once a private fishing camp and now a posh tropical paradise, this 300-room exclusive — and expensive — resort boasts good golf, terrific fishing, and 4,000 acres of park and wildlife preserve. It offers 145 hotel rooms plus a varying number of accommodations in condominiums and villas. There are 7 restaurants and 5 lounges, as well as an Olympic-size pool. If you're into high-style living and have the pocketbook to back it up, this is the place for you. 31 Ocean Reef Dr., N. Key Largo, FL 33037 (phone: 305-367-2611 or 800-741-REEF; fax: 305-367-2224).

Pier House, Key West In the heart of the restored Old Town area, this deluxe property has 5 dining rooms (the *Pier House* restaurant is first-rate), a separate health spa (see *Sybaritic Spas* in DIVERSIONS) with 22 of the 142 rooms, a manmade sand beach (with a section for topless bathers), a pool, and a deck for sunset watchers. 1 Duval St., Key West, FL 33040 (phone: 305-296-4600; 800-432-3414 in Florida; 800-327-8340 elsewhere in the US; fax. 305-296 7569).

Tour 9: Everglades National Park

If you've had your fill (for a while, at least) of sea and sand, venture 21 miles west (about a half hour along the Tamiami Trail) from Miami to the Shark Valley entrance of Everglades National Park (visitors' center phone: 305-221-8776) or 10 miles southwest of Homestead to the main entrance for access to the more interesting areas of Royal Palm and Flamingo.

In most of America's national parks there's little more to do than arrive and open your eyes to be impressed. The Everglades is far more demanding. Here you must know something about ecology, and something about what you're looking at, to appreciate the full splendor of this magnificent swamp wilderness.

In 1992, Hurricane Andrew devastated the northern parts of the park: Trees were uprooted, flora destroyed, and the landscape left in virtual ruin. The entire park closed for 4½ months, mostly because of the unsafe conditions for visitors. And although the park reopened early last year, it will take Mother Nature quite a while to restore it to its former state. Happily, there still is much here to lure visitors.

The Everglades is America's only subtropical wetlands. Fed by the waters of southern Florida's huge Lake Okeechobee, the entire southern tip of the state was once more or less as the Everglades is today — a huge tract of mangrove swamps, seas of sawgrass, hammocks of hardwood trees, and millions of birds, fish, snakes, alligators, and insects (including 43 species of mosquitoes). As southern Florida developed, the slow-draining waters of Okeechobee were channeled for irrigation and the swamps drained. Bit by bit, southern Florida dried out.

In 1947, alarmed by the destruction of these unique wetlands, the federal government set aside 1.5 million acres 30 miles southwest of Miami as Everglades National Park. Despite various (and continuing) environmental threats, the park survives. It's the third-largest of America's national parks — 2,350 square miles of the world's most delicate ecological system, stretching to Florida's southern and western Gulf coasts. Although the Everglades is considered the nation's most threatened natural area by the National Park Service and various environmental agencies, there is reason to be optimistic about its future. The Everglades Expansion Act of 1989 added more than 107,000 acres of the East Everglades to the park. South Florida's water management system of canals, levees, and dams is being modified to restore natural water flow and marsh conditions to this critical wildlife habitat. Water entering the park will be cleansed of pollutants as it passes through filtration marshes being created north of the

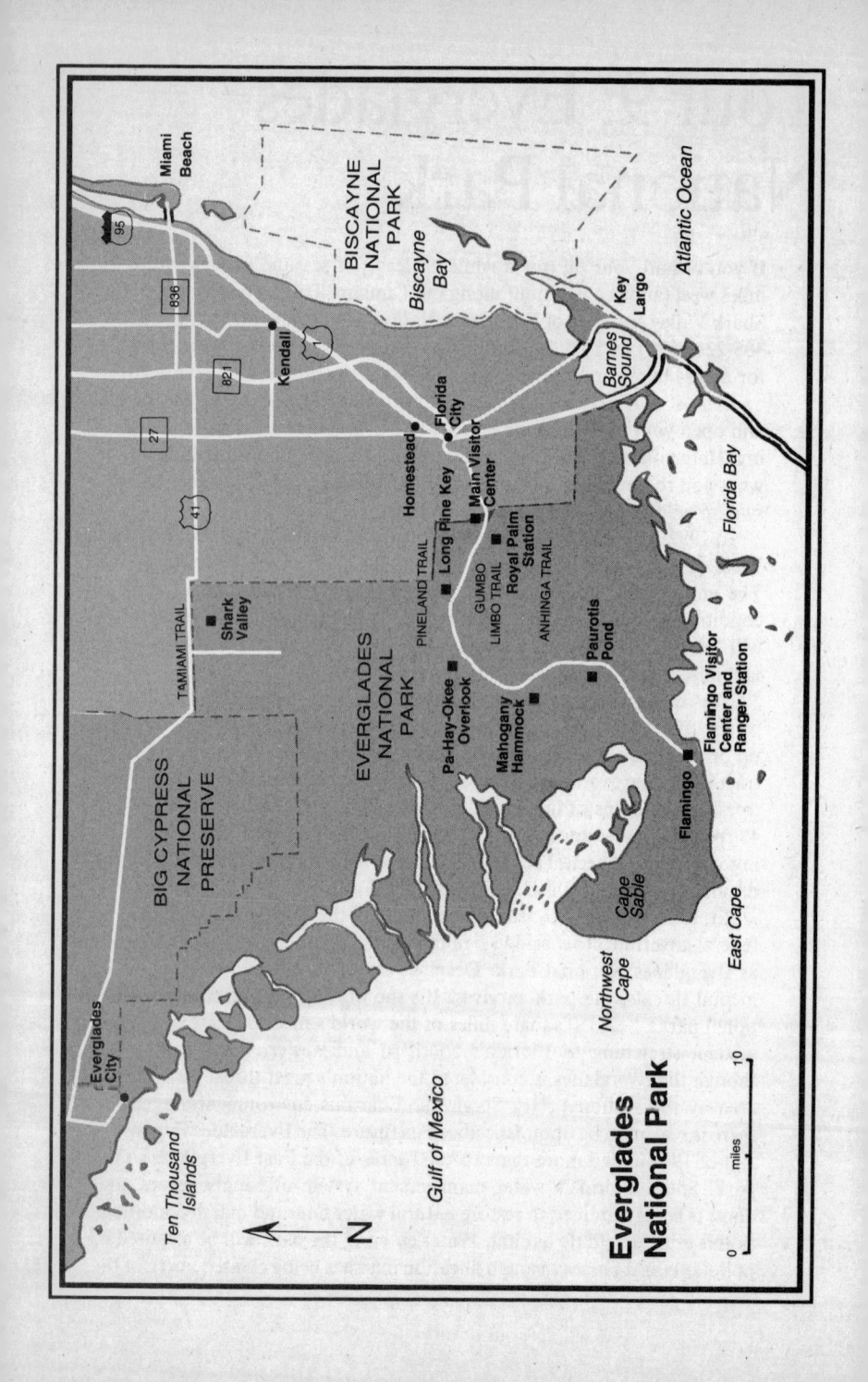

Everglades National Park

park. (There is controversy, however, over whether the efforts thus far have been effective enough.

You must understand the delicacy of the Everglades to enjoy its understated pleasures. It is actually a freshwater river (its Indian name is Pa-Hay-Okee, "River of Grass") 100 miles long, 50 miles wide, and just inches deep. This strange stream travels along an incline of only 3 inches a mile, moving so slowly that a single drop of water takes years to reach the Gulf from Lake Okeechobee. The slow river provides nourishment for a vast and complex system of life, and is a perfect laboratory in which to see the interdependence and sensitivity of an ecosystem. Where the earth rises as much as 3 inches, the plant life in the Everglades changes from sawgrass to hardwood forest. Where ripples appear in a pond, a small fish is eating mosquito larvae; a large fish, a bream perhaps, will dine on the larvae-eater; bass hunt the bream; gar will feed on the bass; and the gar is fodder for the alligator who originally made (or deepened) this pool by digging in with his tail during the winter.

About 200 miles north of the Tropic of Cancer, the Everglades is the meeting point of subtropical and temperate life forms. In this, it is unique in the US: Here you see mangrove, West Indian mahogany, and the poisonous manchineel tree, and in a nearby hammock rising from the sawgrass, pine and hardwood trees. Alligators, crocodiles, and white-tailed deer share the same stomping ground.

Plan to visit the Everglades during the winter, just about the only time to avoid being consumed by mosquitoes. Indeed, in summer, some areas are so infested by these offensive insects that a pleasant visit is nigh impossible. Always carry insect repellent, regardless of the time of year (if you forget, you can buy it at the visitors' centers). Although the Shark Valley area is most accessible from Miami and Ft. Lauderdale, and offers several ranger-led walks and tram tours, the main entrance to the Everglades is on Route 9336, about 10 miles southwest of Homestead; admission charge. Route 9336 ends at the park entrance; from here follow the main park road for a 38-mile journey through the park to Flamingo, on Florida Bay. (The only food to be found between Homestead and Flamingo consists of snacks and drinks from vending machines, so it's a good idea to pack a picnic lunch or to eat in Homestead before leaving.) There are several ways to see the 'glades: By car, drive to various stops along the road; on foot, follow trails (some as short as half a mile) into the heart of things (with or without ranger guides); by small outboard or canoe, follow the water routes.

No matter how you plan to go, the first stop is the temporary visitors' center at the park entrance to see exhibitions on park wildlife and ecology and pick up information on guided tours, "swamp tromps" (more about these later), and park activities and rules. The main visitors' center suffered severe damage from Hurricane Andrew and, at press time, repair work had not yet begun.

The next stop is the Royal Palm Visitor Center (about 2 miles beyond the center; phone: 305-242-7700), with an exhibit on indigenous flora and fauna. The pond here on the Anhinga Trail is rich in animal life. Anhingas and ibis regularly hang out in the trees; alligators waddle out of the water and loll a few feet from visitors; snakes sun themselves on the grass, gars float in the clear water, and raccoons stroll by. Though the Gumbo Limbo Trail has reopened, it suffered greatly from the hurricane: 80 percent of its hardwood trees were uprooted and many exotic air plants were lost. Mahogany Hammock, a bit farther on, resembles the way the Gumbo Limbo Trail used to look; comparing these two places over time will show the often miraculous ways in which an area can replenish itself.

Beyond Royal Palm, the road runs through pine forests, where many trees were lost to Hurricane Andrew. Continue to the Pineland Trail (beginning about 2 miles from Long Pine Key), where you might be lucky enough to spot the delicate Virginia white-tailed deer. The prey of the Florida panther, their numbers here have been dwindling in recent years.

Even more than hurricanes, fire is a forest's worse enemy. Note the pines along the macadam trail. They manage to survive only because they are sturdily fire resistant. You may see a number of them with fire-blackened trunks. In both summer and winter, fires often sweep through parts of the 'glades. Many trees are killed, but pines burn only on the outside; their corky bark protects them. In summer, the saltwort marshes that flank many of the forests dry out and are torched by lightning, but since it is the rainy season, when water levels are relatively high, these fires do little damage. It is the fires during the winter dry season — usually caused by man — that do the most harm. At press time, the campground here was closed, but is scheduled to reopen early this year.

The Pa-Hay-Okee Overlook, at the next stop along the route, provides some of the best views and bird watching in the park. From here, you can see the expanse of sawgrass that makes up Shark River Slough (pronounced *slew*), where alligators and fowl gather. ("Sawgrass" is actually a misnomer; it is not a grass but a fine-toothed sedge. Despite its delicate appearance, it has mean, serrated edges on three sides that chew clothes or flesh with equal ease, so be careful.) The alligators form an important link in the chain of life in the Everglades. During the dry season — autumn through spring — they settle into sloughs and dig deep holes with their tails. In late winter, as the marshes dry out, fish get caught in these 'gator holes. This is crucial for the wading birds, which nest near these natural fishbowls and are thus assured a food supply. The dead-looking trees here are dwarf bald cypresses, some of them 100 years old, which sprout leaves at the onset of the rainy season.

Seven miles beyond Pa-Hay-Okee is Mahogany Hammock, the largest stand of mahoganies in the US and site of the country's largest mahogany tree. Boardwalks allow you to wander into it. Hurricane Andrew downed about 20% of the trees here, but most of the air plants, including orchids, were lost. You'll still see some Vriesia (bromeliads with red bracts) and Spanish moss growing on trees. After this point, little hurricane damage occurred.

About 4 miles farther is Paurotis Pond, with the area's first mangrove trees. Here salt and fresh water begin to mix, and the mangrove is the only tree that thrives in salt water. It is a great colonizer and lives in a constant drama of creation and destruction all along the Gulf shore. It settles into the swampy salt water of the coast, and as it drops seeds and throws out breathing roots it captures material and actually begins "building" earth bulwarks against the sea. As seagulls and other sea birds collect around it, dropping guano, this earth becomes rich and fertile. Then hurricanes sweep the coast, and everything is ripped out of the swampy ground and thrown inland.

Other ponds and trails beckon along the way. At Mrazek Pond, the water level ebbs as the dry season approaches, and hundreds of birds gather to eat the plentiful fish. Beautiful roseate spoonbills, with bright pink wings, share tree limbs with egrets, white ibis, and tricolored herons, among other species.

The main park road ends at Flamingo, where you'll find another visitors' center (phone: 305-253-2241), a hotel, campgrounds, bicycles and boats for hire (including canoes, skiffs, and houseboats) for excursions into portions of the 'glades accessible only by waterway. Ranger-led canoe trips, which are offered at no charge, should be reserved a day in advance.

Slightly beyond this area is Eco Pond, an 8-acre manmade body of water drawn from the Flamingo Sewage Treatment Plant. The pond is the final stage of sewage treatment; the water is then evaporated and later returns to the Everglades as rain. Meanwhile, it provides a stop-off point for alligators and a variety of fowl, including gallinules, egrets, and anis.

Serious visitors should plan to spend most of their time out of their cars, on marked foot trails (usually boardwalks) or on a "swamp tromp", into the very heart of the marshes. For the less hardy, these foot trails are a comfortable way to have an intimate experience in the 'glades; there also are tram rides available at Flamingo and at Shark Valley off Route 41 (which skims the northern border of the park).

For the more intrepid who would like to meet nature's challenge, there are the frequent "slough slogs" or "swamp tromps" from December through March — walking expeditions led by park naturalists which really get you into things — quite literally. You'll need old clothes and shoes that you don't mind getting muddy and wet; waterproof, high boots are a good idea, for you'll be going into the water up to your knees. And be sure to have plenty of mosquito repellent. There are several possible destinations: out to a 'gator hole, a tree island, or a major mangrove stand. Ask for schedules at the visitors' center.

The Wilderness Waterway is just about the most challenging test the Everglades can cook up for an outdoors person. It is a 99-mile water trail that corkscrews through the Ten Thousand Islands area. Although the water lanes are well marked, there is sufficient room for error that travelers are asked to take all precautions when undertaking this journey. By powerboat it is quite possible to complete the course in about 6 hours. However, any serious nature observer will opt for the canoe and the serenity it offers en route. There are minimally outfitted campsites, each wryly nicknamed, along the water lanes: "Hell's Bay" ("hell to get into and hell to get out of"); "Onion Key," the bare-bones remains of a 1920s land developer's dream; and a crude pit outhouse and fireplace campsite known as "the Coming Miami of the Gulf." Shorter canoe trails, equipped with overnight camping, are also available. Overnight stays require a backcountry use permit issued at no charge by Everglades City (Everglades City Ranger Station, Drawer D, Everglades City, FL 33929; phone: 813-695-4217) or Flamingo Ranger Station (PO Box 279, Homestead, FL 33030; phone: 813-695-3101, ext. 182). The waterways begin at Everglades City and extend to Flamingo.

The somewhat less athletic and daring boater might prefer to take a guided boat cruise. Cruises depart every evening from Flamingo and sail among Florida Bay's islets or keys aboard the open-sided catamaran *Bald Eagle* or the schooner *Windfall*. They provide a fine opportunity to view Florida's blazing sunsets and watch the indigenous birds returning to roost for the evening (admission charge); contact the *Flamingo Lodge* for reservations and information (phone: 305-253-2241). There also are daily cruises from Everglades City to explore Upper Chokoloskee Bay. But the craft most visitors associate with the Everglades is the airboat. Though banned from Everglades National Park (the noise and gas fumes disturb the fragile environment), airboats may be operated outside the park. Near the Shark Valley entrance, daily airboat rides are offered year-round at *Everglades Safari Park* (Rte. 41, about 9 miles west of Krome Ave.; phone: 305-226-6923).

The not-so-visible members of the Everglades family run the gamut from the lowly and much-hated mosquito all the way to the signature 'gator, who is most often spotted when his eyes break water while the rest of him hides beneath the surface. Fish are tropical and abundant, each with a role in the food cycle that maintains the chain of life in the Everglades. Schools of dolphin can sometimes be spotted from the coastal shorelines. Recreational fishing is permitted, but all plants and animals are protected by law from any molestation or harm by man. Information: Superintendent, Everglades National Park, PO Box 279, Homestead, FL 33030 (phone: 305-242-7700).

For an overnight stay that doesn't involve camping out, try the *Flamingo Lodge* in Flamingo, the only place to stay right in the Everglades, with modern, clean, and inexpensive accommodations in 24 cottages and 101 motel rooms (all with phones and TV sets). There's a screened-in pool, too. On Florida Bay, 38 miles from the entrance of Everglades Park (PO Box 900428, Flamingo, FL 33090; phone: 305-253-2241); the restaurant and gift shop are closed May through October. And in the morning, after you've scraped the mud off your shoes, climb back in your car. From darkest jungle to sunlit sand, have we got a beach for you!

Index

Accommodations
　Florida Keys, 113, 159–60
　Ft. Lauderdale, 91–94, 112, 113
　Miami, 56–63, 112
　spas, 111–14
Airplane travel, 11–14
　charter flights, 12
　consumer protection, 14
　discounts on scheduled flights, 12–14
　　bartered travel sources, 14
　　consolidators and bucket shops, 13
　　courier travel, 12–13
　　generic air travel, 14
　　last minute travel clubs, 13–14
　insurance, 16–17
　scheduled flights, 11–12
　　baggage, 12
　　fares, 11
　　meals, 12
　　reservations, 11
　　seating, 11
　　smoking, 11
　transportation from the airport to the city, 14
American Police Hall of Fame and Museum, 44
Ancient Spanish Monastery, Miami, 39, 109

Anhinga Indian Museum and Art Gallery, Seminole Indian reservation, 145–46
Art Deco district, Miami, 32, 35, 104–5, 117
　map, 122
　walking tour, 123–27
Art Museum at Florida International University, 44
Automated teller machines (ATMs), 22

Bahia Honda Key, 156
Banking hours. See Business hours
Baseball, 48, 86
Basketball, 48
Bass Museum of Art, Miami, 34–35, 126
Bayside Marketplace, Miami, 33, 35–36, 116, 129
Beaches
　Ft. Lauderdale, 80, 89
　Miami, 53, 103–4, 117
Bicycling, 48–49
Big Pine Key, 156
Bill Baggs Cape Florida State Park, 34, 132
Boating, 49, 88
　See also Ship, traveling by
Bonnet House, Ft. Lauderdale, 79

Business hours, 22
Bus, traveling by, 40, 81
Butterfly World, Ft. Lauderdale, 78

Calle Ocho (8th Street), Little
    Havana, Miami, 36, 105–6
  map, 142
  walking tour, 141–43
Car, traveling by
  insurance, 15, 16–17
  renting a car, 14–15, 40, 81
Caribbean Marketplace, Miami, 36
Cash machines. *See* Automated
    teller machines (ATMs)
Center for the Fine Arts, Miami,
    36, 44
Charter flights, 12
Climate, 11
Coconut Grove, 31
  map, 134
  walking tour, 133–35
Consumer protection, 14
Coral Castle, Miami, 39
Coral Gables, 31
  map, 136
  tour, 137–40
Coral Gables Congregational
    Church, 109
Cowboy and Indian walking tour,
    145–47
  map, 144
Crandon Park Beach, 53
Credit cards, 21–22
  telephone calls with, 23
Cruises. *See* Ship, traveling by
Cuban Museum of Arts and
    Culture, 44, 143

Disabled travelers, 17–19
Dog racing
  Ft. Lauderdale, 87
  Miami, 49
Driving. *See* Car, traveling by;
    Tours; *names of individual*
    tours

Emergency medical assistance, 24
Everglades Holiday Park,
    Ft. Lauderdale, 76–77, 147
Everglades National Park, 2, 110–11
  map, 162
  tours, 77, 161–67

Fairchild Tropical Gardens, Coral
    Gables, 38, 138–39
Ferries. *See* Ship, traveling by
Fishing
  Florida Keys, 155, 156, 158–59
  Ft. Lauderdale, 86
  Miami, 49–50
Fitness centers
  Ft. Lauderdale, 86, 112, 113
  Florida Keys, 113
  Miami, 50, 112
  spas, 111–14
Flamingo Gardens, Ft. Lauderdale,
    77
Florida East Coast Railroad, 29, 155
Florida Keys, 2, 30, 111
  hotels, 159–60
  map, 154
  tours, 155, 153–60
Florida Keys National Marine
    Sanctuary, 153–55
Football, 50, 107
Ft. Lauderdale, 72–100
  at-a-glance, 74–80
  hotels, 91–94, 112, 113
  local services, 81–83
  local transportation, 74–75, 81
  major colleges and universities,
    84

map, 6–7
museums, 84
music, 83, 90
nightclubs and nightlife, 90–91
restaurants, 94–100, 107–8
shopping, 77–78, 84–86
special events, 83
special places, 75–80
sports and fitness, 86–90, 112, 113
theater, 90
tourist information, 25, 80–81
tours, 74–75
Ft. Lauderdale Historical Society, 84
Fruit and Spice Park, Miami, 38

Golf
  Florida Keys, 159
  Ft. Lauderdale, 86–87
  Miami, 50–51
Goodyear Blimp, Ft. Lauderdale, 79–80

Handicapped travelers. *See* Disabled travelers
Haulover Beach, 53
Health care
  emergency number for medical assistance, 24
  hospitals and pharmacies, 24
  insurance, 17
Henry Morrison Flagler Museum, Palm Beach, 151–52
Hibel Museum of Art, Palm Beach, 151
Historical Museum of South Florida, Miami, 36, 44–45
Holidays. *See* Special events
Hollywood Broadwalk, Ft. Lauderdale, 78

Holocaust Memorial, Miami, 39
Horseback riding, 88, 146–47
Horse racing
  Ft. Lauderdale, 87
  Miami, 51
Hospitals. *See* Health care
Hotels. *See* Accommodations
Houses of worship, 109–10
Hugh Taylor Birch State Recreation Area, Ft. Lauderdale, 78

Insurance, 15, 16–17
International Swimming Hall of Fame, Ft. Lauderdale, 79

Jai alai
  Ft. Lauderdale, 88
  Miami, 51–52
Jet skiing, 52
Jogging, 52
John Pennekamp Coral Reef State Park, 111, 155–56
  map, 154
John U. Lloyd Beach State Recreation Area, Ft. Lauderdale, 78

Key Biscayne, 30, 32, 131–32
Key Largo, 155–56
Key West, 30, 156–60
Kravis Center for the Performing Arts, Palm Beach, 152

Legal aid, 25
Lion Country Safari, Palm Beach, 149
Little Havana, Miami, 31–32
  Calle Ocho (8th Street), 36, 105–6
  map, 142
  walking tour, 141–43

Local services
    Ft. Lauderdale, 81–83
    Miami, 41–42
Local transportation. *See*
    Transportation; local
    transportation *entry under
    names of individual cities*
Long Key, 156
Los Olas Boulevard and Los Olas
    area, Ft. Lauderdale, 80
Lowe Art Museum, 45, 139
Loxahatchee Everglades Tours, Ft.
    Lauderdale, 77

Mail, 22–23
Maps
    Art Deco district, 122
    Coconut Grove, 134
    Coral Gables, 136
    Cowboy and Indian tour, 144
    Everglades National Park, 162
    Florida Keys, 154
    Ft. Lauderdale, 6–7
        John Pennekamp Coral Reef
        State Park, 154
    Little Havana, Miami, 142
    Miami, 4–5
    Palm Beach, 148
    South Miami, 128
Mar-A-Lago, Palm Beach, 149
Marathon Key, 156
Medical assistance. *See* Health
    care
Metro-Dade Cultural Center,
    Miami, 36, 44–45
Metrozoo, Miami, 36
Miamarina, Miami, 35
Miami Marine Stadium, 37, 132
Miami—Miami Beach, 29–71
    at-a-glance, 33–39
    communities, 31–32

dance, 55
hotels, 56–63, 112
local services, 41–42
local transportation, 40–41
major colleges and universities,
    45
map, 4–5
museums, 44–45
music, 42–44, 55
nightclubs and nightlife, 55–56
quintessential, 103–8
restaurants, 63–71, 107–8
shopping, 31, 45–48, 108–9
special events, 42–44
special places, 34–39
sports and fitness, 48–54, 112
theater, 54
tourist information, 25
tours, 33–34
Miami Seaquarium, 37, 130, 131
Miami Youth Museum, 45
Miccosukee Indian Village, Miami,
    37, 44
Money, 21–22
    sending, 22
    See also Automated teller
        machines (ATMs); Credit
        cards; Traveler's checks
Monkey Jungle, Miami, 38
Museum of Art, Ft. Lauderdale,
    84
Museum of Discovery and Science,
    Ft. Lauderdale, 73, 76
Museum of Science and Space
    Transit Planetarium, Miami,
    37–38, 130
Museums
    Ft. Lauderdale, 84
    Key West, 158
    Miami, 44–45
Music

festivals, 43–44, 83–84
 Ft. Lauderdale, 83, 90
 Miami, 42–44, 55

Newspapers
 Ft. Lauderdale, 80
 Miami, 40
Nightclubs and nightlife
 Ft. Lauderdale, 90–91
 Miami, 55–56
Norton Gallery, Palm Beach, 152

Ocean World, Ft. Lauderdale, 78
Older travelers, 20–21
Overseas Highway, 30, 153–55

Package tours, 15–16
 for disabled travelers, 19
 for older travelers, 21
 for single travelers, 20
Palm Beach walking tour, 149–52
 map, 148
Parasailing, 88
Parrot Jungle, Miami, 38
Pharmacies. *See* Health care
Photographing Miami and
  Ft. Lauderdale, 115–18
Plane, traveling by. *See* Airplane
  travel
Plymouth Congregational Church,
  Coconut Grove, 109
Port Everglades, Ft. Lauderdale,
  75–76
Port of Miami, 34

Radio stations
 Ft. Lauderdale, 81
 Miami, 40
Religion. *See* Houses of worship
Renting a car, 14–15, 17, 40, 81
Restaurants

 Florida Keys, 159–60
 Ft. Lauderdale, 94–100, 107–8
 Miami, 63–71, 107–8
Rodeo, 88, 146

Sailing, 49, 88
Sawgrass Mills Mall, Ft. Lauderdale,
  77, 85
Scuba diving
 Ft. Lauderdale, 88–89
 Miami, 52
Seminole Bingo Hall, 145
Seminole Indian Reservation,
  Ft. Lauderdale, 79
Seminole Indian Tribal Fair, 145
Seminole Tribe of Hollywood,
  145–46
Sending money, 22
Senior citizens. *See* Older travelers
Ship, traveling by
 day cruises, 76, 114–15
Shopping
 antiques, 108–9
 duty free, 48
 Ft. Lauderdale, 77–78, 84–86
 Miami, 31, 45–48, 108–9
Single travelers, 19–20
Skating, 52
Sky diving, 52–53
Snorkeling, 89
South Beach, Miami, 32, 104–5,
  117–18
South Miami, 31
 map, 128
 by car (tour), 129–32
Spanish Monastery of St. Bernard,
  Miami, 39, 109
Spas, 111–14
Special events
 Ft. Lauderdale, 83
 Miami, 42–44

Special-interest packages. *See* Package tours
Sports and fitness
 Ft. Lauderdale, 86–90, 112, 113
Sports and fitness (*cont.*)
 Miami, 48–54, 112
 See also names of specific sports
Strahanan House, Ft. Lauderdale, 79
Swap Shop, Ft. Lauderdale, 77–78, 85
Swimming
 Ft. Lauderdale, 79, 80, 89
 Miami, 53, 103–4

Tax, sales
 Ft. Lauderdale, 81
 Miami, 40, 48
Taxis, 14, 81
Telephone, 23–24
 Ft. Lauderdale, 81
 Miami, 40
Television
 Ft. Lauderdale, 80
 Miami, 40
Temperature. *See* Climate
Temple Beth Jacob, Miami, 110
Temple Emanu-el, Miami, 110
Tennis
 Florida Keys, 159
 Ft. Lauderdale, 89–90
 Miami, 53–54, 131
Theaters
 Ft. Lauderdale, 90
 Miami, 54
Time zone, 22
Topeekeegee Yugnee Park, Ft. Lauderdale, 79
Tourist information
 Florida Keys, 156, 159
 Ft. Lauderdale, 25, 80–81
 Miami, 25, 40
Tours, 121–67
 day cruises, 76, 114–15, 118
 guided
  Everglades, 77
  Florida Keys, 155, 157–58
  Ft. Lauderdale, 74–75
  Miami, 33–34, 52
 nature walks
  Ft. Lauderdale, 88
  Miami, 52
 walking and driving
  Art Deco district, 123–27
  Coconut Grove, 133–35
  Coral Gables, 137–40
  Cowboy and Indian tour, 145–47
  Everglades National Park, 77, 161–67
  Ft. Lauderdale, 74
  Florida Keys and John Pennekamp Coral Reef State Park, 153–60
  Little Havana, 141–43
  Palm Beach, 149–52
  South Miami, 129–32
 See also Package tours; *names of individual tours*
Train, traveling by, 41
Transportation
 from the airport to the city, 14
 local, 14
  Ft. Lauderdale, 74–75, 81
  Miami, 40–41
 See also Airplane travel; Car, traveling by; Ship, traveling by
Traveler's checks, 21–22
Trinity Episcopal Cathedral, Miami, 110

Upper Matecumbe Key, 156

Venetian Pool, Miami, 39
Vizcaya Museum and Gardens,
    Miami, 37, 130

Water skiing, 54

Weather. *See* Climate
Windsurfing, 54

Young at Art Children's Museum,
    Ft. Lauderdale, 84